PAST INTO PRESENT

PAST INTO PRESENT

Effective Techniques for First-Person

Historical Interpretation

STACY F. ROTH

The University of North Carolina Press

Chapel Hill & London

© 1998 The University of North Carolina Press
All rights reserved
Set in Minion and Caslon Open Face
by G & S Typesetters
Manufactured in the United States of America
The paper in this book meets the guidelines for
permanence and durability of the Committee on Production Guidelines
for Book Longevity of the Council on Library Resources.

Roth, Stacy Flora.

Past into present : effective techniques for first-person historical
interpretation / by Stacy Roth.

p.   cm.

Includes bibliographical references and index.

ISBN 0-8078-2407-0 (cloth : alk. paper). — ISBN 0-8078-4710-0 (pbk. : alk. paper)

1. History — Study and teaching.   2. Historic sites — Interpretive programs.

3. Historical reenactments.   I. Title.

D16.25.R68   1998   97-36874

907'.1 — dc21   CIP

02   01   00   99   98   5   4   3   2   1

I would like to dedicate *Past into Present*
to three special educators who made history
enjoyable, vibrant, and relevant to me
as a child and young adult:
Anne Hotalen and John "Mr. Z" Zieleniewski at
Abraham P. Morris School in Hillside, New Jersey, and
Julian Thompson, author, educator, and former director of
alternative school Changes Inc., in East Orange, New Jersey.
Their kindness, humanity, and wise guidance nurtured
an independent thinker and responsible adult.

Also, to the late Dr. David Parry,
Director of Interpretive Programmes at the
Canadian Museum of Civilization, a founding member of
International Museum Theatre Alliance, and a talented performer,
storyteller, and musician who left life's stage all too soon.

And to my parents,
Barbara and Richard Roth, who always believed in me
but are still a little awed that someone can make a
living like this.

CONTENTS

ACKNOWLEDGMENTS

Past into Present reflects the mentorship, generosity, patience, and shared expertise of many. I would like to extend my heartfelt appreciation and thanks to my fellow interpreters, friends, mentors, and colleagues:

Roy Underhill, for his enthusiastic support and role as the catalyst for formal publication of this work;

John Kemp, Director of Interpretation at Plimoth Plantation, for his ongoing advice and gentle direction during all stages of manuscript development;

David Perry, Ron Maner, David Van Hook, and Stephanie Wenzel at the University of North Carolina Press for making a first-time author's experience such a painless one;

David Emerson, one of my earliest "informants" and now my partner in every sense of the word;

Harry Needham and Kathleen Cannon, for their willing editing skills and useful suggestions;

Dan O'Connor and James Anderson of Rutgers School of Communication, Information, and Library Science, for providing a visiting scholarship that enabled me to complete library-based research;

interpreters and staffs of Plimoth Plantation, Colonial Williamsburg, Mystic Seaport Museum, Old Sturbridge Village, the Old Barracks Museum, Conner Prairie, Freetown Village, Upper Canada Village, Morristown National Historical Park, Lincoln Log Cabin, and Fort Snelling, plus the independent interpreters who freely shared their tricks of the trade;

and those who shared their sites and special resources: Jay and Jan Anderson, Edward Baker, David Carr, Keith Dewar, D. Stephen Elliot, Jeremy Fried, Robert Gerling, Glenn Gordinier, Conny Graft, Moira Turnan Hannon, David Heighway, Harold Holzer, Jean Jeacle, Cathy Johnson, Dale Jones, Tom Kelleher, John Krugler, Cindy Kupiainen, Ann Lane, David Lowenthal, Gary Machlis, Ronald McRae, Christy Matthews, Margaret Piatt, Lawrence Schmidt, Kate Stover, Charlie Thomforde, Ron Thompson, Andy Thomson, Lisa Whalen, and Ken Yellis.

PAST INTO PRESENT

Ever wish you could step into the past? Trade witticisms with Benjamin Franklin? Walk in the shoes of an explorer? Prevent your worst enemy's ancestors from ever meeting? If you opened this book of your own accord, I would be surprised if you've never daydreamed about time travel. No, we cannot venture back to the past in a time machine — at least not yet — but that limitation has not stopped tens of thousands of people from painstakingly researching and simulating their favorite periods in history. They roll the dice over strategic board games, line up hand-painted miniature soldiers over tabletop battlefields, build models and dioramas, resurrect ancient dramas, reproduce antiques, refight numerous wars, and re-create the actions and events of people of earlier ages. A fictional girl from Colonial Williamsburg named Felicity spawns a cottage industry. Films and documentaries on historical themes draw significant audiences. Reenacted American Civil War battles seem to have almost as many participants as the original events. Clearly, the past becomes more popular with every passing day.

Why? What larger meaning does such a trend bode for modern culture at the millennium? In 1984 Jay Anderson identified three key reasons that attracted living history enthusiasts to the past: a need for escape from the present, a nostalgic preference for earlier epochs, and a curiosity about everyday life in earlier times. Many of Anderson's informants quested after a magical "moment in time," a transcendent experience when environment and mindset fuse into a physical and mental sense of oneness with the past.[1]

History is continually being recycled by those in the present. Goethe, for example, cheerfully watched Roman Carnivale participants sporting about in historical masks and costumes; officers under British general William Howe threw their commander a grand farewell party dressed as medieval knights, with their female guests as Turkish maidens; and pageants and parades accented by costumed impersonators have always been popular features of celebrations, such as the nineteenth-century New England Fourth of July celebration that featured a reenacted "Deborah Sampson" (the noted Revolutionary War soldier who was later revealed to be a woman).

The difference between historical simulation then and now is twofold: First, it has become far more technical. Today there is a much greater concern for authentic detail, fidelity to documentation, and the appropriate application of research (including social, seasonal, and geographical aspects) to resulting presentations. Second, our needs and purposes for simulation have evolved.

The seductive foreignness of Plimoth Plantation accentuates the illusion of time travel.
(courtesy Plimoth Plantation)

In the late eighteenth and early nineteenth centuries, philosophers admired the democratic ideas, visual balance, and reason of ancients as a model for society. In the late nineteenth century and for much of the twentieth, our worship of colonial and frontier forefathers was highly celebratory, nostalgic, and self-affirming of Anglo-American values. Today, simulators are motivated by an academic thirst to unlock the secrets of the past and a search for personal identification and deeper meaning.

Perhaps the evolution of the way we manipulate the past symbolizes a reaction to modern mental overload that still cannot escape the pervasiveness of an information-age techno-mentality. Perchance it reflects a need for personal control of a selective microenvironment in a world where most of us are interdependent on the actions and decisions of countless others around the globe. Obviously, the social and psychological implications of the manipulation of history, particularly in the second half of the twentieth century, is an area ripe for further study.

While this book is not about the psychological motivations of living history enthusiasts, it does address the behavioral implications of a specific segment of people who animate history. There is another level of consciousness to re-creating the past, one that only a minor portion of history simulators experience. It is the Interpretive Impetus. Individuals affected by the Impetus have an evangelical calling to transform their personal relationship with history into an interpersonal one. They draw enjoyment from making history meaningful to others. Many of these people gravitate to museums and other education-based professions. Others can be found reenacting or volunteering at historic sites. Yet not all teachers, museum personnel, volunteers, or re-enactors automatically possess this quality. Those affected have transcended their own clamor for private revelation and are on a mission to translate — or interpret — what they have learned.

Past into Present explores how people with the Interpretive Impetus re-create the past through first-person interpretation, a challenging living history education method in which interpreters transform themselves into people of the past. There are many variations of first-person (also known as roleplaying and character interpretation). Some interpreters present characters in a dramatic context, allowing visitors to eavesdrop on a scene between several people, or perhaps taking the stage as a famous person for an hour, then answering questions at program's close. Another style commonly found in living history museums encourages visitors to roam at will and encounter interpreters in realistic situations and activities. Visitors engage them on a personal level, letting conversation flow where it may and perhaps participating with a chore or assuming a role themselves. It is this latter interactive method of roleplay that is the primary focus of this book.

A special group of dedicated interpreters has made first-person their livelihood. Many work at places such as Plimoth Plantation, Colonial Williamsburg, Mystic Seaport Museum, Conner Prairie, Upper Canada Village, and the Canadian Museum of Civilization. There is also a growing cadre of freelance companies, theater troupes, and individuals who hire out historical character services to museums, historic sites, festivals, and schools. In addition, countless museum volunteers, reenactors, and history hobbyists portray historical characters for personal enjoyment and community service.

Roleplay is a vital and important educational method. It is flexible. Its content and presentation can be varied according to audience, individual, and group interests. Because it personalizes history, it creates a greater sense of empathy and emotion than lectures, guided tours, and third-person description. It tweaks the imagination and fosters a sense of play in both interpreters and their visitors. First-person complements modern trends in education that encourage multisensory learning methods, creative problem solving, familiarity with daily life and important events in the past, the understanding of differing perspectives, and the application of the past to the future. It augments traditional academic skills with concrete participatory experiences that galvanize concepts and foster retention. Its scalability adapts well to the leisure learning needs of senior citizens and families, two of the most sizable museum-going populations. Famous personalities, re-created events, and specialized demonstrations provide visitor draw for heritage tourism, supplying color and activity that reinforce the historical identity of destinations.

First-person interpreters are more visible now than ever, but no one umbrella organization unites all of them for training or theory purposes. There is no shortage of printed matter on the subject, but it is diffuse, difficult to locate through public avenues of research, and highly specific to employee, volunteer, or reenactor groups. The best materials are nonpublished or privately distributed, such as looseleaf collections of training documents, site training manuals, guidebooks that are issued to National Park Service employees, and the proceedings of the Association for Living Historical Farms and Agricultural Museums. The reenactor press generates plenty of character development information, but — with a few exceptions — much of it centers on achieving an appropriate sartorial and material appearance, rather than on how to engage the public.

Other works have addressed issues in first-person interpretation, particularly Stephen Snow's *Performing the Pilgrims*, which describes first-person interpretation (as practiced at Plimoth Plantation) as a subdiscipline of theater. Although he devotes considerable space to analyzing visitor types and their motivations, Snow emphasizes theatrical analogy such as the dramatic aspects of character portrayal, the "backstage" feel of "behind the scenes" places such as the interpreters' lounge, and the personality traits coincident to actors and selected staff. The interplay between interpreters and visitors is used as supporting evidence for the theatrical model. *Past into Present* complements rather than refutes Snow's thesis. It acknowledges a theatrical side to many first-person presentations but explores an alternative body of first-person interpretive methods that sublimate dramatic techniques to communication- and education-based styles.

Although the portrayal of historical characters is a common device in film, theater, and other types of performance, its presence at museums and historic sites has been both championed and derided. Many detractors simply dislike the concept of costumed simulation because it can never be a perfect reproduction of the past. Other critics have drawn attention to examples of interpreters' smart-alecky or rude remarks, characters who claim they don't understand visitors' questions, and the audiences' difficulty interacting comfortably with those in role. Challengers' comments were not always misplaced. Character interpretation, like acting, teaching, and any other skill-demanding endeavor, requires aptitude, study, and practice. Unlike other arts, it presents a unique set of communication challenges that must be met with special techniques if it is to succeed as a thought-provoking, educational medium that the public will enjoy and appreciate. First-person has had some time to grow and develop since its first appearances at historic sites in the mid-1970s. Today's best interpreters sparkle, inspire conversation, entertain, and provide a compelling sense of the past through methods, for the most part, of their own development and initiative. This book focuses on their genius at circumventing the challenges and pitfalls of a relatively new genre.

Back in June 1990, at a conference of the Association for Living Historical Farms and Agricultural Museums, I met Ken Yellis, then director of public programming at Plimoth Plantation, who discussed with me his own efforts to codify the crucial philosophical elements for planning first-person programs at historic sites. In his series of "Real Time" essays, Yellis threw down the gauntlet to historic sites to make the public's encounter with first-person programs "seductive rather than threatening, pleasant and intriguing rather than uncomfortable and bewildering."[2]

The challenge inspired me. I had been enchanted with first-person since my first encounter with "soldiers from the Continental Army" at Morristown National Historical Park in 1975. Later, visits to Plimoth Plantation left me absolutely mesmerized. It felt as close as one could come to really stepping into the past. The environment and the knowledge of the "Pilgrims" combined to offer a magical experience. What potential! One could ask those people *anything* about life in 1627. The dialects and speech patterns, too, were fascinating. I sought out other first-person programs — and decided to become a person of the past myself.

As a connoisseur and practitioner of the genre, I realized that some interpreters were very adept at creating believable historical characters and stimulating spectators; others, less so. Additionally, there was much style variation from one site to another and from one interpreter to the next. Would it be possible to identify a set of theories on which first-person interpretation should be based? Are there particular behaviors that work consistently? Are there certain methods grasped by those especially magical interpreters but not by the less successful ones?

The answer is more complex than a simple "yes." Readers will follow along on a quest for the secrets of first-person, a search that led me through literature on interpersonal communication, body language, visitor behavior, learning theory, audiences with special needs, theater, anthropology, popular travel news, evaluations, and interpretive training texts and manuals. However, the most meaningful sources were not those in print but hundreds of hours of discussions, questionnaire responses, and observations of both interpreters and visitors. In the following pages, readers will discover with me the range of techniques practiced by interpreters whose characters evoke the flavor of a realistic past, galvanize audience interest, stir the emotions, and stimulate thought, inquiry, and positive responses.

Past into Present is divided into four sections. The first defines important concepts and terms that are used throughout the book, examines the goals of the genre and reviews the debate that surrounds costumed historical simulation, and offers an overview of first-person's history and development. The second section examines the foundations for successful programming, dissects recent opinions comparing first-person to theater, and investigates the qualities for creating characters that possess depth, interest, and plausibility. The remainder of the book explores the practical side of interpreter-visitor interaction. Section three discusses the unusual communication situations that provide special challenges for interpreters, examines the context of audiences' leisure experiences, and looks at some of the many ways that interpreters can capture attention, maintain interest, and "read" their listeners and themselves. Section four investigates techniques for relating to various audience subgroups, with special attention to the requirements of children at different stages of maturity and the simple tips that can improve the enjoyment level of handicapped visitors. The final chapter is devoted to the delicate nature of the interpretation of controversial topics and conflict. We'll look at the type of advance preparation necessary, along with the many creative solutions available for minimizing public misunderstanding and outrage.

Whether you are a professional interpreter, reenactor, museum volunteer, actor, museum administrator, program planner, interpersonal communication or behavioral specialist, graduate student, or just plain interested in living history, I hope that you will find food for thought and practical information within these pages.

New Approaches to History

An Overview

{ 1 }

The Terminology of Living History and First-Person Interpretation

One of the challenges of describing activities related to living history is the lack of a fixed terminology. It is not uncommon to find two different writers describing first-person interpretation yet referring to vastly different presentations. This chapter establishes definitions for roleplay and related activities based on the terminology of interpreters themselves. On occasion I have coined terms for methods or techniques that lacked common description and hope that fellow interpreters will find them appropriate.

Museums communicate with visitors in many ways: through exhibits, multimedia programs, special events, brochures and books, labels, guided tours, and more recently — especially over the last thirty years — living history interpretation. Living history programming encompasses a palette of methods: demonstration, discourse, roleplay, reenactment, and theatrical performance.

Jay Anderson has defined "living history" for those of us in heritage-dependent disciplines, industries, and avocations as a simulation of life in another time for the purpose of research, interpretation, and/or play.[1] In its most encompassing sense, living history can be anything that evokes a link with the past: cultivating heirloom plants, singing a song learned from grandmother, re-creating a battle or trekking through the mountains in buckskins, collecting antique cars, preparing an old recipe, hiking an old trail, attending a religious service, or cutting the capers of a morris dance. If it touches a connective chord with the past, be it mystical or deliberate, it is history expressing itself in vital form.

What is an "interpreter"?[2] Readers associated with museums and parks recognize the term immediately, while the rest of humanity assumes that an interpreter translates foreign languages. For the layman, an interpreter, as defined by those in our field, translates material culture and human or natural phenomena to the public — as Freeman Tilden implied — in a meaningful, provocative, and interesting way.[3] In living history programming, presenters employ a combination of discourse, demonstration, and interaction within a historical or simulated environment. Living history interpretation is a complex art that requires a combination of skills from many areas, including — but not limited to — communication, history, practical technology, and theater. Its practitioners must possess both a broad and a specific understanding of history, material culture, and related subjects, and they must convey that information effectively to the visitor.

This book focuses on living history's most dramatic technique, first-person interpretation, and in particular its interactive mode, in which interpreters encourage audiences to converse or participate with their historical characters. Interactive first-person is found in a variety of situations; however, its most likely venues are living history museums, public reenactments and other special events, and in museum theater programs.

Living history museums and living history sites re-create past material culture, technology, and behavior. Although most stress educational purposes among their official objectives, their role extends far beyond education. People visit them for many reasons. Teachers escort their charges to them in the hope that students will learn about the past in ways that complement their classroom studies. Families seek outings that are both fun and educational. Others enjoy historical settings, wish to immerse themselves in the past, seek authentic experiences, feel nostalgic, or simply want a new experience or a diversion.[4]

On their grandest scale, living history museums are dedicated to re-creating convincing environments, such as the Pilgrim Village at Plimoth Plantation. These re-creations vary in scope and content from a single event in a fixed location (such as Mayflower II, where it is always the same day in March 1621 onboard the ship, no matter what the time of year outside) to a wide band of time and more than one geographic location (Old Sturbridge Village in Sturbridge, Mass., for example). Many sites tell the story of specific historical figures or events. Others focus on agriculture, technology, movements, religious or ethnic groups, or daily life in specific historical situations. Because it is both impossible and impractical to replicate thoroughly an entire world down to the last detail, most re-creations emphasize features that underscore their educational purpose and deemphasize those that are visually or socially repugnant to twentieth-century sensibilities or hazardous to health. (The impact of such choices will be discussed later.)

Living history sites are not the only type of museum to incorporate live interpretation. Traditional museums have found that museum theater or gallery drama programs add dimension to art, architecture, science, and other "static" exhibits. Museum theater encompasses dramatic pieces, plays, storytelling programs, monologues, dialogues, and interactive roleplaying as performed in gallery spaces, auditoriums, and other environments. The Science Museum of Minnesota (which launched its own theater department in 1984), the Canadian Museum of Civilization (in Hull, Quebec), and the Science Museum of London are pioneers of the movement, which began in the 1970s. Many other museums have since followed suit. Museum theater is a significant trend within museology, requiring examination far broader in scope than space permits here.[5] Only those programs that stress interactive first-person interpretation will be addressed in these pages.

"Freelance" or "independent"[6] interpreters are individuals (or groups) who contract with museums, sites, schools, and organizations on their own or through a third-party agent. Some freelancers have worked in museums; others come from theater, education, reenactment, public speaking, and other backgrounds. Many offer services for classrooms, libraries, assemblies, festivals, historic sites, promotions, and public events, doing "history for hire" wherever needed.

"Reenactor" describes those for whom living history is both passion and recreation. They frequently belong to re-created military units and other groups that organize simulation events. Their number has mushroomed over the past two decades. Writing in 1985, Jay Anderson predicted that the reenactment movement would double by 1995.[7] If the proliferation of reenactor periodicals, vendors of reproduction clothing and equipment, and computer forums that have appeared over the past decade are evidence of a trend, numbers have more than doubled. Although many reenactors do first-person interpretation as described in this work, the majority opt for third-person or have limited interpretive contact with the public. Some reenactors have become increasingly aware of the function of interpretation in recent years, a trend borne out by newsletter articles that include tips on approaching the public and by the legions of hobbyists who have taken to working with historic sites for special events and weekend programming.[8] Although avocational reenactment is significant within the living history movement, it will receive only peripheral consideration here unless directly concerned with first-person interpretation.

The two major types of interactive living history interpretation are first-person and third-person. Third-person interpretation is the most common form of interpreter-visitor interaction. Using this method, interpreters, often dressed in period attire, describe, demonstrate, illustrate, and compare their

Reenacting — of the battle of Trenton, for example, in this photograph — has become one of the most popular pastimes of the late twentieth century. (photo: Kate Nagy)

subject in ways that effectively communicate its meaning to visitors. Interpreters refer to the past as the past. For instance: "I am cooking a pottage the way a housewife or servant would have prepared it in the seventeenth century. Today, we might call the same recipe 'soup' and simmer it in a crock pot." The public can ask questions that pertain to the exhibit at hand or venture farther afield in conversation. Inquiries pertaining to local services and comfort needs, or questions about the interpreter's background are considered legitimate for discussion.

The method featured in this book is recognized by several names among interpreters: first-person interpretation, roleplaying, and character interpretation. All refer interchangeably to the same style. "Interactive historical character interpretation" and "interactive historical roleplay (or roleplaying)" are additional synonyms, personally concocted but descriptively literal. Incidentally, these terms are virtually unknown to the press and public, who frequently refer to character interpreters as actors, actor-historians, or guides.

In these pages "first-person" and its four synonyms refer to the presentation style encountered on a typical day at the 1627 Pilgrim Village and 1621 Mayflower II of Plimoth Plantation (Plymouth, Mass.) or 1836 Prairietown at Conner Prairie (Fishers, Ind.).[9] I have selected the Plimoth method as the standard because of the pioneer role played by that institution in its development. Variations, of course, are many and will be discussed in turn.

In the prototypical form of interactive historical roleplay, interpreters recreate the daily activities, thoughts, and behavior of real (or composite) historical people. Presentations may be spontaneous or built around scenarios, themes, or specific events. When first-person is responsibly presented, it strives to achieve accuracy in as many facets of a historical culture as research, site constraints, and other modern conventions permit. The interpreters behave in a fashion that evokes, as closely as possible, the behavior, folkways, customs, beliefs, activities, foodways, speechways, tradeways, religions, technology, dress, deportment, and contemporary perspective of the past peoples they represent. By assuming a historical persona, the roleplayer humanizes complex information while performing tasks, activities, or scenes that are within the context of everyday life. First-person interpreters, when in role, avoid discussion of occurrences beyond their character's time. They speak from personal perspective: "I built this house last year"; "My wife and I sleep in that bed." They make conversation as opposed to speeches and monologues. Dialogue is improvised, based on historical sources. Interpretation can venture off in a variety of directions, depending on the interests of the visitor and the skill of the interpreter.

First-person interpretation, as described above, is more demanding of interpreters than third-person interpretation and is also more demanding of the public. It forces the visitor into the role of anthropologist, voyeur, outsider, time traveler, and interloper. Counterbalancing the required effort, it harbors special rewards for the inquisitive, imaginative, and willing player, akin to the thrill of achieving the higher levels of a virtual-reality game.

First-person interpretation can be absolutely spontaneous or built around deliberate themes and concepts. It can incorporate single or multiple scenarios, blocks of preconceived dialogue and activity that develop a chain of ideas; highlight a given subject within the larger interpretive setting; provide additional structure to a free-form presentation; or re-create actual (or typical) events. For instance, Plimoth Plantation frequently punctuates its daily interpretation with prearranged scenario activity. During a three-day period each October, the usual interpretation is overlaid with the re-creation of a trade visit by Dutch dignitaries, which includes mini-events: an opening salutation with greeting speeches and a militia demonstration, a feast, and a trade session with the local natives.

Portions of a scenario dialogue, such as marriage vows during a re-created wedding, may be scripted, while other activities and remarks are improvised, albeit in an anticipated sequence. In a trial scene, for example (a common feature at many living history museums), the "judge" is familiar with historical laws and court procedures. The action unfolds according to common historical custom, directed by the judge and court officers. Those portraying the lawyers, litigants, and witnesses know how one another will support or defend their arguments. Visitors, perhaps, may be recruited to play the jury and are encouraged to question key characters before drawing a verdict.

There are many variations on first-person as described above, developed to meet the special needs of other programs and their unique situations. They are classed below as "mixed interpretive medium," "role acting," the "my time/your time approach," "ghost interpretation," and "museum theater."

A "mixed interpretive medium" approach uses first- and third-person methods in concert. In such a program, a third-person interpreter might prepare visitors for the first-person experience by providing historical background, answering questions that postdate the scope of the presentation, and/ or interacting with the roleplayers. One example, "red T-shirting," is a guided first-person technique developed by the freelance Historical Reenactment Workshop for their programs at various heritage sites in the United Kingdom. The team's third-person interpreters — dressed in distinctive red T-shirts — greet visitors, explain the first-person concept, provide suggestions on how to interact with the roleplayers, and strategically station themselves to interject explanations and become intermediaries as needed.[10] Another example is the

Mixed interpretive media: visitors, as members of the press, question Thomas Jefferson (Bill Barker). (courtesy Colonial Williamsburg Foundation)

placement of "contextualists,"[11] at selected Colonial Williamsburg (Williamsburg, Va.) programs. They introduce upcoming scenes, explain the significance of key issues, and hold a wrap-up session at the end. At Old Sturbridge Village similar content bracketing is conducted by a selected roleplayer who steps temporarily out of character for the task.

The are many creative possibilities for mixed interpretation. At Colonial Williamsburg, random visitors are chosen to play "reporters" at a twentieth-century-style press conference with Thomas Jefferson. They stand in a press box, are supplied with written questions, are prompted to jump up and down with excitement, and are called on in turn by a twentieth-century "moderator." Jefferson, portrayed by interpreter Bill Barker, answers the questions based on actual writings. Following the reporters, the floor is open to all spectators.

Some programs invite visitors to take improvisational roles. This succeeds best with participants who have studied in advance and are well prepared with background readings and role portfolios. Old Sturbridge Village and Plimoth Plantation have run especially successful programs in this area, Sturbridge with junior high and high school students and Plimoth with college classes.[12] Roleplay has long been a popular educational method in classrooms. Many educators enthusiastically declare that role-taking stimulates learning, develops empathy, personalizes historical research, and encourages students to link cause, effect, and partisanship with given issues.[13] To attest to this, I vividly recall portraying a Confederate slave owner in a simulated fifth-grade debate on the abolition of slavery. The process of understanding an alternative outlook widened my perspective on conflict and its causes.

"Role acting," a term coined by Margaret Piatt when she directed living history presentations at Maryland's London Towne Publik House, is an amalgamation of first- and third-person techniques.[14] The method encourages characterization yet sanctions a step out of role when a third-person response seems more effective. At Old Sturbridge Village, where Piatt was more recently assistant director of museum education, role acting is the preferred style of first-person interpretation because it lets the interpreters employ some of the histrionics of standard first-person while addressing a wider range of visitors' questions.[15]

According to its practitioners, role acting reduces the alienating effects of first-person for visitors who fail to catch on and accommodates questions that are outside the scope of historical characters. Aficionados of Plimoth-style first-person are frustrated by role acting interpreters who flip-flop in and out of character during the same conversation. A dilemma is created when one visitor's out-of-period question distracts from the momentum of a compelling story or absorbing characterization. Is it wise to break the continuity for everyone else in the group? Whether or not the average visitor is disturbed by such shifts is a matter worth pursuing by evaluators.

A cousin of role acting is "first-hand interpretation" (author's term), a style common to craftspeople and foodways demonstrators who explain their activities in the present tense — referring to themselves as "master of the shop," for example — but do not assume character roles and answer the gamut of possible visitor inquiries as would a third-person interpreter. Because little characterization is involved, this method will not be a focus of this study.

Tom Sanders of Fort Snelling (Minn.) developed the "my time/your time approach" as a way for first-person interpreters to answer out-of-period questions without breaking completely out of character. My time/your time characters display prescience. They claim to be from the past, but acknowledge the visitors' time period and make post- and pre-period comparisons. The interpreter may make statements such as, "In your time, you watch television for entertainment. In my time we entertain ourselves with songs and stories. Television didn't become popular until the 1950s." Sanders emphasizes that this method works well with young children, senior citizens, foreign visitors, and people who dislike the roleplay premise.[16] Other interpreters from Fort Snelling have enthusiastically embraced the technique.[17]

In certain situations the my time/your time method is a feasible alternative, especially with young children or other audiences cited by Sanders. However, I suspect that teen and adult visitors may feel patronized by it. As with role

"Jumping the Broom." Visitors enjoy the re-creation of a rustic wedding at Carter's Grove slave quarters. (courtesy Colonial Williamsburg Foundation)

acting, it poses a problem when most of the audience appears to be enjoying a realistic character and one person asks a "modern" question.

Bonnie Williams, curator of the Wylie House (Bloomington, Ind.), has experimented with another variant, "ghost interpretation," inspired by Sanders's my time/your time approach, but with an additional twist. In ghost interpretation, the historical character confronts his or her visitors in the present. Williams developed this method to compensate for Wylie House's small staff and its many anachronistic features, such as electric outlets and a security system. She thought, too, that standard first-person made visitors too uncomfortable and could not reflect the change over time that seemed so integral to the site.[18] Her character, Elizabeth Wylie, greets guests herself at the door and escorts them into the parlor. Miss Wylie, drawing on her "memories" and employing the descriptive arts of a storyteller, recalls the charm of a garden that has since been buried by pavement. She tosses off a query about the burglar alarm without ducking: "I asked Mrs. Williams and she told me it was a burglar alarm! I told her that when I was a girl, our 'burglar alarm' was the dog."[19]

Williams's presentation charmed me. Another interpreter, Eric Olsen of Morristown National Historical Park (Morristown, N.J.), portrays Revolutionary War soldier Joseph Plumb Martin as a ghost. Olsen, too, relies on storytelling. But can the ghost technique lend itself to other styles and settings or be used with multiple interpreters? Would too many ghosts counteract its effectiveness? Only experimentation will tell.

"Order in the Court." Trial scenes are a natural source of human drama.
(courtesy Colonial Williamsburg Foundation)

Vignettes and monologues that are more akin to traditional theater or public speaking than the above methods also fall under the banner of first-person. Such presentations are often preceded by an introduction and/or followed by a question-and-answer session with the participants, either in or out of character. Examples include a play about the incidents that influenced Benedict Arnold to change his allegiance, performed at Morristown National Historical Park;[20] Plimoth Plantation's "Cursed Tenets," a dramatization of Puritan/Quaker antagonisms in the 1660s; and a "jumping the broom" wedding ceremony at Carter's Grove. Independent interpreters, such as Sarah Grant Reid, Robert L. Spaeth, and William Kashatus,[21] use monologue as a vehicle for one-man or one-woman shows, evoking the popularity of Hal Holbrook's *Mark Twain Tonight!* Reid refers to herself as a "character speaker," reflecting her own emphasis on the techniques of public speaking rather than acting.

"One-person shows" and staged scenes are effective because they convey historical information in an enjoyable format familiar to audiences. They allow viewers to assume a more passive role than interactive interpretation and enable the portrayal of characters, time periods, events, or situations that are not a regular part of a site's standard interpretive programming. Their self-containment can be transplanted to settings not conducive to elaborate re-created environments. However, because public interaction during playlets and monologues is limited, its inclusion here will be limited to examples where active verbal participation by the audience is a factor.

Although several first-person approaches were defined in the preceding pages, this work targets techniques described earlier as the prototypical style of interactive historical roleplay, drawing occasionally on the others. Please assume that I am discussing that form unless I specifically refer to variations.

This book is not a defense of first-person but an exploration of an interpretive vehicle now standard at historic sites and other venues as an engaging way to present history. Like any other method, it has its benefits and its drawbacks. By capitalizing on what it does best and examining its shortcomings as "communication challenges," this work identifies techniques devised by skilled interpreters to maximize its effectiveness as a catalyst for encouraging audiences to explore the past.

{2}

Goals, Benefits, and Drawbacks

The goal of first-person interpretation is to relate the past and relate *to* the past in a way that personalizes and humanizes it.[1] First-person is particularly suited to the depiction of human feelings, attitudes, beliefs, and social interactions. Presented as an unfolding of events, emotions, and processes, rather than as a lecture full of facts, it promotes understanding rather than memorization, empathy rather than detachment. Like other forms of media, it can portray the lives of people from the anonymous to the well known, and material surroundings from folk culture to high style. It can be dramatic, or it may be understated.[2]

Despite critics' charges that first-person cannot depict a complete picture of the historical record, suffers from sins of addition and omission, and is colored by nostalgia — charges that could be leveled at almost any media — it is for many a stimulating adjunct to more time-honored methods. First-person interpretation complements the Bradley Commission's suggested curriculum goals for history education, which encourage children to "perceive past events and issues as they were experienced by people at the time, [and] to develop historical empathy as opposed to present-mindedness."[3] It encourages speculation of alternative denouements to historical situations, thereby sharpening pertinent problem-solving skills and underscoring the role of choice not only in the past, but in the present. Combined with techniques of historical archaeology and/or anthropology, it fosters insight into the motivations and behaviors that affected the practices and processes of those who went before us.[4]

First-person initiates a dialogue between past and present on many levels.

It links the modern visitor and the historical environment. Intergeneration-ally, it unites families and friends who experience living history together and share their own perspectives of their place in history with one another.[5] In addition, it harbors special meaning for those working within the medium who seek to understand the past and hope that they have done it justice. It challenges us not only to resurrect the past through the study of ancient words, thoughts, material culture, and emotions, but to invoke the faculty that early eighteenth-century thinker Giambattista Vico called "Fantasia," that stretch of the imagination without which the past cannot be fully compre-hended.[6] As Isaiah Berlin summed up Vico's view of Fantasia, he emphasized that while Vico maintained the need for critical methods of verification, he also believed that "without *fantasia* the past remains dead; to bring it to life we need, at least ideally, to hear men's voices, to conjecture (on the basis of such evidence as we can gather) what may have been their experience, their forms of expression, their values, outlook, aims, ways of living; without this we cannot grasp whence we came, how we come to be as we are now, not merely physically or biologically and, in a narrow sense, politically and insti-tutionally, but socially, psychologically, morally; without this there can be no genuine self-understanding."[7]

THE DEBATE OVER FIRST-PERSON INTERPRETATION

The debate over first-person interpretation has been raging ever since the method first appeared. Its detractors argue that the attempt to re-create the past is quixotical, misleading, incomplete, inaccurate, lopsided, rude, embar-rassing, nostalgic, phony, too entertaining or theatrical, too shockingly unlike the present, or alternately, too homogeneous with the present.[8] Its champions counter that it is thought provoking, educational, multisensory, emotion in-voking, appealing, entertaining, useful to academic inquiry, and fun.[9] Others are in the middle of the road, weighing equally its benefits and drawbacks.[10]

Many challengers voiced legitimate complaints, but first-person's defenders have strong arguments, too. Over the past two decades, first-person interpre-tation has had some time to "grow up," to become more refined in its tech-niques, historical integrity, and "visitor friendliness."

One of the first problems in discussing the critical literature of first-person is confusion over vocabulary. Meaning must be inferred from context rather than actual usage. Often, writers use the term "living history" when they really mean "first-person interpretation." Occasionally it is unclear whether writers are referring to one or the other.

Rich Sokup portrays Stephen Douglas in a 1994 re-creation of the Lincoln-Douglas debates.
(courtesy Rich Sokup)

A storm of debate followed in the wake of the publication of two books by Jay Anderson: *Time Machines* in 1984 and *The Living History Sourcebook* in 1985.[11] Anderson — whose writings encompass third-person, first-person, historical archaeology, hobbyist reenactment, literature, and film — suggests that living history serves three purposes: as a way that museums can teach about the past, as a research tool, and as a hobby. Anderson believes that experimentation with historical simulation is "one of our generation's contributions to the field of history (and ultimately to society)" and that it is successful because it incorporates our society's traditional methods of cultural expression (including ritual, ceremony, pageant, folkways, theater, games, sport, festivals, and celebration) in a way that is playful, experimental, and memorable.[12]

David Glassberg blasted *Time Machines*, via a book review in *American Quarterly*, for not asking "tough questions" about "living history," using that term to refer to first-person interpretation more often than not. He criticized Anderson for ignoring issues such as the relationship between living history and other forms of historically themed popular entertainment, or the impact of business values and corporate (or government) sponsorship on the presentation of content. Glassberg also chastised Anderson for failing to question why living history appealed to certain ethnic groups more than others, how it served or reflected present social and political concerns, and the significance of the types of demonstrations most commonly exhibited.[13]

In Anderson's defense, *Time Machines* was a broad introduction to the entire living history movement rather than a searching investigation into its sociocultural implications, and first-person was not the focus of the work. Glassberg did, however, raise important questions that could form the core of an entirely new study about late twentieth-century uses of the past, encompassing phenomena such as the Bicentennial, reenactments, the emergence of minority history, the popularity of the Civil War, and living history museums. I hope that Glassberg himself is planning to undertake such a project as a sequel to his insightful *American Historical Pageantry: The Uses of Tradition in the Early Twentieth Century.*

David Lowenthal has raised thought-provoking concerns about the impact of living history (including first-person). He reminded readers how the "spell" of the past affects the present and that modern attempts to restore and re-create that past reshape it by inflicting modern aesthetics, tastes, and comforts on it. Lowenthal asked if living history museums mislead the public when they fashion pasts too much (or too little) like the present, conflate time, or are too uniform to one another.[14] Lowenthal also observed that visitors can be offended or appalled at portrayals that are "too authentic." They may become incensed at "misogynistic" or bigoted comments or faint at the sight of a recently butchered animal.[15] This happens occasionally, but not as often as critics would like to think, and the problem is not limited to first-person programs. The confusion stems from many visitors' inexperience with "historical understanding" on one hand and sponsors' inadequate orientation or follow-up on the other. Programmers faced with potentially offensive subject matter have choices: omit sensitive issues from interpretation, present the material with discretion, or support delicate subject matter with solid orientation to minimize misunderstandings.[16]

To be sure, interpretation of the past is shaped by the present, as T. H. Breen has documented so well in his *Imagining the Past: East Hampton Histories.* He demonstrates how historians of successive eras have distilled starkly different messages from the same primary documentation to create patriotic, nostalgic, religious, and economic meanings. We would fool ourselves if we thought we did not do the same. History is not "the past." It is an interpretation of the past, ever shifting because our uses for it change. We would have to abandon the entire practice of history if we allowed guilt over our inability to uncover the absolute truth to dismay us.

Edward Alexander suggests that roleplaying, in certain cases, restricts minorities (as well as women) to a proscribed variety of roles or leaves them out of the picture entirely.[17] He has a good point. Race- and gender-specific casting do present serious employment limitations, as they do in theater and film. Since Alexander wrote that criticism, more programs that feature women and minorities have been launched. However, that still leaves countless sites with limited casts of characters that preclude any pan-ethnic representation if first-person is the sole interpretive technique, unless race-blind casting is permitted.

John Fortier, who, in general, supports living history, condemns the interactive form of first-person[18] interpretation, preferring instead fourth-wall vignettes and scenarios. When he was the superintendent of Fortress Louisbourg in Nova Scotia in the 1970s, he felt that the first-person approach led to visitor confusion and convoluted the message of the museum. Unfortunately, the shortcomings of first-person at Fortress Louisbourg probably had more to do with the mechanics of the infant program and the approach of its interpreters, rather than the medium. Visitors' first contact with roleplay was an *unexpected* challenge at the front gate by "soldiers" who put them on the defensive and made them uneasy.[19]

Fortier also feels that first-person entertains rather than educates, that it is too difficult to do well (many quality programs contradict both charges), and that the average visitor is not up to the verbal parley with interpreters. He does, however, raise valid concerns about the ethical obligations in re-creating someone's life.[20] *Past into Present* will, I hope, dispel the persistent belief that first-person *has* to make visitors uncomfortable or place them under a burden. A skilled roleplayer knows how to manipulate the interaction so that those who wish to participate may do so comfortably while others may contentedly watch.

Critics contend that first-person (when compared with third-person) places a heavier burden on visitors, who must figure out the rules of participation for themselves.[21] They may be intimidated or shy about asking questions. I maintain that proper orientation and perceptive interpretation can circumvent discomfort. The focus of interpretation should be on the interpreter and his or her presentation, not on the visitors. The interpreter, like a skilled winter fisherman, should quickly break through the ice and perceptively cast out hooks and bait that will be eagerly pursued by quarry.

Indeed, first-person is more demanding of staff than other types of interpretation and more difficult than third-person to present effectively. It requires interpreters to know their historical information, technical processes, and a vast range of peripheral facts. It requires more research, training, and authentic detailing than third-person. It demands proficiency at communication, teaching, and (frequently) theatrical skills.[22] It can only be as good as its interpreters. But is the requirement for specialized interpretive skills any more of a drawback than the need for curators or exhibit designers to possess specific qualifications for their positions?

Tom Sanders observed that certain groups of visitors, including the physically and mentally handicapped, youngsters under nine or ten years old, senior citizens, and foreign visitors, may have difficulty with first-person.[23] These groups present challenges, as they do with other forms of interpretation, because their special needs require programs that are designed specifically for them. Seniors, I might add, have become less of a problem audience since the days when first-person was new. Today they are well traveled, sophisticated, and energetic, and they are not afraid to add their own two-cents' worth to a conversation. Nevertheless, interpreters have developed ways to include young and special visitors into general programming, particularly with the use of multisensory and hands-on involvement. Many of these techniques will be revealed later in the text.

In his 1988 article in *History News*, David Peterson, curator of the Otter Tail County Historical Society in Fergus Falls, Minnesota, called for the practitioners of first-person interpretation[24] to face their "flaws." He criticized Jay Anderson and others for not realizing the limitations of their medium. Peterson complained that historical re-creation was fruitless and imperfect, inadequate at interpreting complex and controversial topics such as slavery and domestic violence, and too removed from historical realities such as poor diet and harsh living conditions. Peterson, too, scolded the adherents of first-person interpretation for not addressing its ramifications.[25]

Ken Yellis penned "Real Time" as a rebuttal to David Peterson. Over subsequent revisions it became less rebuttal and more theory about the practice of first-person as developed at Plimoth. Yellis reminded the critics that few practitioners of living history or first-person claim that it is the "best" way to teach history, as the detractors have so often insinuated.[26] Even John Fortier noted that most of the hype about "stepping back in time" comes from promoters and the media rather than interpreters.[27]

Most recently, Kevin Walsh condemned first-person interpretation as an approach that "falls short of competent history, which should be concerned with contrasting the past with the present."[28] Proponents of first-person agree that past-present comparisons are difficult to incorporate and that the line between fact and conjecture cannot be delineated as it can in third-person.[29] Even first-person supporter Ken Yellis draws attention to the misinformation generated when interpreters are asked about out-of-place architectural features and other inaccuracies in the physical site.[30]

Walsh's comments prompt the larger question, "Is first-person interpretation 'history'?" Dr. John Krugler, associate dean of the Department of History at Marquette University, has thoughtfully pondered this question, surmising that first-person is a unique form of history, but more akin to historical fiction or historical drama than the academic form.[31] While first-person should incorporate scholarly methods, it differs from academic history because its audience is fundamentally different. Therefore it must have popular appeal and age appropriateness. Certainly, as Krugler notes, many presentations assume the appearance of drama. However, many interpreters employ a participatory-Socratic rather than a dramatic approach, actively "teaching" history. The relationship of first-person and drama will be discussed later in more detail.

Advocates of roleplaying admit that the method is not everyone's cup of tea. However, this particular form of leisure learning remains popular among many history buffs, tourists, and teachers. Educator Charles C. Cole Jr. summed up the feeling of most first-person enthusiasts when he wrote, "A program in which the past is re-created in the present is not a substitute for reading good history. But one's understanding of history can be enhanced by doing more than merely reading about it. One may discover more dramatically those values associated with past cultures by participating in a living history project."[32]

The practitioners of first-person interpretation are more aware of its limitations than anyone else, critics included. Tom Vance's piece for the Association for Living Historical Farms and Agricultural Museums is a good example. It emphasizes the pitfalls as well as the benefits of the medium. Vance does not claim that roleplaying is a panacea, but it is one of many teaching tools that can enliven the study of history.[33]

To those who emphasize the imperfections of first-person and accuse it of quixoticism, why not gaze into the mirror?[34] What medium can completely portray the past? None. Not books, not film, not guided tours, not even multimedia exhibits can produce an unbiased, true-to-life, compelling product that will appeal universally to all learning styles or leisure proclivities. That is why many of first-person's supporters advocate the liberal use of complementary interpretive media.

Critics' claim that first-person does not portray unpleasant and controversial topics was once true, but no longer. Conner Prairie, Plimoth, and Old Bethpage Village (in Old Bethpage, N.Y) conduct funerals. Colonial Williamsburg portrays slave life, including the recent portrayal of slaves on the auction block. Outcast characters such as Conner Prairie's Baker family, Plimoth's Billingtons, and Washburn Norlands's (Livermore, Maine) local indigent, Mercy Lovejoy, are conspicuous residents in museum "communities." Old Sturbridge Village depicts alcoholism, and interpreters at Mystic Seaport Museum (Mystic, Conn.) castigate Irish immigrants. In fact, from what I gathered from my informants, there is almost no topic that is so taboo that it will not be discussed if a visitor is willing to inquire about it.[35]

Ken Yellis recognizes that first-person sites appeal to visitors who like to think for themselves. While no form of interpretation is free from bias, participants at a first-person program such as Plimoth Plantation's must shape their own opinions. They play detective. They are presented with a less pedantic version of "the facts" as they roam at will and ask questions, fitting together the pieces of the puzzle. Information is absorbed affectively as well as cognitively. The senses and the emotions, as well as the intellect, are an integral part of the experience.

Little is known about the implications of teaching history through historical simulation, a topic that calls for more balanced and reasonable study. Assessment of long-term learning is difficult at best, complicated by the varied backgrounds and learning styles of visitors. A common feature of historic site evaluation is to test visitor recall of facts and themes. But are factual details of primary importance to visitors? While accurate information is crucial for the presenters, audiences tend to absorb only those "facts" that are directly related to personal interests. Sensory, social, and emotional components of a visit have a far more lasting impact.[36]

In her thesis "An Oral History of a Field Trip: A Study of Participants' Historical Imagination in 'Action' and 'Artifact within Action,'" educator Vicki Ann Green collected the memories of her former students' field trips to Barkerville, a Canadian living history site that featured first-person roleplay. The students, fully a decade after their visit, recalled with enjoyment "knowing the characters" of Barkerville because they conveyed a sense of story about the place. They remembered the anxiety of panning for gold with the miner, the realism of the disagreement between the miner and the carpenter over claim jumping, the nervousness of pleading a case before "Judge Begbie," and the excitement of meeting personalities they had studied in class. Green said that one theme came out again and again in her interviews: a feeling of emotional involvement and connection with the past, which was stimulated by activity and immersion in the simulated environment. Green's study underscored the special nature of learning at living history sites: tangible experiences and environments breathe life into the abstract concepts read in books and taught in classrooms.[37]

Several sites have conducted evaluations of their first-person programs. While results reflect positive opinions by the public and indicate that short-term learning and new understandings of history occur in the minds of visitors, it is still impossible to judge the medium as a whole. Studies such as Green's, in which visitors are interviewed after a period of time has elapsed,

Youngsters at the Old Barracks Museum summer camp spend one week experiencing eighteenth-century life. Camper Peter Nagy (far left) repeated camp several times and eventually "went native."
(photo: Stacy Roth, courtesy Old Barracks Museum)

will be crucial for estimating the long-term impact of first-person. New questions must probe for deeper meanings. Does first-person stimulate further interest in history or related subjects? Do people seek out other roleplay experiences? Do programs alter previously held perceptions of the past, or are they simply enjoyable social events with little impact on historical awareness?

Existing program evaluations do not elaborate on the quality of interpreters' presentation skills, yet visitor reaction is inescapably related to the talent and ability of the interpreters themselves. At the Old Barracks Museum (Trenton, N.J.), for example, many teachers schedule their class trips for days when specific roleplayers are slated for duty, and evaluation responses frequently include praises for the ability of particular staff members to enliven the past for their students.[38] References to individual interpreters were prominent in visitors' statements for Colonial Williamsburg's "Becoming Americans" theme evaluation.[39] In the Canadian Museum of Civilization's study, the skill of the "actors" was the most common reason for watching a presentation through to its conclusion, illuminating the importance of interpreter prowess in attracting and holding a transient crowd.[40]

First-person interpretation is a popular form of history lesson that is here to stay. Its practitioners continually seek to improve its effectiveness as a teaching method and an accurate reflection of the past. First-person has weaknesses, but it also has strengths. There will always be topics it cannot cover, visitors that are not well served by it, and people who just do not care for it. That is the price we pay for a medium that is exciting, alive, and effective for many audiences. Identification of drawbacks is the first step toward mediating them. Later chapters will translate many of these drawbacks into communication challenges that must be overcome by interpreters if first-person is to be engaging and accessible to the widest possible audience.

{3}

Development of First-Person Interpretation

First-person interpretation did not spring up fully grown of its own accord. At historic sites it evolved as a logical extension of its predecessors, which included craft demonstrations, costumed third-person interpretation, and historical pageantry. Its pedagogic roots go back to the Williamsburg-inspired re-creations of the mid-twentieth century, the first "natural" arrangements of artifacts in the period rooms of the Essex Institute in Salem, Massachusetts, and the open-air museums of nineteenth-century Europe, most notably Skansen, in Sweden.[1] The reenactment of historical behavior, however, goes back to time immemorial. It is the stuff of religious rites and of nationalistic propaganda, the soul of social custom, the heart of theater, and a refuge for the nostalgic and those out of synch with their own time.[2]

The current burst of energy in today's living history museum movement grew out of the desire for a more accurate, holistic way of presenting a history that went beyond the lives of the rich and famous to include the disenfranchised. The movement accompanied an outgrowth of scholarship in the 1960s that centered on the history and culture of ordinary people, guided by an influx of "new social historians" such as Cary Carson and James Deetz into the museum field.[3] Complementing this burst of pro-proletarian enthusiasm, new generations of museum-goers became increasingly interested in the history of everyday people.[4] The trend gathered strength from the founding of the Association for Living Historical Farms and Agricultural Museums in 1970. The association's national and regional conferences and publications serve as a forum for exchange and debate among museum professionals and others who use living history. One of its specialized subcommittees serves the interests of first-person interpreters.[5]

First-person interpretation had more than one birthplace. Its techniques developed within the National Park Service (NPS) and the private museum world. A few NPS sites began to animate their programs with third-person costumed staff as early as the mid-1930s, with the practice becoming fashionable in the 1960s.[6] First-person interpretation was incorporated as early as the late 1960s, according to ranger reminiscences and the appearance of handbooks that provided advice on its execution. During the early 1970s the park service produced two manuals on living history demonstrations (which included roleplaying) aimed at its own historic sites and their interpreters. The first, William Kennon Kay's *Keep It Alive! Tips on Living History Demonstrations* (1970), stressed qualities that are still considered sound today: accuracy, a broad knowledge base, assimilation of a worldview, ability to tie demonstrations to larger economic and social issues, and concern for visitor needs and interests.

Four years later the NPS introduced Gordon Hilker's *The Audience and You: Practical Dramatics for the Park Interpreter*. Hilker advocated a much more theatrical approach than did Kay. He suggested hiring professional writers, selecting dramatic backgrounds with dramatic lighting, practicing dialogue and blocking, including song and dance, and choosing simple themes over complex ones. While not all of Hilker's advice was bad (some degree of theatricality or awareness of theatrical technique *is* necessary in good interpretation), the work seemed like a step backward in the development of realistic interpretation. Another hindrance to realism in those early days arose from the agency's concern with maintaining a clean-cut family image (evident in both Kay and Hilker), which precluded the presentation of controversial material or even an understarched appearance.

In the 1980s the NPS discontinued many of its first-person presentations, citing expense, high staff turnover, and public discomfort as key reasons.[7] In many cases it was a wise decision, since a quality first-person program requires ongoing support and continuity. Morristown National Historical Park, for instance, relied on first-person as a standard feature of its program during the 1970s and 1980s, but the park has since sidelined it to an occasional feature. But first-person is far from dead in the NPS. Several sites have continued successful programs, including Chatham Manor in Fredricksburg (Va.), Gettysburg National Military Park (Pa.), and Appomattox Court House (Va.).[8]

In 1990 the NPS produced another guide to living history presentations, this one by Temple University speech professor Donald H. Ecroyd. Ecroyd developed what Kay had begun in 1970, focusing on the importance of good interpreter/visitor communication, the necessity of setting objectives and goals, and recommendations for careful evaluation for both the staff and the site. Ecroyd continued the NPS preference for clear themes and simplicity rather than "too much detail."[9] The idiosyncrasies of seasonal staffing and the nature of federal budgets strengthen the park service's rationale for keeping it simple. Conversely, private museums such as Plimoth, Colonial Williamsburg, and Sturbridge Village, while also employing themes as an intellectual focus, prefer to immerse the visitor in richness of detail: lots of objects, offbeat as well as pertinent information, and variety.

While the NPS reduced the scale of first-person programming, other sites developed its techniques even further. Private museums picked up where the park service left off. Sometimes the tail wagged the dog. At places such as Plimoth and Old Sturbridge Village, the interpretive staffs began experimenting with roleplaying techniques independent of any administrative prompting. It became fashionable among interpreters to dress as authentically as possible, to speak in dialects, and to compile background documentation that substantiated interpretation. At Conner Prairie, which adopted first-person around the same time as Plimoth, the impetus to institute first-person was an early administrative decision.[10]

Plimoth Plantation took the lead in comprehensively developing, implementing, and disseminating the theory and practice of first-person interpretation. Staff were inspired by the leadership and active scholarship of archaeologist James Deetz and historian David Freeman in the late 1960s and early 1970s.[11] Several interpreters experimented with dialects and dramatizations of historical scenes, which in turn evolved into improvised dialogue or roleplaying.[12] By 1977, staff member Robert Marten had developed methods for training interpreters in the new techniques. In 1978 the museum officially decided to rely on first-person as its sole form of interpretation in the Pilgrim Village. The final say came not from Deetz but from his successor, Thomas A. Young, who moved from the position of director of exhibits to assistant director.[13] Deetz's writings at the time seem to indicate that the new method was well entrenched when he departed: "It occurred to us that the live interpreters ought to be re-creations at Plimouth [sic], too. We had them speak in period dialect, which we were able to research, in the first person. At that point the visitors became interpreters, and we started calling the interpreters 'cultural informants.' It was as if the visitors coming into the exhibit were anthropology fieldworkers going in to experience a community and elicit from it what they could."[14]

However, according to John Kemp, current director of interpretation,

Deetz actually doubted that a total first-person program could work success-fully. On a recent visit to the plantation, Deetz was pleasantly amazed to see how well it actually turned out.[15] The transition at the museum was not with-out its shake-ups. Many of the old interpreters, uncomfortable with or unable to adapt to the new style of interpretation, left the plantation or changed posi-tions within the museum.[16]

If Plimoth's new interpretation was an electric current, "worldview" was its groundwire. The worldview philosophy, defined by Jim Baker as "the cultur-ally determined perceptual context in which each individual meets the world," was developed in tandem with the new interpretive method at Plimoth and was incorporated into interpreter training as early as 1977. For Plimoth's Pil-grim characters, worldview included knowledge such as Galenic medicine, vernacular architecture, astrology, Ptolemaic cosmology, alchemy, Aristote-lian physics, magic, and early modern social hierarchy. Pilgrim worldview be-came the basis for interpreter dialogue and demeanor and gave staff a set of assumptions on which to formulate their replies to visitors.[17]

Warren Leon and Margaret Piatt reported that Plimoth's early attempts at first-person were not always successful. The talent of the interpreters varied, some visitors were confused, and other visitors felt that interpreters were con-frontational because they did not answer anachronistic questions.[18] At times, some interpreters' methods of portraying true-to-form Pilgrims included re-flecting some of the seventeenth-century Englishman's xenophobia. Ken Yellis refers to this as the "surly pilgrim problem" but contends that surly Pilgrims have always been in the minority.[19] As time progressed, staff developed tech-niques for making visitors more comfortable.[20]

Yellis maintains that converging factors led to the evolution of the first-person program as practiced at Plimoth Plantation today. He identified Plim-oth's clearly defined mission, focus, story line, and intellectual boundaries; commitment to detail, authenticity, and ongoing research; and the develop-ment of interpretive worldview. He also noted the importance of supporting a critical mass of people and things, exclusion from modern distractions, methods for evaluation and criticism, and response to visitor needs.[21]

Another strain of historical character interpretation, the "celebrity mono-logue," developed independently from the museum world. Its roots sprang from theatrically inclined Lyceum and Chautauqua platform speakers of the late nineteenth and early twentieth centuries who introduced dramatic tech-niques to audiences that customarily shunned "scandalous" stage produc-tions.[22] Helen Potter, active in the 1870s and 1880s, presented impressions of popular actors and lecturers performing extracts from plays and well-known speeches. Potter impersonated men as well as women, diligently re-creating their physical, vocal, and sartorial characteristics. Her subjects included Susan B. Anthony, Edwin Booth, Fanny Kemble, and Oscar Wilde.[23] The earliest known Abraham Lincoln impersonator, Ben Chapin, emerged in the 1880s, evoking revulsion from Lincoln's son Robert and awe from Mark Twain.[24]

During the first half of the twentieth century, impersonators such as Cissie Loftus and Dorothy Sands continued the trend with perceptive mimicry of contemporary theater personalities and their famous scenes.[25] Costumed readers such as William Sterling Battis, who animated selections from Dickens's Lyceum lectures and writings, were also popular with audiences.[26] By 1950 such one-person shows had cast aside their association with Chautauqua and were firmly entrenched as theater. Welsh actor Emlyn Williams created stage shows based on interpretations of Dickens's and, later, Dylan Thomas's writings, but although he wore the historically appropriate dress of each author, the stories, not the authors, were the focus for characterization.[27]

One actor in particular, Hal Holbrook, catapulted the popular appeal of historical character portrayals. Holbrook first experimented with the character of Mark Twain in the late 1940s for one segment in a series of historically based vignettes. Early performances featured Holbrook as the great author and Holbrook's wife Ruby as an interviewer. The two-person sketch evolved into a solo act, *Mark Twain Tonight!*, which ultimately made it to Broadway in 1966. Holbrook appeared as a seventy-year-old Twain making the rounds of the lecture circuit, pontificating and reading his own famous writings.[28]

Although *Mark Twain Tonight!* was conceived as a theater piece, one cannot read Holbrook's own account of how he built his dramatization of Twain without recognizing that he possessed the same sense of mission as a first-person interpreter. The actor spent years developing the character. He studied the author's writings and letters, analyzed secondary accounts, and viewed photographs and videos. He applied makeup and chose props that encouraged audiences' association with Twain and his era. Holbrook the social critic selected material that would not only personify Twain but would echo Holbrook's own agenda — his educational objectives, so to speak — on topics such as racism and environmental pollution. He carefully balanced the timing of humorous and serious material for its greatest impact. *Mark Twain Tonight!* was not a single set script but varied nightly from a repertoire of pieces, much as a storyteller composes a set. The strategy enabled him to tailor each performance to anticipated audience types. In addition, the premise created a situation that placed theatergoers in a comfortable role as an audience rather than as voyeurs intruding on a private scene. Many interpreters, especially those who speak to large groups and auditorium audiences, have adopted this style.

Norman L. Jackson analyzed the success of Holbrook's presentation, attributing it to the actor's coincidental adherence to Aristotle's canons of rhetoric and modes of proof. Holbrook/Twain displayed virtuousness of character through common sense and humor, demonstrated superb mastery over his material and the ability to observe and adapt to his audience, selected topical examples with which listeners could identify, and exuded a natural demeanor. Such characteristics persuaded audiences to embrace Holbrook's (and Twain's) viewpoints — which are, coincidentally, the aims of the traditional rhetorician.[29] It would be interesting to see if other successful portrayals conform to similar parameters. If so, it would help to explain why this form of character interpretation enjoys greater commercial success than those where laudable views and persuasion of personal beliefs are not the aim of the character/interpreter.

Because monologue-based interpretation frequently relies on scripting and minimizes audience participation, it is beyond the scope of this book. However, today's first-person interpreters owe Holbrook a debt of gratitude. His excellent performances paved the way for the public's — and museum administrators' — acceptance of the simulation of people of the past.

The 1980s found the practitioners of first-person interpretation refining and improving many aspects of the medium. In addition to ongoing efforts to increase accuracy through research,[30] first-person interpreters and their sponsors sought more effective ways of communicating with their visitors (including many of the alternative and spin-off methods discussed in Chapter 2),[31] developed storytelling and scenario techniques, increased the presentation of conflict and controversial issues, and heightened their awareness of the needs of special audiences.

The staff at first-person sites have become increasingly aware of how interpreter behavior affects visitors' experiences. Many realize that positive interaction is crucial to the success or failure of the interpreter/visitor encounter, and ultimately to repeat visitation and future ticket sales. Lisa Whalen, site supervisor at the Pilgrim Village at Plimoth Plantation, recognized a transition in interpretive focus at the site, first on style, then content and, more recently, on visitor contact. "In trying to improve interpreter training in communication & visitor empathy," she says, "we have been moving away from a theater/entertainment or an educational model towards a business/sales model." She cited the "Filene's Five" (after the Boston department store) as an example of such thinking: "Meet them, greet them, assess their needs, meet their needs, ask them back again."[32]

One manifestation of this shift is the incorporation of interpersonal communication topics into interpretive training. Plimoth's "sensitive '90s" innovation is the staff's annual viewing of *If Looks Could Kill: The Power of Behav-*

ior, produced by Video Arts, Inc., a humorous film on interpersonal relations in the business world. Its message, "behavior breeds behavior," has inspired more than a few "Pilgrims" to adopt a sympathetic view of the visitor and make special efforts to ensure that visitors have a positive experience.[33]

"Scenarios" are another popular development at museums since the 1980s.[34] These flexible pods of performance provide structure to highlighted themes. Scenarios have also been embraced as a way of enlivening standard interpretation or static exhibits by sites where most programming is not in first-person. They vary in size from one-person sketches to large productions and in format from tightly scripted to outlined to improvisational. The subjects are as diverse as the sites. Examples include town meetings, court hearings, slave life, celebrations, animal auctions, and even murder mysteries.[35]

The field of interpretation has witnessed significant breakthroughs since the mid-1980s through the incorporation of sensitive and controversial topics, portrayals of formerly overlooked populations such as minorities and the poor, and deeper insights into the private lives of historical people. These days, interpreters openly discuss slavery, alcoholism, domestic quarrels, sex, death, and a plethora of other issues absent from living history museums in the 1960s and 1970s. The emergence of this material is due to the influence of new social history and the public's willingness to accept and even embrace proletarian history and "myth-busting." The movement counteracts living history critics' well-founded complaints of museums as "peaceable kingdoms." Unquestionably, there are topics that remain too sensitive to broach with certain (or even most) audiences, and there are still many visitors who cling to a nostalgic view of the past and do not take readily to such innovations.[36] Nevertheless, an unromanticized view of history legitimizes rather than trivializes first-person programs.

The art of storytelling has also inventively worked its way into the repertoire of many interpreters, though it tends to be more naturalistic and less stylized than traditional festival and library presentations. Storytelling is a universal form of communication, used in a variety of situations from formal tale-telling to teaching to normal conversation. As lexicographer/humorist Leo Rosten wrote in his classic *The Joys of Yiddish*, a good story is "an excellent pedagogic peg on which to hang a point."[37] First-person interpreters comb primary sources such as diaries, letters, journals, and newspapers to create their story lines. Anecdotes are related in an incidental, conversational fashion in keeping with one's character. Mystic Seaport Museum embraced storytelling as its primary style of roleplaying during the 1980s, a tradition that continues to this day.[38] Although skilled storytelling requires practice and a degree of inborn talent, it is a relatively simple process to transform contemporary writings into anecdotes.

Another growing area of concern among interpreters is how to meet the needs of visitors with handicaps. First-person sites, in particular, are challenged to find workable compromises between historical accuracy and accessibility for those with limitations. Interpreters find that the interactive, hands-on aspects of living history sites lend themselves to serving the disabled. Recent "consciousness raising" has inspired individual interpreters to surmount communication problems associated with handicaps.

First-person has indeed grown and changed since its early days. The innovations of the 1980s and 1990s have transformed it into a more potent and "spectator-friendly" medium. Looking back on the past few decades of its development, three fundamental elements for successful programming are clearly recognizable: purposeful planning and research, thorough character development, and strategies and techniques for audience-appropriate interaction.

Foundations for Historical Roleplaying

Before Interpretation Starts
Planning, Research, and Development

Proper planning, thorough research, and adequate training and preparation are essential to interpretive success. Planning begins with the assessment of academic, physical, and human resources, educational goals, and intended audience. The focus year, basic themes and issues, fictional or historical characters who will illustrate the story, material requirements, and logistics are built on — and consistently refer back to — such foundations.

Likewise, individual interpreters must anticipate and plan their personal strategies. Interpreters need a repertoire of ideas, activities, stories, and skills that fulfill program objectives and create a deeper understanding of the historical era for the visitor. These are developed from research materials and the ability of interpreters to draw from primary and secondary sources to create dialogue and activity.[1] Museums and sites must establish a training system to indoctrinate efficiently a large staff and new employees in historical background and related skills. It is particularly important to make research materials available in a convenient format that will promote consistency, highlight important information, and reduce duplication of effort.

For independent interpreters, preparation and training habits vary, but most read widely on their eras, amassing walls full of books and cabinets full of files. Of those who perform without set scripts, some speak entirely extemporaneously, some draw up outlines, and others write examples of dialogues. Many immerse themselves in reference materials in the days before a performance. Some feel that they must spend months working on a character before its debut, and others trot them out on short notice.

Obviously, each program has a unique set of variables that drive decision making. David Emerson[2] and I, as freelance duo History on the Hoof, begin each new project by establishing educational goals and selecting characters that both represent a body of historical viewpoints and suit the range of personalities that we can portray convincingly. Next we draw up a rough outline of what we plan to say and do, perform the necessary research that uncovers real anecdotes and provides a historically valid framework, work up a final outline, and estimate our clothing and prop needs. We find it helpful to sketch out life histories of our characters and to compose sample conversations. As we become comfortable with the program, the amount of improvisation increases. Like a Native American stew that adds new ingredients to the old, our programs evolve as new information and fresh anecdotes season the existing pot.

Good interpreters anticipate a variety of visitor behavior and are prepared to direct their activities in an appropriate direction.[3] With on-the-job experience a predictable range of visitor interests and reactions become apparent. Seasoned interpreters usually have a storehouse of surefire techniques that stimulate expected responses. Such tricks are especially handy when stamina is flagging or as counterweights to experimental interpretation.

In programs with more than one character, participants should meet regularly to discuss and coordinate their ideas. Not only is this essential for keeping story line details consistent and improving logistics, but it is conducive to the creation of new ideas. Brainstorming sessions are a great way to stimulate group dynamics, too. (It is helpful to record and distribute meeting notes to recollect suggestions and decisions.) Such sessions create a forum for coordinating common topics of conversation. Take, for example, the interpreters at Lincoln Log Cabin who were abuzz with the news of a neighbor's barn that had burned down. Visitors could hear how each member of the community reacted to the incident and assemble the story from the different perspectives.[4] By thrashing through ideas beforehand, interpreters become familiar with the views of other characters, pick up new ideas, and reinforce what they already know.

It is always helpful for ensemble interpreters to corroborate the "facts" of their selected stories or the gist of the day's interpretation with other characters shortly before performance time. At Old Sturbridge Village, Parsonage roleplayers often spend the first half-hour of the day discussing what their characters are "doing."[5] The staff of Plimoth's Pilgrim Village also holds a short morning meeting to discuss logistics, such as which household is under-stationed for the day and requires periodic character visitors, or to coordinate specific activities that must be completed, such as milking the cows.

Ken Yellis, Tom Vance, and other writers have suggested criteria for first-person programs at living history sites.[6] The following list of principles is inspired by these earlier writings:

Appropriateness and purpose. Programs should dovetail institutions' missions, educational and interpretive goals, and topical focus. Interpretive efforts should be structured around — but not limited to — specific goals and objectives that will shape the visitor's experience.

Interest potential. Programs' subjects should bubble with good story lines and/or themes that help to focus the direction of interpretation and research[7] and are likely to draw public interest.

Sufficient documentation. Adequate primary and secondary source materials should support programming. Interpretation should be grounded in documentation, ensuring historical validity.[8] Internalization of a well-researched seventeenth-century worldview, for example, helps Plimoth interpreters construct reasonable conjectural replies to questions that have no absolute answer.[9]

Institutional dialogue. A productive relationship between personnel of various responsibilities (such as interpreting, researching, marketing, or curating) is crucial to coherent and harmonious programming.

Suitable setting, costume, and working equipment. Environments should support first-person activities. Vance, Yellis, and Fortier contend that the ideal living history setting should be as historically pristine as possible. Of course, such perfection is often unaffordable or unattainable. Interpreters and planners have devised methods, such as ghost interpretation, for coping with inherited site anachronisms. However, such techniques will not work effectively in all situations. Surprisingly, though, when programs are performed in completely foreign settings such as gallery spaces and classrooms, anachronisms hardly matter because the focus is on the interpreters and not on the surroundings.

Training. A system for indoctrinating new interpreters should be in place. Source documentation and synthesized informational materials should be readily available to interpreters via libraries, reference files, and training manuals. Training should include historical information, suggestions for first-person interpretive techniques, educational learning theory, technical skills, especially pertinent documentary evidence, and site rules and regulations.

Orientation. Visitors must be incorporated into the programmatic matrix with as little confusion as possible. Brochures and pre-encounter media should acquaint newcomers with the first-person premise and suggest ways to "play along." Within the program, there should be obvious clues that emphasize visitors' roles.

Balance. Program personnel must establish an equilibrium between educational goals and visitors' interests and preconceived expectations. Interpreters should not be so intent on pushing their own agenda that they miss opportunities for revelation. Institutions should know the characteristics and needs of their audiences.

Muse factor. There should be methods for stimulating visitors to think about historical change and its causes and consequences, either from within the program or by incorporating supporting interpretive services such as third-person closure or post-visit activities.

Evaluation procedures. A system for evaluating the staff, the program, and visitor response should be part of a strategy for ongoing improvement.

Perpetual commitment. Once a program is initiated, it requires ongoing research, staffing, training, and upkeep of material resources.[10] A means for maintaining high standards of accuracy and attention to detail in both verbal and physical presentation is essential.

Freelance interpreters often work without a fixed site, performing in so many different formats and venues that it is difficult to generalize the elements for success. As with any type of interpretive endeavor, independents' programs should be appropriate and meaningful to their audiences, inspire personal learning and discovery, possess historical validity, and appear interesting and cohesive as presentations.

Many of the criteria suggested above for living history sites also apply to freelance individuals and small groups. Freelancers can be compared to sites in miniature, with similar concerns over resources, documentation, and audiences. Their entrepreneurial nature also demands quality, reliability, and flexibility. While independents often have more freedom than institutions, they must justify their fees with top-quality performances, they must be accountable for showing up promptly and delivering as promised, and they must be willing to make occasional program adjustments to achieve compatibility with their sponsors or address special requests. In any contract situation, both parties must discuss what the hiring institution expects from the freelancer and what the contractee can deliver. From a marketing standpoint, a well-defined program or presentation is much easier to describe — and sell — to potential clients.

There are common questions that all planners need to ask themselves when developing a new program: Who is the audience? What do we want them to know about our characters, era, and theme? What methods will work successfully with a particular audience? If the focus of the presentation is a famous character, which anecdotes best illustrate that person's life? If the focus is a theme, what type of character(s) and stories will best personify it? How much will the audience participate and how can we involve those who do? How do we work out the logistics of prop use or demonstrations? Are pre-visit or preparatory materials needed? How comprehensively should a topic be covered and how much background information needs to be included in the presentation?

The research needs of first-person programs are wide ranging, yet research is not an end in itself. It must be organized in formats that interpreters can easily use, such as training manuals, character profiles, research reports, and research briefs. Training materials should suggest not just what but *how* concepts can be incorporated into interpretation.[11]

Interpreters can often pinpoint information that they need on the front lines. They should not be overlooked when developing training resources and should be encouraged to collect information that augments the existing canon. No matter who produces the research materials, sites should set requirements for documentation so that sources are traceable.[12] Mystic Seaport Museum, for instance, has a card system and controlled list of topic headings that standardize interpreter research and footnoting.

Training systems vary widely from site to site.[13] Some sites run intensive blocks of classes, others hold sporadic meetings, and still others rely on manuals and self-training. The process, of course, never ends but is ongoing, much of it taking place on the job and through additional reading. Ideally, training should include at least the following elements: immersion in site and period history, geography, and culture (including plenty of exposure to primary sources); examination of main concepts for interpretation; development of technical skills; character development (including speech and deportment, if applicable); interpretive and communication techniques; site rules and regulations; a full tour of the entire site, including offices and personnel; and role-play practice. In addition, each site will have a variety of topics and skills that are specific to its programs. Some sites, for instance, will add training sessions in religion, trades, domestic skills, child raising, period perspective, or ethnic culture. (For more topic examples, see Appendix 2.) As a program acquires veteran interpreters, training should be expanded to accommodate advanced skills. Eventually, parts of the training may need to be directed at newcomers or veterans only.

Every site should make an interpreter's manual available to its staff. The manual (or manuals) should be well organized, clear, concise, and indexed. It should contain information that relates directly to the site and the program, consisting of summarized information rather than lengthy reports and photocopied journal articles. (The latter belong in easily accessible research files and bound collections). Tom Vance suggests that a manual should include general information on the program; background on the site and its development; information on the site's characters and their history; information on interpretive skills, dialects, clothing, crafts, and activities; and other information pertaining to site and period history. Actual manuals from sites with first-person programs include some of the elements suggested by Vance, plus time lines, bibliographies, maps, theme lists, scenarios, subject information reports and memos, first-person philosophy, calendars of contemporary and seasonal events, lists of prices, and warm-up and rehearsal exercises.[14] In addition, many site interpreters, ever inquisitive, will add supplemental material to their manual.

Rehearsals benefit interpreters who roleplay infrequently or who do extended monologues or dialogues. They are also useful for perfecting dialects and as preparations for programs in which timing and partial scripting are prominent. Interpreters who work on the front lines five days per week say that on-the-job experience itself eliminates the need for rehearsal and warm-up. Claire Gregoire and Betty Frew confided that the Old Sturbridge Village staff rehearses its nonscripted roleplay very little. Conscious attempts at rehearsal, they related, usually end up stiff and self-conscious. The visitors, Claire added, are necessary to create energy. Sometimes, though, staff warm up with roleplaying just before visitors arrive. Their impending presence adds the nervous tension that a planned rehearsal lacks.[15] Nevertheless, rehearsals are laboratories where interpreters can experiment with new ideas before committing to them. Scenarios and scenes should be well "talked through" if not rehearsed. Dialects should be perfected before springing them on the public. Plimoth Plantation interpreters re-create over a dozen dialects from four dialect areas of England plus several other European locales. During training periods, each dialect group rehearses separately. The challenge comes when an interpreter uses one dialect while a coworker speaks in another.

Margaret Piatt and Dale Jones recommend opening rehearsals with vocal and physical exercises that extend tonal range, bring out expressive qualities in the voice, and loosen up the body, such as muscle and back relaxers, shoulder shrugs, head rolls, facial exercises, voice projection, and vocal range warm-ups.[16] Theater games and improvisational exercises help interpreters improve spontaneity, stimulate creative thinking, and promote effective movement and emotional expression, especially when combined with group brainstorming tactics.[17] At a workshop at the March 1991 Union of Spirits Conference for Interpreters at the Farmers' Museum in Cooperstown, New York, Margaret Piatt led participants through an exercise in which a newspaper clipping was transformed into a roleplay presentation by analyzing the story and transforming it into a scene. Donald Ecroyd suggests that it is also helpful to ask friends to play museum visitors at rehearsals.[18] Interpreters can take turns doing this, too, but they need to refrain from playing "the visitors from hell."

Although most of the historic site interpreters interviewed admitted that they rarely rehearsed or ran through vocal exercises immediately before meeting the public, many of them "psyche up" right before the visitors appear, much the same way an actor gets into a role. Some of this prepping includes reciting in dialect, internalizing the personality of the character, reflecting on the character's past, or simply thinking about what one is going to say and do.

When Chris Creelman of Old Sturbridge Village, who portrays actress Fanny Kemble, is anticipating her entrance, she "recalls" notable events in her character's life and imagines an "incident" that "occurs" just before the interpretive story picks up. She warms up by reading primary sources in period dialect, practicing period phrases, and planning appropriate gestures.[19] Sarah Grant Reid, who classifies herself as a "character speaker," presents a variety of one-woman shows featuring unusual famous women (including Madame Tussaud and Empress Josephine). She begins daily rehearsals and visualizations of her programs about a week before an appearance, listening to taped performances and mentally walking through her presentation in her head. She keeps the actual number of run-throughs to a minimum, to conserve her voice and her energy.[20] Rick Jenkinson, Old Sturbridge Village potter, mentally reviews his interpretive story line, assembles his props, and paces back and forth a bit. "I just react to situations, rather than 'act,'" he says.[21]

The ritual of dressing in period clothing has a transforming effect for many. To Eric Olsen of Morristown National Historical Park, slipping on eighteenth-century clothing and shifting into dialect helps him "get psyched."[22] On the other hand, Dave Cloutier of Old Sturbridge Village admits to feeling "a little different" in his "work clothes," but he believes that his knowledge of background information helps him feel more like a nineteenth-century person than does the costume.[23] Perhaps this phenomenon affects those whose costumes are radically different from our modern dress. A set of tight stays or a

Oh what we do for historical accuracy! Stays and corsets, which are not as uncomfortable as they look, affect the posture and mindset of distaff interpreters. (courtesy Plimoth Plantation)

hoop skirt has a much greater impact on the psyche than a loose, flowing shirt and a pair of comfortable trousers.

To summarize, a first-person program requires adequate planning, research, and training before interpreters ever go before the public. Planning should take into account educational goals — and entertainment considerations, where applicable — as well as resources, logistics, and material requirements. Research and training need to be holistic and thorough, encompassing intellectual issues, material requirements, practical considerations, and communication needs. Living history sites and group presentations need to develop a balanced representation of differing perspectives on the site story or program theme. Interpreters should be well prepared with fleshed-out characters, documentable activities, and anecdotes. A substantial portion of program research for first-person interpretation involves character development, the subject of Chapter 7.

Is First-Person Interpretation Theater?

We don't want to *seem* like we're acting.
Lisa Whalen

We want to educate, but if you are boring, what's the point?
Moira Turnan Hannon

I go down there, I dress in clothes I'd never wear anywhere else, talk in a way I
wouldn't talk anywhere else, [and] tell people I believe in things that I think are
wholly full of shit. If that's not acting, I don't know what is.
Larry Erickson

The combined effect of evocative setting and persuasive interpretation can be labeled
dramaturgy, atmospherics, and mise-en-scene. If this is entertainment, it is
entertainment with purpose and coherence, whose elements — focus, bounding,
physical and sensory accuracy, story line, worldview, critical mass — give visitors a
powerful sense that all the pieces fit together, that the presentation is all-
encompassing, coherent, seamless.
Yellis, "Real Time," October 1, 1990

It is an acting job. . . . The performance goes on all day.
Peter Cazaly

I am not an actor and resent being called one.
George Chapman

Raising the subject of the relationship between theater (or entertainment) and
first-person interpretation around a group of interpreters can be as incendiary
as bringing up politics at the dinner table. Interpreters at one end of the spec-

trum consider themselves strictly educators and/or historians; they blanch at any insinuation that they are acting. Those at the opposite pole claim first-person is theater. In the middle are those who describe it as a hybrid that marries history and education with effective performance technique. Discussion of the controversy reveals the considerable scope of first-person styles and the array of opinions on comparisons to theater.

Two scholars, Stephen Eddy Snow and Richard Schechner, have suggested that first-person interpretation is a "form" of theater.[1] Richard Schechner, exploring the "points of contact" between theater and anthropology, pronounced first-person interpretation an environmental theater method, dubbed "restored behavior."[2] Snow, a former interpreter at Plimoth Plantation, drew analogies between interpreters and Stanislavskian[3] actors. He classified first-person, as practiced at Plimoth, as a "new genre of cultural performance," drawing examples from the site's scenario work, special events, and multi-interpreter dialogue as evidence.[4]

Schechner and Snow provided valuable insights into the theater-inspired side of first-person; however, they emphasized extraordinary spectacles and celebrations rather than the ongoing interactions with visitors that comprise the meat and potatoes of day-to-day interpretation. They overlooked or side-stepped interpretive styles that fail to fit a dramatic formula. Commonalities abound between first-person and theater, but some methods of interpretation emphasize alternative strategies and downplay performance.

Admittedly, theater and roleplay converge indecipherably at times. Scenarios, monologues, scripted scenes, event re-creations, and the individual style of many roleplayers do indeed reflect the blurred genre described by Schechner and Snow. The public, too, unfamiliar with the concepts of heritage interpretation, does not distinguish interpretation from performance. Still, it seems theater-centric to proclaim it all "theater."

At least five characteristics define the ultimate timbre of first-person interpretation: the individual style of the interpreter; the format (for example, scripted scenario, monologue, discussion, process demonstration); the passive or active role of the audience; the subject matter; and the venue. The more declamatory the interpreter, the greater the amount of monologue, the larger and more passive the audience, and the less the environment resembles a living setting, the more interpretation blends into theater.

At Plimoth, the bulk of everyday interpretation — the relating of life's more humdrum tasks — is not, in itself, performance-oriented drama when presented by interpreters who are conversational and actively encourage participation from listeners. Some individuals are naturally more dramatic than others, approaching first-person from the theoretical background of drama professionals. Others adopt a pedagogic or incidental style, concentrating on educational, inspirational, and/or communicative aspects more than on conscious characterization. Ideally, skilled interpreters pick and choose from all available techniques, depending on the situation, invoking, for instance, broad projection and movement with a large outdoor group, gentler tactics for more intimate settings.

The more a presentation assumes the appearance of a performance, the less visitors will contribute — they tend to stand back and watch. When there are a lot of visitors, a performer-audience relationship may be preferable. But when the goals of interpretation are to promote participation via thoughtful questions or activities, to encourage involvement, and to reinforce concept comprehension, the interpreter must apply the techniques of many disciplines in concert with dramatic characterization. The presentation must suit the vehicle and its purpose. When a program enjoys the luxury of a large staff, it is beneficial to offer a range of personal styles. A mixture of techniques stimulates a wider array of visitor experiences than a staff that uniformly holds one philosophy.

The similarities between first-person interpretation and theater are many. Both genres reenact human behavior.[5] Both require participants to play someone other than themselves; therefore character development is a common factor. Both are performed before spectators and respond to audience reaction. Each asks viewers to suspend disbelief — at least somewhat — during their experience. Most audiences know they are not really talking to people from the past, yet we hope they play along with the program, just as theatergoers become involved in a play even when they know the ending. And the sequence of preparation, performance, and cooldown — including rehearsal, warmups, getting into character, performance, and post-performance decompression — is frequently shared by both.[6]

Improvisational theater has the most in common with first-person, particularly in spontaneous or planned-but-unrehearsed dialogues and scenarios. Both involve approaching a situation from the skin of a character and interacting with other characters, the environment, and a set of relationships or issues. Dramatic progression is crucial to improvisation when its purpose is entertainment, but it is not uniformly demanded in interpretation. It can give structure and flow to roleplay scenarios, particularly in the portrayal of conflict, where it can keep interpreters from stepping all over each other, wandering verbally, or heading off in unintended directions. A situation such as two women preparing a meal at an open hearth, on the other hand, does not necessarily require breach, crisis, and resolution.

Theater and first-person interpretation often differ in intent and execution.

First-person programs, particularly when associated with a museum or historic site, are usually anchored to an educational message. Skilled presentation and inherent interest are desired, but commercial entertainment value is usually not the primary consideration. Theater, likewise, can be educational and impart socially significant messages, but its criteria for success are weighted differently. An actor is understandably concerned about the quality and believability of his or her performance, but an interpreter, by definition, has a primary responsibility to relay a message.

Traditional theater produces a more polished product. Scripts ensure uniform presentation. Its actors perfect lines and emotions through rehearsal. It demands dramatic focus, peak of action, resolution of plot, and a clear and tidy ending. Sometimes first-person includes one or more of these features, but not as a rule. Some programs are highly structured; others are more organic.

First-person interpretation, in its attempt to mimic real life, does not necessarily have the heightened concern over economy of thought and movement and the adherence to dramatic convention that theater demands. George McCalmon and Christian Moe, in their *Creating Historical Drama: A Guide for the Community and the Interested Individual*, suggest that effective historical drama revolves around dramatic events and characters, situations in which obstacles have been overcome and a significant change takes place among the main characters, and that conflict and decision making are key elements in a story.[7] They contend that while historians have to work with the facts before them, the playwright must consider dramatic focus along with historical accuracy, choosing material that creates a "vivid, meaningful and truthful dramatic experience for an audience."[8] These theories are echoed by Peter Stone and Sherman Edwards, authors of one of my favorite musicals, *1776!*: "To quote a European dramatist friend of ours, 'God writes lousy theater.' In other words, reality is seldom artistic, orderly, or dramatically satisfying; life rarely provides a sound second act, and its climaxes usually have not been adequately prepared for."[9]

Museum theater consultant Mark Giesser also summed up the difficulties of presenting factual history as effective drama: "Good dramatic structure requires the compression and consolidation of details in order to provide focus and power, but it is this very process which can get in the way of communicating scrupulously accurate information. Conversely, emphasis on communicating accurate historical detail often results in dialogue composed largely of laundry lists, boring the audience. The more complex the subject matter, the harder it is to maintain the balance."[10]

Does that make first-person "bad theater"? It can, when open-ended first-person is not suited to its venue and its audience. Dramatic structure and progression are invaluable especially when audiences are large and/or their participation is limited. A framework helps define the message and keeps interpreters from rambling or missing important points.

In first-person interpretation, historical fidelity drives the choice of behaviors. The roleplayer is expected to keep within the limits of documented facts and plausible conjecture, avoiding ingenious or surprising improvisation for the sake of dramatic interest. The ability to sustain such fidelity underscores the need for interpreters to understand history and related subjects.

Interactive first-person of a free-form nature, such as one might encounter walking into a Pilgrim's house in Plimoth, goes beyond the confines of drama if it so chooses, allowing a visitor to "look up the footnotes" of a conversation or explore new topics. While some situations are naturals for dramatic treatment, others are not — and probably do not need to be. Must the goodwife add histrionics while demonstrating and explaining how to prepare a goose for the pot? Would visitors be disappointed if their conversation with her meandered casually into the uses of herbs or how to make cheese? Visitor observation indicates the contrary. And consider this: if interpreters do not adopt foreign-sounding dialects as they do at Plimoth, does the public still perceive task-oriented first-person as theater?

This type of interpretation encourages a much different interaction from its audiences than does theater. Audience response and participation affect mood and energy in both, but first-person commonly adjusts content to visitor interests. Can the same be said of theater?

Authenticity of setting, clothing, and accoutrements also sets first-person apart from theater. Roleplayers often perform with living scenery and fully working props that illustrate historical material culture, whereas in most stage performances the props are visual rather than functional. Activities and reactions take place in real time, regardless of the audience's schedule.[11] The real time of first-person often takes visitors — so accustomed to twentieth-century instant satisfaction — by surprise. For example, some visitors watching brewing or baking activities expect to return in about an hour for a taste when the product is done. They look astonished when the interpreter tells them that the bread won't be ready for hours because it needs to rise, or that the beer requires five weeks to ferment. Year-round immersion in a historical environment makes the historic site interpreter's knowledge more firsthand than that of an actor in a historical drama, so that his or her rationale for actions is based more in fact than feeling, more in experience — however simulated — than imagination. Many actors, of course, realize the value of real-time experience, immersing themselves in situations similar to an unfamiliar new role.

While touching on the subject of education in the context of theater and museum interpretation, it is important to note that roleplaying can be an educational and enlightening process for the practitioners as well as the visitors. Not only do interpreters increase their understanding of the effects of historical events, but they gain insight into the workings of human nature and develop empathy for their predecessors. The practice of first-person, for many, has a humbling effect on one's view of the present. The personal revelations stimulated by physical and mental re-creation of the past are among the most significant benefits of the method. The challenges and demands of first-person contribute to professional motivation in a field with limited monetary rewards. Anthropologists Victor and Edith Turner summed up the emotional value of experimenting with the ethnographic re-creation in an issue of *Drama Review*. To them, it promoted "understanding of how people in other cultures experience the richness of their social existence, what the moral pressures are upon them, what kinds of pleasures they expect to receive as a reward for following certain patterns of action, and how they express joy, grief, deference, and affection, in accordance with cultural expectations." [12]

Despite denials that roleplaying and acting have much in common, certain performance techniques, especially those related to projection and blocking, can improve the quality of interpretation. First-person interpretation certainly loses its effectiveness when, for the sake of flawless "reality," visitors can neither hear what is being said nor see what is going on, or if they feel excluded from the action. Mystic Seaport Museum's training materials encourage selected dramatic maneuvers. Roleplayers are reminded to initiate dialogues with other interpreters at a distance of fifteen feet or more, making obvious the start of a public conversation. During dialogues, they are advised to face visitors partially with an open posture and to employ confidential "asides," creating a sense of welcome involvement. [13]

Admittedly, too much theatricality can make interpretation seem contrived, and surprisingly, even good acting can actually undercut a program's educational message. Kate Stover observed how frequently visitors concentrated on the acting rather than the content. [14] First-person excels at adding an emotional dimension to the presentation of history, but when emoting obliterates the message, it ceases its interpretive purpose. Anyone who enjoys watching skilled actors knows this is a tough problem to solve. Who wants to sabotage something that succeeds, even if for the wrong reasons?

Drama techniques can aid and improve character development. Claire

Gregoire of Old Sturbridge Village, who earned a master's degree in theater arts, believes the study of acting helps interpreters put themselves in role and maintain character. Others, such as Claire's coworker Betty Frew, prefer the "natural" approach: "It's probably a good thing that I don't have a theatrical background — I'd have my head all full of what I should and shouldn't be doing. I do what I'd do if I were in my own home — but in terms of a nineteenth-century person."[15]

Improvisational theater exercises help sharpen roleplayer awareness, quicken the ability to respond to visitors and other interpreters, and improve ensemble interaction. By concentrating on concerns such as building audience interest, resolving conflict — especially when it gets to an uncomfortable level — and maintaining direction during improvisation, interpreters improve the overall cohesiveness of their presentations.

In short, there are a variety of opinions on the relationship between theater and first-person interpretation and the influence of dramatic skill on living history presentations. There is increasing awareness and acknowledgment of the benefits of performance technique for training and character development. But while selected methods improve roleplayer-visitor communication and are well worth incorporating into the canon of interpretive techniques, first-person interpretation cannot be defined wholesale as a subdivision of theater. Even if, as Stephen Snow concluded, it is a blurred genre, it is one mixed from the pigments of many disciplines, among which theater is sometimes dominant and at other times muted.

Developing a Character

Every good character has a legend.
Peter Ryan

What goes into a character?

The characters in a first-person program are the envelope in which the interpretive message is delivered. At historic sites where first-person is a primary exhibit, the variety of characters in a given program should be varied enough to present the spectrum of perspectives composing the site story. Even when identifying and assigning characters is the responsibility of program planners and researchers, the real development falls to the interpreter, since he or she is the one who breathes life into a collection of facts. Independent interpreters who are not tied to specific sites have much more choice in adopting a character. Some choose figures they admire, some select or create a character that underscores a theme, and others establish a persona around an existing skill or available costume. Whatever the case, the roleplayer is the one who thinks for the character — the one who takes two-dimensional information and creates three-dimensional thought and action — and the one who literally interprets the evidence.

Every character needs a history, a personality, and a perspective (or worldview, as it is called at Plimoth). There are two kinds of characters: factual, an individual who once actually existed, or fictional composite, a representative based on selected biographical, cultural, occupational, and other characteristics. Choosing which type to portray depends on the purpose of the program, available documentary evidence, the need to find a good character "fit" for the interpreter, and education and/or entertainment goals.

Fictional characters can be desirable — and more flexible — if the goal is to highlight typical occupations or subcultures rather than specific people. Even so, fictional or semifictional (real people for whom documentation is scanty) characters require histories and personalities, too, and should be compiled from logical circumstances. Composite characters afford advantages such as the opportunity to incorporate existing interpretive skills and the leeway to manipulate a character's past to serve programmatic objectives.

Playing a person who once lived has its particular challenges. Sometimes documentation simplifies the reconstruction of an individual's history and personality. If the subject was famous and prolific, portrayal can be downright daunting. More often so little is known about ordinary lives that details must be pieced together from reasonable conjecture, based on related examples. Many interpreters feel ethically obligated to make every effort to ensure that the words they put in the mouths of those who once walked the earth are truly representative. For John Kemp, director of interpretation at Plimoth Plantation, the words of Pilgrim minister John Robinson, who urged his flock to "daily renew our repentance with our God, special for our sinnes knowne, and generall for our unknowne trespasses," present an ironic double meaning for him and his staff.[1]

Incorporating worldview — a synonym for "past contemporary perspective" or "historical mindset" — can reinforce documentation or support conjecture for both fictional and factual characters. It is impossible to underestimate the importance of developing a worldview. Worldview is the filter through which people view their surroundings, how they navigate their existence. It helps interpreters understand not only what characters are thinking but what they are incapable of thinking.[2]

According to Ken Yellis, "Worldview is the intellectual, emotional, moral, spiritual, perceptual context in which the story is told, the sense the actors made of themselves and the universe in which they acted. Worldview is the almost-totally-unconscious-because-taken-for-granted way of seeing, understanding, speaking, thinking, processing information, adapting to change, and interacting with other people and the physical world, that uniquely characterizes each culture."[3]

This concept can be illustrated by recalling phenomena commonly taken for granted in our own lives, such as indoor plumbing or electric lighting. These now-simple technologies affect an entire chain of attitudes and responses. Electric lights enable us to see despite the darkness outside, prompting us to work through the night or to arrange our furniture with little thought to tripping over it in dim light. Today we light candles in our homes to create a romantic atmosphere, heedless of the need to snip the wick every few minutes or endure the smell of burning animal fat, as did our ancestors. Why do some of us step into the shower every morning? Late twentieth-century standards of cleanliness, indoor heating that prevents a chill, or the sheer pleasure of the water waking up the soul were unthinkable 100 years ago.

Worldview itself is not a totally new concept. Cognitive anthropologists Ward Goodenough and Anthony Wallace promoted related theories in the 1960s. Goodenough suggested that members of a society possessed an internal "mental template" of their culture, which enabled them to negotiate their world successfully. Wallace's "mazeway" theory posited that an individual's cultural behavior is governed by an internal "cognitive map" of social roles.[4]

So what does a first-person interpreter need to know? The first-person interpreter must portray a character — fictional, real, or a combination of both — with depth, validity, and a wide range of knowledge that pertains to his or her world. The best roleplayers can create a believable person out of research, conjecture, and characterization. A well-developed character has a relationship to other characters and economic, social, political, and physical forces.

In the list that follows, I propose a framework for character development based on five spheres of knowledge: personal, local, occupational/domestic, stational, and worldly.[5] In Appendix 2, an expanded version of this outline includes further details and suggestions for conceptualizing personal histories.

Personal sphere includes what a character knows about himself or herself: place of birth, birthdate, immediate family and household relationships, genealogy, residences, education, income, personal habits, personal belongings, sexual habits, personal health, travels, personal events (for example, marriage, crossing the Atlantic, or first job), and personal social skills and traits.

Local sphere is knowledge that a character shares with others of his or her region, neighborhood, or ethnic enclave: local geography, local events past and present, social class (perception of place in the social order), ethnicity, religion and religious customs, neighbors and friends, local people of importance, local economy (how trade and business occur), communication (how one gets his or her news), health and illness (perceptions of, superstitions about, and treatment and maintenance of), speechways, custom of dress, local customs, weights and measures, foodways, deathways, local agriculture, flora and fauna, local weather, and local material culture.

Occupational/domestic sphere encompasses traditional employments that are a main source of income, partial occupations (such as dairying or

Interpreter Chris Hall at both ends of the social spectrum: as the well-connected Isaac Allerton (left) and the notorious John Billington (right). (courtesy Plimoth Plantation)

midwifery), avid interests (such as botany or astronomy), and/or other work that may not be a source of income but may absorb a great deal of the character's time. Housewifery, domestic skills, child rearing, household agriculture, and seasonal tasks are also included here. Within each occupation, its related trades, practices, tools, processes, associations (such as unions, guilds, or professional memberships), wages, prices, terminology, occupational cycles, and sources of raw materials are fodder for consideration.

Stational sphere covers characteristics and habits related to class, including social competencies, cultivated skills (such as dancing, poaching, charm, social ritual, or courtesies), dress and accoutrement, and dining habits.

Worldly sphere addresses awareness of global phenomena and is dependent on the other spheres. It includes world events, well-known figures, world geography, arts, literature, history, science, other religions, other ethnic groups, world economy, trades and occupations, and material culture.

BUILDING A CHARACTER'S PERSONALITY AND LEGEND

First-person gets under the skin of history. Its chief advantage over other interpretive choices centers on its ability to add an emotional dimension to the telling of history. A compelling character has depth, relating not just the facts of key program themes, but feelings, too. It is the goal of the first-person interpreter to create a character who "has hopes and fears, one who complains and gossips, one who remembers the past and looks forward to the future."[6] In a sense, one creates another ego, a second personality. An interpreter internalizes opinions, prejudices, and emotions and incorporates them seamlessly into a coherent presentation.

In our own lives there are events both public and personal that stand out in our consciousness. Many adults today might clearly recall, for instance, what they were doing when they learned of President John F. Kennedy's assassination, their political orientation during the 1960s, Neil Armstrong's first steps on the moon, the birth of a first child, the death of a loved one, or the influence of a mentor. Likewise, opinions on common issues such as religion, politics, and sex; friends and neighbors; or raising a family shape our personality and behavior.

Personal perspective is one of the secrets to believable first-person. Interpreters improve the depth and quality of their character by developing responses to crucial events in their character's past, present, and even future. Primary and secondary sources (including diaries, letters, and local, national, and world histories and newspapers) help flesh out narrative details. Every character should have a biographical legend that defines his or her place in time. It can be a tale of travel, social mobility, adventure and adversity, or even monotony, but its construction, in addition to the internalization of worldview, supplies a basic framework for responding to visitors' more thoughtful and unusual questions.

Donald Ecroyd, in his living history guide for the National Park Service, recommends that interpreters draw on their own personality and background to add realism to historical characters.[7] The caveat in transferring skills and special knowledge is to deploy them appropriately. Responsible interpreters make reasonable characterization a priority, restraining fantasies and resisting the temptation to show off impressive but out-of-place skills and knowledge.

Nancy Caouette recalls childhood visits to the mill where her mother worked when she describes a textile mill to students in Old Sturbridge Village's "Farm to Factory" program. She remembers the clunking machines and the awful occasions when a worker's hair tangled in the gears. Nancy believes that by drawing on experiences like these, her interpretation sounds more realistic.[8] Claire Gregoire, also of Old Sturbridge Village, remarked that some interpreters assign their fictional characters a familiar place of origin so they are comfortable describing it; they feel it rings truer to visitors. One of her own characters attended a female academy in Providence, Rhode Island. Claire grew up there and knew just where the academy was. Her description of the area became more vivid as a result.[9]

On the other hand, when armed with maps and local histories, it is possible to create the illusion of familiarity with a character's place of origin. At Plimoth, researchers have compiled an archive on the local origins of the Pilgrim emigrants, enabling interpreters to create a mental image of their former homes in England and Holland. Plimoth's "Origins Project" also specifies structures and features that still exist, as well as attractions that postdate 1627, so that interpreters can recognize names of places where a more recent structure has replaced an old one. Interpreters can convince even natives that they "remember" their neighborhoods. David Emerson recounted how, upon discovering visitors were from Wotton-under-Edge, his character's hometown, he would muse that he had heard that a pie-powder court and market had moved into the almshouse that was built by Lady Warwick (a well-known local landmark).[10] Foreign visitors to Plimoth are often happily surprised to find that interpreters have been so thorough in doing their homework.

Some interpreters choose a character who appeals to their personality. David Barto, a teacher from Bucks County, Pennsylvania, developed a first-person portrayal of Henry David Thoreau for his high school classes. He chose Thoreau over other inspirational writers specifically because he identified with him. He thoroughly researched Thoreau the man, as well as the behavior, dress, philosophy, and speech of the writer's era, and he carefully selected anecdotes and stories that would translate lesson objectives to his students. The portrayal was so popular that it took on a life of its own, and Barto was invited to visit other schools.[11]

William Kashatus III, the director of religious studies at William Penn Charter School in Philadelphia and independent interpreter via Dr. K's Living History Programs, confessed that he needs to admire the characters that he presents. They include George Fox, William Penn, Thomas Paine, Eddie Collins, and Underground Railroad president Levi Coffin. Kashatus once experimented with a characterization of William Franklin, the last royal governor of prerevolutionary New Jersey and disaffected son of Benjamin Franklin. But no matter how much he rehearsed, both he and audiences had difficulty relating to the character, and Franklin was dropped from his repertoire.[12] Steve Gulick, another local (Philadelphia) interpreter who specializes in Quaker living history, confided that although his characters were initially launched because of requests, he has continued to develop them because their personal philosophies appeal so strongly to him.[13] Gulick has dubbed his independent venture Peace Meal Player. His Quaker characters discuss the Friends' history of concern for nonviolent conflict resolution. In selected programs Gulick's characters transcend time barriers à la my time/your time to discuss modern issues. As gentle antislavery crusader John Woolman, Steve has brainstormed with students on possible ways of negotiating with Saddam Hussein — from Woolman's point of view, of course.

In summary, creating a well-fleshed-out and believable character who has feelings, perspectives, and a personal history makes the difference between an ordinary presentation and one that convinces visitors they are talking with a person of the past. An interpreter achieves this through the building of a personality framework and personal legend, ongoing research that adds meat to its bones, an ability to select memories that provide a sense of depth and touch the emotions of listeners, and the reliance on a period worldview for shepherding responses.

Interaction across the Centuries

Communication Challenges

First-person interpretation poses peculiar challenges for interpersonal communication. In common third-person interpretive conversation, the speaker, influenced by knowledge, attitude, energy level, and audience assessment, sends verbal and nonverbal messages to the receiver-listeners, who process the information through personal filters of background knowledge, mood, attention, and surrounding stimuli. Feedback is returned via body language and verbal responses to which the original sender again responds.

The message path between sender and receiver during first-person interpretation is complicated by the adoption of a character personality by the sender (and perhaps by the receiver, too); the internalization of a historical worldview different from that of the receiver; and speech, vocabulary, and/or dialect differences. And what of the premise of twentieth-century visitors stepping into the past? Interpreters and visitors together must relish the game of time travel for the best experience. It is an artificial — yet familiar — contrivance, one that people have dreamed about for ages and pursued through books, films, and other media. But alas! Should our fantasies come true, we would discover that people of most historic communities would fear and suspect us, imprison and interrogate us, perhaps even put us to death. This sets up a dichotomy for interpreters, who are traditionally expected to encourage and comfort audiences while fostering informal learning. Thus, the true art of first-person interpretation is to render compelling portrayals without idealizing or falsifying the past, an ethical tightrope walk that requires a careful balance between historical authenticity and the communicative and pedagogic needs of heritage educators.

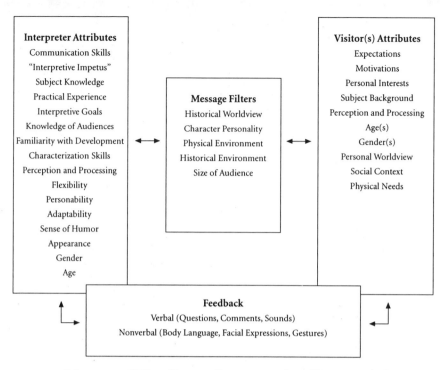

Interpreter Attributes	Message Filters	Visitor(s) Attributes
Communication Skills		Expectations
"Interpretive Impetus"		Motivations
Subject Knowledge		Personal Interests
Practical Experience	Historical Worldview	Subject Background
Interpretive Goals	Character Personality	Perception and Processing
Knowledge of Audiences	Physical Environment	Age(s)
Familiarity with Development	Historical Environment	Gender(s)
Characterization Skills	Size of Audience	Personal Worldview
Perception and Processing		Social Context
Flexibility		Physical Needs
Personability		
Adaptability		
Sense of Humor		
Appearance		
Gender		
Age		

Feedback
Verbal (Questions, Comments, Sounds)
Nonverbal (Body Language, Facial Expressions, Gestures)

Diagram of First-Person Interpretation Characteristics

First-person communication process

Just how comfortable must visitors be to have a successful experience? Can they learn more about the past by feeling at odds with it, or must they be helped along by familiarity? Ken Yellis suggests that to encounter an alien worldview "is to be disturbed out of the lazy, comforting notion that one understands the past and is somehow connected to it."[1] Many first-person interpreters, as crusaders for new social history, are enthusiastic myth-busters and proud of it.[2] Visitors are often surprised — but not always pleasantly — to learn that the past was not really like the history lessons of elementary school. John Kemp, drawing on his experience at Plimoth Plantation, suggests that the "dissonant condition" between the Pilgrim world and the visitor "is an essential stage in the visitor experience."[3] Other museum professionals, such as Old Sturbridge Village's Margaret Piatt, contend that visitors patronize museums for a variety of reasons, including family entertainment and enjoyment; thus dissonance and harsh reality do not serve all clientele.[4] Each view is valid. Each has a place. Obviously, museums (and freelancers, too) must base decisions concerning the aspects and degrees of historical reality in programming on mission, objectives, research, resources, and the audiences they target.

Roleplayed realism requires a modicum of mediation. Characters who treat newcomers with historically appropriate suspicion or xenophobia jolt visitors into the illusion of encountering a foreign culture, but sustained hostility negates the benefits of the lesson. The "surly approach" of Plimoth's early programming cast the visitor in the role of perpetual outsider and created an adversarial relationship between the interpreter and the visitor[5] — hardly a way to encourage repeat customers. At the larger living history complexes especially, many staff are sensitive to media comparisons that lump them with amusement parks. As a result, there is still a wide swing of opinion on the balance between accuracy and visitor comfort.[6]

The social restrictions imposed on historical gender and class communication must also give way to the needs of interpretation. Women, servants, slaves, and children would not — in the distant past — freely address strangers as would free men, especially in the presence of characters who are portraying their "betters." For the sake of explaining the lives they portray, interpreters are far more candid. They must devise ways to relate content while conveying the essence of their social roles. One of the most successful methods for overcoming social communication barriers is to treat visitors as confidantes with whom privileged information is shared. For instance, "I really shouldn't say this behind the Master's back, but I trust you won't tell." Techniques that compensate for alienation but still create a sense of foreignness encourage visitor identification with common characteristics of human nature while minimizing intimidation.

Another dichotomy is created because first-person interpretation borrows from a variety of disciplines, and the techniques of those disciplines often contrast or conflict with one another. As a communicator, the first-person interpreter is an educator, a public speaker, and an actor, rolled into one. The interpreter draws some, but not all, techniques from each of these roles to compose a new set of communication behaviors called first-person interpretation. Because it is a medium with so many creative variants, it has no single prescription for success. The secrets for effectiveness are derived from broad concepts applied perceptively to a variety of situations.

Public speakers facilitate the transition of ideas by analyzing the needs of their audience; establishing common ground by providing information that is within the means of the listeners' hierarchy of values, interests, and beliefs; and estimating the moment of harmony when listeners are in agreement, then supplying them with new information that expands current understanding. Listeners form their own personal analogies and consolidate old information by comparing it with the new.[7] Freeman Tilden incorporates this advice into his principles of interpretation, particularly commandment one: if interpre-

Despite his down-at-the-heels appearance, Eddie Grogan, shown here portraying Prairietown's resident ne'er-do-well (top and middle), mesmerizes audiences with deadpan folksiness and a little fiddlin' around. Outcast neighbor Ma Baker (bottom) takes a puff on her pipe and speaks her mind. (photos: Stacy Roth)

tation does not relate to the "personality or experience" of the visitor it will be "sterile."[8] This does not mean that roleplayers must act like modern people and speak current slang. It means they must find links — material, emotional, sociological, ecological, psychological, or economical — to establish a common interest, a reason for listening.

Of course there are significant differences between public speaking and first-person interpretation. A public speaker is usually not trying to convince his listeners that he or she is someone else. Despite the occasional exception, most first-person interpreters seek to transform receivers' points of view but not to that of the character or the culture they represent (even though individual characters play at such persuasion). It is the illusion, not the message, they wish believable. First-person interpretation introduces audiences to historical views, habits, customs, beliefs, and material culture in hope of affecting perceptions of not only the past but one's place in the spectrum of humanity. Its intent is to provoke the visitor to further exploration rather than purposefully to encourage twentieth-century people to adopt historical beliefs.

An interesting exception to the foregoing is the first-person style of Ralph Archbold, Philadelphia's busiest Benjamin Franklin impersonator. Archbold's bread and butter is the conference and convention market, where he presents motivational talks to business and professional associations. Archbold considers himself a public speaker by profession and works within the trade's traditional formula, noted earlier. Each Franklin appearance is carefully synchronized with the goals of corporate clients, drawing on real examples of Franklin's values such as his frugality, his use of Socratic inquiry for problem solving, and his negotiation skills. Archbold selects illustrative maxims, writings, and anecdotes that best persuade listeners to embrace a central message. He carefully edits the length and curbs the level of detail to interest — but not bore — audiences whose appetite for history is limited.[9]

Communicators are advised to start from a point within the listener's experience, but what happens when subject matter is far removed from present-day consciousness? Can we decode archaic terminology and worldview for the contemporary visitor without resorting to modern comparisons? Skilled interpreters overcome such hurdles by casually "double-explaining" their own comments. The word "receipt," a colonial term for "recipe," flies quickly to mind as an example. A concept such as "I'm making this receipt for lamb" is better understood when broached as "I'm making this receipt for lamb — I found it in mother's book of receipts along with instructions for such things as gingerbread and syllabub." It reinforces and clarifies the word and may in turn stimulate a question about "syllabub."

A rather embarrassing (albeit humorous) interpretive moment happened to a colleague portraying a military officer from the American Revolution at an encampment. He intended to include a nearby visitor in a conversation with several other "soldiers," so he politely turned and asked, "Do you have any intelligence?" (that is, military intelligence). Absorbing a rather shocked look from the recipient, the impact of his statement dawned on him, and he quickly clarified the intent of his words.

Conversely, visitors often ask "untranslatable" questions in modern terms, as the interpreters at Plimoth will attest. To an inquiry such as, "Is that your plate?" (to a Pilgrim sitting near a wooden trencher), the interpreter could literally answer the question as a seventeenth-century person, for example, "Nay, I own no plate, for I be far too poor," which is accurate but potentially confusing. Or she could answer the visitor's question without making a fuss but possibly adding the correct term: "Aye, that be my *trencher*," which supplies an answer and *might* have an impact on the questioner's discovery of historical terminology. Or she could rephrase the visitor's question in a way that provides clues to the difference, such as "Oh do you mean 'Is this *my trencher*?' Aye. In truth it doth belong to my husband. Alas, silver *plate* is for them that's got more wealth." The point is that difficult and potentially confusing terms *must* be explained in some fashion or misconceptions are inevitable — and opportunities to enhance understanding of the past are forfeited.

Interpreters need not always be sticklers about terminology but should read visitors and adjust responses accordingly. Freelancer and Colonial Williamsburg interpreter Carson Hudson suggests, "Sometimes it's educational to get them [visitors] to explain their question in more detail. . . . And sometimes it's beneficial just to cheat a little bit and answer their question." [10]

Unavoidably, interpreters must discuss issues that are removed from visitors' experiences. Some encourage imagination with verbal devices that draw substitutive relationships. "I went to sea for the first time when I was about your age" or "A little boy — no bigger than yourself — was herding swine to the market" are examples. Interpreters can also link character episodes to more general experiences of the visitor, such as travel hardships, memories of family or work, or raising children.

Many historical concepts are complex. How does an interpreter translate, for example, the role of a seventeenth-century Quaker woman minister to those with no background in Quakerism and little understanding of historical attitudes toward gender — and Quakers? On one level, most visitors hear the word "minister" and think of a person who leads a congregation; on the other hand, they are often unaware of the relative progressiveness of early Quaker women as compared with other sects. While some visitors occasionally ask how a woman could possibly be a religious orator, they rarely inquire about the term "minister," because they already "know" what it means. To promote visitor understanding, it is helpful to interpret how Quaker ministry differs from other Christian ministry and why Quaker women are encouraged to speak publicly where women of other sects are not.

Nonverbal and tonal cues also have an impact on message reception. Educators, public speakers, and actors vary tone, movement, and expression in unique ways shaped by each profession's goals. Tour guides and teachers must cultivate speech and tone that command respect and emphasize their authority. Public speakers desire traits that promote audience identification and persuade listeners to accept their viewpoints.[11] Actors manipulate body and voice to project believable emotion, convincing audiences they are someone other than themselves. The actor's range of permissible behavior differs from that of the public speaker and the educator. Speakers, teachers, and third-person interpreters must speak and move in ways that maintain authority and control because they are "the expert," "the leader." Actors may invoke "negative" traits; they have the freedom to express actions or words perceived as dissonant with a listener's ideal of speech and behavior as part of a character.

Where does this leave the first-person interpreter, who combines the techniques of public speaking, education, and theater? First-person interpreters aim to introduce visitors to a past culture in a way that intrigues, interests, and inspires further investigation. On the other hand, the first-person interpreter is also portraying the thought processes and historical perspective of a past culture that may or may not appeal to visitors. Occasionally, visitors confuse the traits of interpreters' characters with the beliefs of the interpreters themselves. It is this very communication gap that often causes discomfort with first-person. Ken Yellis remarked that first-person interpretation is both "seductive and gross" at the same time. As the dissonance between visitors and the culture portrayed widens, so does the potential for misunderstanding.

Visitors are familiar with lectures, stage plays, guided tours, and third-person interpretation; these are pervasive forms of presentation in popular media. First-person interpretation is much newer and much less familiar. Surprise contact can be unsettling for unsuspecting first-timers, especially when their only reference points are traditional media in which the audience's role is passive. As first-person becomes commonplace — and I do believe this is happening — audiences will realize and capitalize on its great potential for creative learning. However, the situation is compounded by the variety of ways that first-person is presented, by its confusion with "living history," and by the unfortunate circumstance that a good deal of unskilled interpretation is unleashed on the public by sites and individuals who have undertaken such programming without realizing the complexity and skill required for the medium to be effective.

How can those of us in heritage professions assist the transformation of public perception? Sponsors must truthfully promote the benefits and "playing directions" of their programs via thorough orientation and aggressive marketing; mass media as helpful handmaiden will continue to spread the word. Potential audiences should be advised that first-person is not necessarily gracious entertainment; they should be introduced to its deeper purpose and prepared for its challenges. Popular magazines such as *Early American Life*, *Historic Traveler*, and *Americana* can be first-person's best friends. Their editors have kept up with changes and trends in the living history world, and they do a credible job informing their readers about what to expect at the sites and events their readers visit. Old standbys such as *Better Homes and Gardens* and *U.S. News and World Report* periodically print features on living history sites.[12]

Visitor studies authority Dr. Lynn Dierking stresses the need for museums with first-person programs to provide visitors with a sense of what to expect and a clear idea of how they fit into the social context of the program.[13] Pieter N. Roos and Carolyn B. Wilkinson, in their aptly titled article "Operating Instructions for the Visitor," echoed this advice. Orientation, they explain, should also introduce key themes, fit a site's story into a broader historical background, provide basic instructions for negotiating the terrain, and explain how to make the most of the experience. Likewise, independent interpreters will avoid misunderstandings by supplying pre-visit literature that defines their methods and suggests tips for enhancing interaction.

In 1989, Video Tours released a thirty-minute video highlighting Plimoth Plantation, addressing not only the seventeenth- and twentieth-century history of the site but the philosophy, research base, and training that contribute to making the museum such a special experience. The film takes the viewer behind the scenes to "visit with the Pilgrims" and to introduce the roleplayers, too. The video explains what roleplaying is and how wide is its scope, in the words of both the narrator and the interpreters. It suggests that the more visitors know about what goes into the museum's program, the more they can elicit from a visit. Interpreters themselves explain to the camera that roleplayers are more educators than actors, armed with knowledge and historical understanding, who hope to inspire visitors to see the seventeenth century from a seventeenth-century point of view. The film also warns viewers that twentieth-century people have many misconceptions about the Pilgrims and that the museum sets out to dispel them. It pays to reason that visitors who watch this video are less likely to be confused and offended and more likely to take advantage of interpreters' special knowledge than those who miss it.

In the meantime, first-person interpreters must strike a very delicate balance between the behavioral requirements of public speaking, teaching, guiding, and theater, based on their ability to read visitors in each interpretive situation. There is no set formula for this. Ken Yellis observes that when a program and its support are highly developed, occasions for compromising conventions such as breaking character decrease dramatically. Conversely, interpreters in smaller-scale, less-developed programs may need to rely on techniques that are more harmonious with twentieth-century sensibilities. In personal experience I have found that to be the case. But it must be remembered that interpretive latitude also depends on personal charisma, subject matter, audience composition, orientation, and the amount of programmatic variety offered during a visit.

The Role of the Visitor

From a business angle, interpreters provide a service and visitors are the consumers. While such a statement sounds crassly commercial and clinical, it is a notion that cannot be ignored by anyone who earns a livelihood from historical interpretation.[1] It separates the professional from the dabbler. Admittedly, many interpreters forget or ignore this responsibility. But the concerned professional interpreter, salaried or independent, and the serious hobbyist or volunteer care about the visitor experience.

Catering to visitors is a daunting task. They do not fit into neat categories. Background knowledge varies from person to person; so does personal perspective and impetus. Only a magician could satisfy them all. No, we cannot please all of the people all of the time, but an understanding of factors that urge people to leave the comfort of their homes to visit the places interpreters work and perform provides insights for adapting and relating to a heterogeneous clientele. Analysts of visitor behavior have developed theories of heritage tourist motivation.[2] Margaret Piatt mentions that visitors come to historic sites such as Old Sturbridge Village for a variety of reasons, including relaxation, family experiences, nostalgia, entertainment, and education.[3] John H. Falk and Lynn Dierking observed that the interplay of three contexts — social, physical, and personal — affect museum visits.[4]

The gospel of "authenticity" is sacred to many first-person interpreters, but what of its importance to visitors? Visitor perceptions of authenticity have been a focal point of several studies. Gianna M. Moscardo and Philip L. Pearce found it an important element of the visitor experience at two Australian living history museums.[5] The desire for believability was also reflected in a sur-

Orientation on wheels: visitors to Mystic Seaport Museum tour the village on one-horse power. (photo: Edward Baker, courtesy Mystic Seaport Museum)

vey at the Canadian O'Keefe Ranch, where 97 percent of respondents deemed it germane to their appreciation of the site,[6] and in another study at Old Sturbridge Village, where 100 visitors rated the importance of "a sense of the past" a score of 6.38 on a scale in which 1 was "not at all important" and 7 was "extremely important."[7]

In *The Tourist: A New Theory of the Leisure Class*, Dean MacCannell theorized that tourists were propelled by desires for authentic "back regions," places where mandated public decorum and studied performance are absent and the "natives" are free to be themselves.[8] MacCannell concluded that because most tourist destinations staged or artistically enhanced real native behavior and activity, very few tourists could actually see the very type of experiences that originally motivated them to travel far afield in the first place.

Both Erik Cohen and P. L. Pearce took exception to MacCannell's theory, creating broader motivational models. Cohen developed a five-mode scale that is based on physical desires at one end, intellectual on the other.[9] Pearce's "traveler career scale" superimposed leisure motivations on Maslow's hierarchy of needs. Individuals either graduated through the continuum to the ultimate stage or fixated at one of the lower levels. Pearce insisted that neither MacCannell's nor Cohen's theories could accommodate the living history site

Erik Cohen's Five Types of Visitors

Recreational: seek amusement and physical satisfaction

Diversionary: want escape from daily boredom

Experiential: appreciate others' lifestyles

Experimental: desire to sample alternative lifestyles without total commitment

Existential: search for intense inner meaning

---

phenomenon because neither considered tourists' desires to see *reconstructed authenticity.*[10]

Stephen Eddy Snow adeptly discusses and applies the theories of Cohen, MacCannell, and others and posits his own typology of visitors to Plimoth Plantation in the "Pilgrims and Tourists" chapter of *Performing the Pilgrims.* Snow divides Plimoth's tourists into three types: those seeking recreational or diversionary entertainment (Snow says most visitors fall into this category); experiential visitors who hunger after educational and aesthetic experiences (Snow classes them as the "best" visitors); and those looking for religious or cultural identification or affirmation (Snow's "modern pilgrims").[11]

Perhaps visitor typologies classify us too rigidly, but they certainly underscore the reality that audiences with a many-hued spectrum of interests, motivations, intellectual development, learning styles, and moods attend public programs. Such models alert us to the social, psychological, and intellectual roots of visitor behavior, articulating what perceptive interpreters absorb from experience. Layer on the dynamics among individuals in visiting social units and the effects of physical and environmental circumstances, and one realizes the importance of flexibility, resourcefulness, and empathy. Contact is brief, but impressions can be lasting; the interpersonal characteristics of the encounter will remain long after the content fades from the visitor's memory.[12]

At living history sites, most visitors are strangers, unfamiliar with the rules and customs of the place they have just entered.[13] They require a period of adaptation, as does anyone who negotiates a foreign environment. It is easy to overlook visitor disorientation while caught up in the myriad of details required of first-person, yet interpreters must project themselves into their place. John Kemp, director of interpretation at Plimoth Plantation, cautions that interpreters should not be too quick to judge visitors on initial comments. Unfamiliarity can prompt visitors to ask questions or make statements that are perceived by interpreters as "stupid." (It can also make some visitors so anxious that they are afraid to say anything.) A little more effort on the part

P. L. Pearce's Traveler Career Scale

Maslow's Needs	Tourist Characteristics
Physiological	Want escape from routine to indulge in food and exercise
Security/arousal	Desire stimulation and novelty
Love and belongingness	Seek social rewards from group activities with family and friends
Self-esteem	Wish to attain cultural and intellectual skills for self-development or prestige
Self-actualization	Desire to develop own potential, seek inner peace, relate to the wider world, or transcend oneself

of the interpreter may trigger an interest that ignites a great conversation.[14] I agree with Kemp and urge interpreters to humble their assumptions about visitors who "don't know their history" by recalling their own experiences with insurance agents, lawyers, or auto/appliance/computer repair technicians (or pick your own favorite area of ignorance).

Visitors will better enjoy a first-person program if they know what their role is — not necessarily what character to play, but what they are supposed to do. Are they time travelers, anthropologists, or contemporaries, or can they choose an identity? If visitors are not instructed beforehand on any particular strategy, then it is important for interpreters themselves to provide adequate clues. Visitors need to know they belong in the scene and are expected to play along.

Interpreter opinions diverge on what type of role to assign visitors. Many place them in their characters' own era and in the position of likely callers — often combined with a classification suggested by the sex, age, and/or twentieth-century appearance of the addressee. Thus tradesmen and shopkeepers greet their potential customers, schoolmasters welcome new or prospective students, ministers see members of their congregation, and recruiting sergeants look for likely cannon fodder.[15] Glenn Gordinier and Bettye Noyes of Mystic Seaport Museum both commented that they view the visitor as a "neutral contemporary," someone from the year 1876 but not assigned or imagined in a particular role. "It's different with kids," added Gordinier, who will place children in a particular role, such as that of a potential cabin boy.[16]

Some interpreters employ unique casting techniques with their audiences. One schoolmaster at Conner Prairie addressed all of his listeners as "scholars," no matter what their age.[17] He gestured to one thirty-something woman and referred to her as a sixteen-year-old who would soon be finished with her studies — which elicited a rather tickled grin from the subject. Larry Earl hopes that visitors will empathize with the role of slaves. He occasionally addresses groups of listeners as "fellow Africans," regardless of their color. "It is very interesting to see the expression on peoples' faces, and then after that, how they react to the bigger picture."[18]

The role of transient, guest, or newcomer is apt for visitors.[19] When interpreters inquire if visitors are prospective settlers or on a journey, visitors can assume a comfortable identity and know that their unfamiliarity with the local milieu is expected. A nonspecific question presents options, unlike "Why are you here?" or "Who are you?," which puts people on the spot to come up with an answer.

In some programs, basic roles — and even specific personas — are assigned. At Beechwood, Caroline Astor's home in Newport, Rhode Island, visitors were asked for their names by an unctuous butler as he greeted them at the door; then he grandly announced them to everyone else in the room as an honored guest of the Astors as they walked inside. It was startling at first, but it certainly set everyone into the appropriate "400 Club" mood. Washburn Norlands Living History Center in Livermore, Maine, parcels out complete 1870 identities to weekend overnight visitors, who are introduced to other members of their "family" as they arrive at the site. Participants in the program stated that the opportunity to immerse themselves in a role added to the program's effectiveness.[20]

A few interpreters simply let visitors select their own identities, be they historical or modern. Scott Atwood (Plimoth Plantation) said, "Visitors are foreigners, guests in my home, are paying my salary. I treat them accordingly."[21] Some visitors naturally choose the role of time traveler. Many parents teach their children about the differences between past and present by asking anachronistic questions (such as "Do you know what an airplane is?") or by encouraging their children to ask them. Many interpreters feel that such questions detract from the historical mood. Unfortunately, interpreter-baiting visitors deliberately ask anachronistic questions in jest, accounting, in part, for the hard feelings. A skilled interpreter should take a moment to discern the true purpose of an anachronistic query and respond appropriately, taking advantage of opportunities to link out-of-period questions to corresponding historical topics. For example:

Child: Do you know what an airplane is?

Interpreter: Airplane? What do you do with that?

Child: Fly through the air in it!

Interpreter: Now why would you want to do that?

Child: To get from one place to another that's far away.

Interpreter: Oh. When I travel a long ways away, I ride in a coach drawn by horses.

Because first-person interpretation is a relatively new form of museum medium, surprise first-time encounters can be startling, confusing, or intimidating. Living history sites that feature first-person should introduce it during orientation, draw attention to it in printed publications, and/or erect prominent signs at key entry points that proclaim visitors will step into another era. Wording should clearly indicate that staff are in character and that interaction is welcome, if that is the case. Advice on question-and-response strategies can give newcomers added courage.

For example, Conner Prairie displays a three-case exhibit where those in the admission queue can see it. Labels define living history and first-person interpretation and explain why it is forever the year 1836 in Prairietown and why the site has chosen this presentation method. The text reminds visitors that Prairietown and its characters are fictional but based on facts, and that staff portray a representative sample of the people who lived on the Indiana frontier. It encourages visitors to ask questions of the interpreters and relates that characters' knowledge stops at 1836. In addition, on the day that I visited the site, a staff member greeted tour group visitors at the close of the orientation slide show and illustrated the types of questions that we could ask of the Prairietown inhabitants.

One of Plimoth Plantation's brochures includes a map of the village's houses, provides information about each village household, and encourages visitors to "become acquainted with the 'colonists' — portrayed by costumed museum staff, who . . . answer your questions from their seventeenth century perspectives."[22] This special brochure clearly indicates that the interpreters in the village are in character, while those in the adjacent Hobbamock's Homesite are in twentieth-century time.

At Mayflower II, a Visitor Services staff member personally informs each group of visitors that the costumed people on the ship will behave as if the year is 1621, and that if visitors have any other types of questions they can feel free to stop back and ask. The Pilgrim Village, on busier days, stations a greeter at the entrance to the reconstructed village for the same purpose. Mystic Seaport Museum places a sandwich board outside the roleplay venue that announces that inside, the year is 1876. Colonial Williamsburg uses the phrase "A Person of the Past" in its *Visitor's Companion* listings to alert visitors that certain presentations are in first-person.

Despite brochure explanations, signs, personal greetings, and other media, visitors can still miss the instructions. In a novel place, they are bombarded with many other messages that compete for their attention. They can't absorb everything. A disaster? No. However, it means that interpreters will continue to be some folks' first encounter with the rules. Even when visitors have prior contact with first-person, styles and methods differ so widely between sites and interpreters that guidance and clues are still necessary. If first-person is done well, most onlookers catch on very quickly.

We in heritage professions work with an increasingly enthusiastic public. Both interpreters and the popular press concur that visitors have become more sophisticated in recent decades, with a concurrent appreciation for historical accuracy and detail, and that they are enjoying roleplay destinations in increasing numbers.[23]

Visitor opinion of first-person programs is an area that begs for further study. Several sites have conducted evaluations using questionnaires, interviews, and behavioral observation. However, an overall analysis of the medium's effectiveness based on evaluation data has yet to be written. Many, many questions ache to be answered: Are first-person programs able to efect changes in visitors' prior perceptions of history? How does first-person compare with third-person in its capacity to aid the retention of historical knowledge? What types of visitors tend to enjoy first-person? Do such programs inspire further study of topical material or encourage visitors to engage in participatory history themselves? Do marketing and advertising methods present a public picture of the site that works for or against the goals of roleplay programs in shaping visitor expectations? These questions are but the tip of the iceberg.

Breaking the Ice and Encouraging Interaction

You want them to feel relaxed — let them know we are not threatening.
Betty Frew

From the moment visitors and interpreters see each other, communication begins: sizing each other up, making judgments based on appearance and prior experiences, and thinking of what to say. Next, they engage in what — for many — is one of the most difficult activities in interpersonal communication: starting a conversation.

When visitors enter an interior space that is occupied by an interpreter, there is an air of curious anticipation. Some expect a performance. Many are reserved, concerned at first about intruding. They stand at a distance from the interpreter, not certain if it is permissible — or prudent — to move closer. They could be thinking, "What if I get 'stuck' here? How will I escape?" Sensitive interpreters put visitors at ease, employing body language, eye contact, and verbal cues that signal a willingness to engage in conversation.

"Breaking the ice" is an important social convention in many cultures. It is an exchange of social niceties that soften the edges of an encounter. Ice breakers rarely address conversational intentions or important themes. They signal friendliness and break the tension of silence. They announce, "Open for business," "Welcome stranger," "Howdy friend." They can set a mood and provide orientation. Interpretive ice breakers have one rule of thumb: the subject of conversation should be something to which visitors can respond easily.[1] A few examples include common "How do you do?" greetings, comments about the weather, or a word of sympathy for the visitor's transient state ("New to these parts?"). Tacking period terms onto a greeting ("How do you do, *Mistress*") reinforces the aspects of roleplay. "Of course," reminds interpreter and assistant site supervisor Jeff Scotland, "visitors use ice breakers, too."[2]

Many interpreters stress the importance of establishing friendliness during initial contact and throughout the interpretive exchange, especially if they want visitors to converse freely.[3] Moira Turnan Hannon personally greets many of the visitors who enter "her house" at Plimoth.[4] She and Betty Frew, of Old Sturbridge Village, fit what Moira calls the "gracious host" style of interpretation. Betty feels, too, that greetings are a highly individual activity, dependent on a character's personality.[5] When an interpreter is already engaged in conversation, interpreters should acknowledge newcomers with a glance, a nod, or a smile. Even brief eye contact improves perceptions of inclusion and welcome and quells fears of exclusion.[6]

Ever hear of a phenomenon known as the "eyebrow flash"? It is a split-second upward jump of both eyebrows, usually accompanied by a smile. It occurs unconsciously when close friends converse, but people with a naturally friendly nature do it more frequently. Paul Risk observed the impact of this minute but devastatingly charismatic movement. The flash influences people who receive the signal to become more relaxed and open in their conversation than they would otherwise. Risk discovered, quite informally, that an interpreter acquaintance, extraordinarily popular with visitors, tended to "flash" most of the people he met. Risk concluded that perhaps interpreters should practice becoming "flashers."[7]

Flashing aside, every theory in first-person interpretation almost always has exceptions, and some of these will be discussed here and in the section on presenting conflict and controversy, later in the text. For instance, not all interpreters believe it is necessary to be friendly. Some devise alternate ways of initiating conversation that they feel are more in keeping with their character. One key to success with a not-so-friendly first encounter is to stay within the bounds of empathizable subject matter. Claire Gregoire of Old Sturbridge Village, for example, occasionally launches into the "flustered housewife." As the visitor walks in, she complains about the minister's unruly children and other domestic frustrations — something twentieth-century visitors immediately relate to. Visitors take comfort in the recognizable humor of the situation, and the interpreter has not even made an obsequious attempt to be neighborly.[8]

Scott Atwood, who plays Francis Cooke and other characters at Plimoth Plantation, sympathizes with visitor disorientation and plays on the commonalities between them and the original settlers. "Pretty strange isn't it? I thought it was pretty strange too when I first came here."[9]

Techniques for breaking the ice are somewhat different when roleplayers initiate encounters with the public, rather than the other way around. Roving roleplayers on the street, characters who visit classrooms, and gallery interpreters who make surprise entrances are examples of this. Such interpreters must quickly provoke interest, garner attention, and make their arrival welcome. Popular ways to do this include a straightforward introduction and explanation for one's presence, a startling pronouncement, or a request to the visitor to help solve a problem.

Colonial Williamsburg character interpreter Jack Flintom, as King's Attorney John Randolph, springs an ingenious flattery tactic on strolling visitors: "I know I know you, but your name escapes me. I should know a woman of your quality."[10] His colleague Susannah Badgett introduces herself as the Widow Hay, then asks people if they knew her husband and broaches other subjects from there.[11] Introducing oneself early is a good habit. Sometimes visitors are too inhibited to ask for identification, and it is easy to forget to identify yourself when encountering large numbers of visitors.

According to Glenn Gordinier, the outdoor interpreter's primary aim is to involve visitors in the roleplayer's activity or discussion. He likes attention-grabbers like "Excuse me, I'm looking for a sailor who deserted from my ship. Have you seen him? He looks like . . . ."[12] Gordinier senses that some visitors may feel threatened by people in strange costumes approaching them on the street, particularly the gruff, bearded, sailor-types like some of the male interpreters at Mystic Seaport Museum. He advises his staff to remain conscious of this potential reaction.[13]

Two Plimoth interpreters who worked the village street devised unusual entreaties. One, portraying a visiting diplomat from the Dutch settlement of New Amsterdam, stopped visitors near the gun mount in the center of the settlement and asked them how many cannons they counted in the village, because he was attempting to verify if the Pilgrims had as much ordnance as they had claimed. Another, playing a stranded sea captain, begged tourists to find room for him on their vessel so he could get away from the strict New England settlement and head for his original destination — Virginia.

Some interpreters like to catch visitors off guard, then bring them around, but such techniques require personal charisma and the ability to manipulate an audience. When David Emerson portrays a Revolutionary War recruiting sergeant at the Old Barracks Museum, he occasionally opens his portion of the "Meet the Past" program by striding up to school groups and bureaucratically demanding to see their papers. When they respond with "What papers?" he accuses them of spying for the British, which they deny. Then, with a great big smile, he says, "Well, if you are not spies you must be here to join the Continental Army, so I'm just the man you're looking for."

There is one type of initial contact that is almost guaranteed to fail. It is practiced by the nontalkers, the interpreters who go about their business, ignoring the visitor, not looking up from their task, and not saying a word until the visitor asks a question (or glances around and leaves). Such an approach makes visitors feel intrusive and uncomfortable.[14] These same interpreters often reply to inquiries with a short, flat answer. A friend and I recently visited one historic house summer kitchen where three "servants" were puttering around. Even though we were the only spectators in the room, no one said a word. About three minutes passed, so I asked, "What are you making here?" "A sweet pudding," came the reply. Then more silence. Unfortunately, Silent Sal and Wordless Will are met all too frequently, thinking themselves authentic but appearing, instead, uncommunicative. Interpretation is a profession for talkers and explainers. The old adage "silence is golden" does not apply here.

How does one portray a character whose personality or station is traditionally deferential or silent? Some might claim that silence is appropriate behavior for certain characters. However, if the character is one who traditionally only speaks when spoken to, interpreters must bridge the gap for the sake of imparting information. Solutions — such as treating visitors as confidantes — were suggested in Chapter 7.

In common communication, silence can be a means to exert control, demand attention, force inquiry, and plant uneasiness.[15] Christy Coleman Matthews, the director of African-American Interpretations and Presentations at Colonial Williamsburg, plays a character named Cate, a slave of the Powell family. Cate is sullen, frequently silent, and displays irritation with visitors. Matthews uses this character to evoke emotions and reactions that intensify feelings toward the dehumanizing effects of slavery. Cate will be discussed further in the chapter on conflict and controversy, but she is introduced here to underscore the reaction of many visitors to negative behaviors. According to Christy, her colleagues, and visitors themselves, onlookers feel discomfort, anger, and confusion. Even those who appreciate and understand the impact of her presentation often feel incredibly uncomfortable.[16]

Once the silence is shattered and the channels are open for interpreter/visitor interaction, it is time to feast on the meat of interpretation. There are many ways interpreters "hook" visitors into participating. They ask questions, cast out verbal lures, demonstrate activities, involve onlookers in tasks, wear or use an object that elicits curiosity, and start dialogues with other interpreters. Hooks stimulate interest from the visitor and provide focus for conversation. They are devices that attract attention and/or set up the visitor to discuss interpretive themes.

Some visitors have no desire to interact. Perhaps they are uncertain about what to say, are shy, or just want to listen unobtrusively. All are perfectly acceptable preferences. Some visitors are not shy and jump right in. More often, interpreters must initiate conversation. There are advantages to speaking first. It affords more content control and permits interpreters to vary subject matter and keep things fresh. Frequently a roleplayer is bursting with some newly learned information that he or she is just dying to relate to the public. Betty Frew of Old Sturbridge Village was half-kidding when she said, "You try to draw them [the visitor] into talking about something *you* want to talk about."[17]

Many interpreters stimulate conversation by asking questions; however, a query that requires a simple yes or no answer may fail to stimulate further conversation.[18] Interpreters must be sensitive to the discomfort that some visitors feel when the burden of participation is placed on them;[19] therefore, an inquiry that cannot be answered incorrectly is the most tactful choice.[20] While most visitors are not ready to do a period repartee, they can relate to timeless human conditions and form opinions when given enough background information by the interpreter; they will almost always respond to invitations to make comparisons or judgments.

Some interpreters avoid questions that ask visitors to explain themselves — such as "What brings you here?" — because it may put the visitor on the spot. Yet there are no hard and fast rules. The "Where do you come from?" or "What do you do?" ploy is commonly used to evoke a response, but it is a technique that can have variable results, depending on both the purpose of its use and the involvement of the visitor. It can invite an anachronistic answer, either unintentionally or on purpose. There are some skilled interpreters, however, who ask such questions to investigate visitor orientation, to make visitors comfortable, and as a jumping point to related topics.

Scott Atwood poses the "Where do you come from?" inquiry to test visitor willingness to "play along." If they respond with answers such as "I'm from a place you never heard of" or "I'm from New Amsterdam," he knows that visitors understand what's going on and are willing to participate. If they say "I'm from Texas" and expect him to know where that is, Scott knows he is dealing with someone who hasn't caught on or is making sport. He can adjust his approach accordingly.[21] Plimoth interpreters — whose characters would be at a loss to identify the hometowns of most U.S. visitors — take great delight in asking people where they are from and surprising those from places such as Boston, Massachusetts, by "assuming" they are from Boston in the mother country. Those with particularly good knowledge of British Isles geography take special pride in their ability to discuss the points of origin of visitors from the United Kingdom.

B. J. Pryor of Colonial Williamsburg, who portrays the recently emigrated Reverend Henley, asks visitors where they are from so he can spout oft-unflattering impressions of what their unsophisticated, rustic hometowns must be like, reflecting the attitudes of an English country clergyman. Tom Hay, Colonial Williamsburg's William Lane, sergeant of the city, draws on his extensive knowledge of eighteenth-century geography to take visitors on a guided imagery tour of frontier Virginia and the Ohio Valley, incorporating his character's memories of exploring those places during the French and Indian War.

Questioning is just one way to stimulate participation. Another successful tactic is to salt conversations, using a strategy that Jeff Scotland (Plimoth) calls "verbal prospecting." With this technique, the interpreter initiates a monologue that strikes on several subjects. Aided by perception or perhaps luck, one of the ideas may correspond with the visitor's interests or experience. The first part of verbal prospecting, says Jeff, is the greeting.[22] "One greets people to open communications — to say 'let's sit down and talk.' One offers a greeting and waits for a rejoinder. You can see the eyes light up [if it's working]." Jeff always keeps several subjects in mind to stimulate conversation after the initial exchange: "I will try to say something 'curious' so that the visitor might ask another question. Often, I will try to fit several different subjects or references into the opening of the conversation, so that the visitor can pick up on something that interests him. I also try to read the individual and suggest some subjects that might interest them in particular."[23]

The technique is effective for Scotland. Observing him in action on site as Governor Bradford confirms this. Other interpreters use related strategies. Tom Hay sprinkles his sentences with unusual phrases and startling words. When replying to "How long have you been a Sergeant?" Hay might say, "I've been a sergeant since right before the Stamp Act 'riot,' summer of '64." The response is often "What Stamp Act *riot*?"[24]

B. J. Pryor is a masterful manipulator of the hook, throwing them in like hand grenades and then quickly dashing onto another topic. His Reverend Henley casually remarks, "I arrived not long after that dreadful incident regarding young Mr. Byrd, but you don't want to hear about that." Then he switches the subject. Anyone who is the least bit nosy is going to stop him in his tracks and grill him for the juicy story.[25] The incident's details then become a reward for the intrepid visitor.

Unusual objects, displayed in obvious places, can spark conversation. Christy Coleman Matthews wears a pouch around her neck in which her slave character Hattie stores valuables. Visitors frequently ask about it, thinking that it may be an object related to voodoo ritual. When visitors inquire about the nails that are poked through Tom Hay's hat, they learn that one of his duties as sergeant of the city is to nail prisoners' ears to the pillory.

A good interpreter should be prepared with plenty of things to do or say if the visitor has no questions.[26] As Nancy Caouette, a museum educator at Old Sturbridge Village, points out, the visitor often has little frame of reference from which to ask a question, is shy, or is afraid of saying the wrong thing.[27] Other visitors simply do not want to interact. Many stick to "safe" questions, such as "What are you doing?" or "What is that thing over there?"

Educator Lois Silverman observed that visitors usually want roleplayers to take an active part in the interaction process; therefore, it is crucial for the roleplayer to initiate and maintain conversation.[28] Moira Turnan Hannon of Plimoth Plantation, for instance, will launch into a description — but not a complete one — of her activity of the moment when confronted with a quiet visitor. For example, she will say, "These spices come from far away," in an effort to prospect for questions about the spices themselves or their origin.[29] Lisa Simon Walbridge, also from Plimoth, discourses on objects or subjects that elicited frequent inquiries from past visitors when no questions are forthcoming.[30] David Emerson rhetorically asks what he wishes visitors would ask, then proceeds to answer the questions himself: "I can see by your faces that you're thinking, 'Why should I join the Continental Army? What's in it for me?' Well, I'll tell ya . . . ."[31] David believes — and rightly so — that it is the business of the interpreter to dispense provocative information and make sure that the delivery sounds fresh no matter how many times it has been said that day.[32] A skilled monologuist can go on indefinitely, if need be.

Many veteran interpreters avoid hooks that pick out visitors' anachronistic clothing and modern gadgetry unless such ploys serve as springboards to meaningful interpretation; otherwise they are a waste of time. Question a visitor about the "funny gizmo" around his or her neck, and you may have to listen to five minutes on the functions of a camera. Eddie Grogan of Conner Prairie has a distinct mindset on the matter. He thinks to himself, "Yeah, you people are dressed funny, but I'm too polite to mention it."[33] Again, every theory has its exceptions. Someone portraying a tailor or seamstress can effectively sneer at visitors' curious hemlines, but in general, it is better to steer clear of the temptation. Why rely on a cliché when there are so many other engaging topics?

One of the easiest ways to pique the interest of a visitor is to demonstrate an activity.[34] This promotes curiosity and active inquiry. Even chores as mundane as washing clothes or dusting can spur interaction.[35] Who can resist asking the housewife busy at the hearth, "What's in the pot?" As with verbal ice breakers, activities should be departure points for deeper meaning rather than an end in themselves. What is the reason for the activity? Its place in the family? The community? The general economy? How does the character feel about the activity? What would happen if the activity was not completed? Could the visitors see themselves doing the task day after day or season after season? Interpreter Dee Ashpaugh at Conner Prairie, for instance, uses her needlework to relate class differences to visitors. Her wealthy character, Mrs. Campbell, has the time to do "fancy work," whereas the poor Widow Bucher will do plainer pieces because her livelihood requires that she be production minded.[36] David Emerson, as Stephen Hopkins at Plimoth, would sit outside "his house" working on a fishing net, offering visitors the opportunity to do a few loops, shifting the topic to the importance of fishing for Plimoth colonists, and segueing into his character's former trade as a weaver and the reasons why he abandoned the profession in the new colony.

Activities encourage visitors to come closer; they want to see what's going on. Even those who are not in the midst of complicated trades can attract attention with action-based hooks. Tom Hay polishes Colonial Williamsburg's fire engine rather than simply standing next to it. Eddie Grogan, seated on a neighbor's porch, hauls out his fiddle during a lull at Conner Prairie and starts to play. Jean Jeacle, as Flora MacPherson, Upper Canada Village's secretary of the Total Abstinence Society, decked out in a sash with the word "ABSTI-NENCE" blazed across it, launches into a temperance song, and Larry Earl's slave preacher Gowan Pamphlet springs into an impromptu street sermon.

Activities acquire more meaning when visitors participate. Once a visitor is engaged in a project — whether they sit on the shaving horse to make a spoke, practice mustering with a broomstick, join the chorus of a song, or recite lessons off the schoolhouse blackboard — they become involved. Hands-on techniques are especially effective with children, who love to volunteer for demonstrations.[37] Lois Silverman observed that when the roleplayers at Penns-bury Manor asked visitors to assist with a process, such as working flax, the participation response was 100 percent.[38] Adults, too, can be just as eager to try their hands at historical activities and should not be overlooked. One grown-up visitor to Plimoth confided in me that he wished he could rent a costume at the entrance gate and play along with the Pilgrims.

Intra-interpreter dialogues are a natural attention-getter for audiences and provide a forum for complex contextual interpretation. Two or more role-players stationed together can provide contrasting perspectives, illustrate so-cial order, and/or show family and community relationships. New avenues of interpretation are created by varying character combinations. Multiple char-acters naturally arouse a sense of activity, especially when roleplayers "float"

Carson Hudson's colorful foot puppets commonly draw curious onlookers on the streets of Colonial Williamsburg. (photo: Stacy Roth)

Interpreters at Lincoln Log Cabin check to see if the "leather breeches" beans are dry. (photo: Stacy Roth)

between stations. Unexpected arrivals stimulate natural curiosity about new characters and the introduction of "news."[39]

Many interpreters enjoy working in tandem, too. Jeff Scotland and Lisa Simon Walbridge, as Governor and Mistress Bradford, described the benefits of stationing a male and a female interpreter together. The combination permits a wide variety of gender issues and perspectives and presents a more complete picture of a historical scene.[40] John Kemp adds that intra-interpreter dialogue allows the characters at Plimoth Plantation to "relate to each other as a community" — something the staff has been doing with greater intensity in recent years.[41] The interpreters at Plimoth frequently plan visits to their "neighbors." Some visits allow for micro-events and gossip to unfold at a set time, while other visits are designed to break up the day for an interpreter who is alone at a station.[42] David Emerson and I visit classrooms as a Revolutionary War recruiting sergeant and a Quaker traveler in "The Times That Try Men's Souls." My character encourages students to question the sergeant about the realities of army life by raising objections and seeking the opinions of the students, and by circulating among them and suggesting questions or comments.

Despite the advantages that a multiple-interpreter situation can add to viewpoint variety and activity, many interpreters prefer to work alone. Some confided that they like to have complete control over their presentations, while others felt comfortable only when working with knowledgeable and well-seasoned colleagues who can improvise without monopolizing the conversation or maneuvering their partner into embarrassing situations. Glenn Gordinier prefers stationing interpreters at Mystic Seaport Museum on their own. Outdoors, especially, Gordinier fears that visitors might mistake intra-interpreter conversations for private discussions. For that reason, Mystic interpreters carefully plan their street engagements beforehand and compensate for visitor apprehension by exaggerating the volume of their conversation and by standing at least 3½ feet apart.[43] Likewise, Plimoth's interpreters try to avoid "Pilgrim bunch-up," a gathering of three or more interpreters that looks too formidable to interrupt. "You don't want to walk up to three guys with axes who are laughing," mused Scott Atwood.[44]

There are other trade-offs to intra-interpreter conversation. Lois Silverman observed that visitors ask fewer questions when they are watching a dialogue and that they tend to spend less time at a station when not interacting themselves.[45] To counteract visitor passivity in such situations, interpreters can instigate visitor participation by soliciting opinions or inviting onlookers to examine an object of discussion.[46] And last but not least, interpreters should be clearly audible to all.

{10}

The Art of Conversation

Once visitors are hooked, interpreters can seize the opportunity to expand listeners' understanding of the interpretive story, a sense of time and place, and the intricacies of the cultural past. How does one proceed from here? This is where advance planning, subject immersion, and the ability to link thoughts together contribute to overall effectiveness. A knowledgeable, well-prepared interpreter can lead a discussion in any number of directions — expounding on current events, folkways, lifeways, anecdotes, familyways, daily activities, processes, or history — provoking the visitor into thought and verbal parley.

Thought linking, the process of relating one topic to another, is essential for maintaining conversation. Novice roleplayers can improve their interpretation by anticipating possible links in advance. With practice, it becomes second nature. The way Jeff Scotland draws visitors into a dialogue is a good example of this technique. One cold rainy morning, a man walked into the Bradford house to warm up by the fire and remarked that the "rain must hinder what you people do all day." Jeff, as Governor Bradford, picked right up on the visitor's observation by mentioning that the foul weather gave him a chance to catch up on "civil matters," such as the colonists' contract negotiations with the Merchant Adventurers. The visitor, intrigued by the contract issue, asked questions and made comments that could concern a legal agreement in any time period, including, "How did you know you could trust the other party?" and "You took a big chance coming over here." He also expressed an interest in Bradford's opinions about the outcome of the situation.

The discussion came to a close with an exchange of small talk and gracious "thank yous" for the hospitality.[1]

I asked Jeff how he chose the topics he broached with that particular visitor. He explained that the nature of his character and chronological events in the village provide the structure for presenting information. Yet, he effortlessly linked a remark about rain into the activities that a rainy day affords one to do, which led into the discussion of Governor Bradford's workload. If the colonists' contract failed to elicit interest, Jeff could have mentioned several other things his character would do on a rainy day; if that didn't work, he would have simply switched to another subject.

Another example is an exchange observed between Stuart Bolton (Plimoth), portraying Master Edward Winslow, and a small boy who was curious about Winslow's sword. Bolton talked briefly about the physical aspects of the sword, then added, "Do you ask about the sword because you fear the Indians? You need not fear the local Indians because they are friendly." This led the conversation onto the subject of Indians. Bolton also peppered his discourse with references to past occurrences and speculations on the near future, adding depth to his interpretation.[2]

The seasoned interpreters at Plimoth are masters at thought linking, which enables them to converse indefinitely. In fact, on days when the site is not very crowded, some visitors sit and chat with the colonists for hours. One reason the Plimoth interpreters are so good at maintaining conversations is their training, which emphasizes a well-rounded view of the world of a seventeenth-century person, both physically and philosophically.

While the ability to keep a running commentary is laudable, interpreters should not run on at a breakneck pace without giving visitors ample chance to squeeze in a question or comment.[3] It is important to watch for physical signs that visitors want to say something: opening the mouth as if to speak, or raising the hand as if to make a point. One should not be afraid to pause slightly *after* a visitor asks a question, either. Having the answer on the tip of one's tongue can be a dead giveaway that an interpreter is not spontaneous.[4] In real life we mull over answers to questions; a thoughtful pause is both a natural and beneficial way to respond to a visitor.[5]

The ability to stimulate the visitor's intellectual involvement goes hand in hand with being a good conversationalist. There are almost as many gambits for doing this as there are interpreters. In addition to the ideas offered above, the staffs at first-person sites have demonstrated their creativity with some of the following techniques:

One is the "help me resolve a dilemma" approach, favored by Chris Creelman at Old Sturbridge Village. This method encourages youngsters to exercise their problem-solving skills and gives adults a chance to offer advice. Her character discusses a personal crisis, such as deciding which of two marriage proposals to accept, then turns to visitors for suggestions. Few can resist bombarding her for more details and helping her make up her mind.[6]

David Emerson has a favorite device for stimulating visitor questions. He discloses information so that it is obvious there's more to tell. For instance, if a visitor asks about the thatch on the roof (at Plimoth), David explains how the roof was thatched, adding, "It's a much better method than the way a neighbor did it back home." He pauses, having baited the hook for the visitor to ask about the neighbor's method. If the visitor bites, he is rewarded with an answer that stimulates yet another question.[7]

Both David and John Kemp at Plimoth are also adept at using a "fill in the blanks" technique, where the interpreter pretends to forget the name of something visitors might know, allowing them to display their own knowledge. In one example of this, David's character Stephen Hopkins dislikes "that scribbler from Stratford who writes all them plays — oh, what was his name?" It takes a great deal of restraint for any visitor who knows the answer to keep from interjecting, "You mean Shakespeare?" This kind of baiting also gives a sense of confidence and satisfaction to the respondent.[8]

As mentioned earlier, stationing both a male and a female interpreter at a location helps to balance the presentation of men's and women's issues. Of course, such staffing is often impossible. When interpreting solo, Effie Cummings (Plimoth) is noticeably alert to the importance of pitching her presentation to both sexes without dwelling solely on the women's activities that she is constantly involved in. She will use a segue such as "I am cooking this dinner for my *husband*," describe something that pertains to her husband's sphere, then refocus on feminine activities.[9]

Many interpreters insisted how earnestly they desire to portray the "foreign country" aspects of the past, as well as its commonalities with the present. To Eddie Grogan it is important to illustrate both continuity and change. "Change," he said, "is much more obvious and easy to portray. Continuity gets a little more subtle." [10]

One way of indicating change is to say something that challenges preconceptions of the past or startles visitors into realizing that many views in the past were radically different from our own. The historical position of women is an overwhelmingly favorite topic. Additional topics observed to startle visitors include historical medical beliefs, referring to modern mainstream religious groups as riotous radicals and heretics, and matter-of-fact acceptance of slavery and servitude (by both blacks and whites).

Grogan, who periodically portrays Prairietown's doctor, is frequently visited by young girls inspired by the television series "Dr. Quinn, Medicine Woman" who do not realize the enormous struggle that a woman had to face in order to practice scholarly medicine in the nineteenth century. They proudly announce that they, too, plan to be doctors when they grow up, just like Dr. Quinn. Grogan's character eyes them suspiciously and asks them if they think they can find a doctor to apprentice them, what their husband will think about such a career, and how they are going to care for their own sick children when a patient needs them ten miles away.[11] Interpreters realize that personifying real historical attitudes can be troublesome, particularly if visitors have not grasped the intent of first-person — but more on that later.

Continuity is far less startling, though visitors may be surprised to learn that "some things never change." A topic that has universal or modern parallels enables visitors to connect their own experiences with the past, rather than feel at odds with it. For example, B. J. Pryor's Henley asks listeners, "Ought a representative to do what his constituents demand, or ought he to employ his own judgement and understanding? Is he to be a puppet on a string to be pulled by every Tom, Dick or Harry, or is he to do as he judges best regardless of the popularity of his decision?"[12]

Many of the interactive techniques for encouraging conversation work best with small groups of visitors. For groups of more than eight or ten people, interpreters tend to do more monologue-style interpretation. John Kemp, discussing interpretation at Plimoth, related that a one-sided conversation is handy for speaking to larger audiences where there is less one-on-one discussion: "It carries better and makes a broader point that can be grasped by a large number of people who are milling around."[13] A monologue (or storyteller) style permits questions from individual listeners, but the interpreter will address the answer to the entire group.

Many roleplayers incorporate storytelling and short anecdotes into their interpretation, and in fact those who specialize in speaking to auditorium audiences (including Sarah Grant Reid, William Kashatus, and Bill Barker) consider storytelling an essential part of what they do. Storytelling is a very effective way to illustrate themes, illuminate abstract concepts of culture and attitude, evoke vivid images, and "make the characters seem like real human beings," whatever the size of the audience.[14] Public speaking expert Dorothy Sarnoff has said, "Anecdotes involve your listener. When you tell one, your listener sees a real scene."[15] First-person interpreter B. J. Pryor agrees, employing personalized narrative whenever possible: "Any point that can be turned into an anecdote is superior to a merely abstract point. If [my character, Reverend Henley, is] asked how Baptists are regarded or how the students [at the College of William and Mary] are disciplined, I tell of an instance. These are often actual documented events. I will often narrate a conversation or argument I have had with someone; thus conveying two 18th century opinions at once."[16]

First-person storytelling tends to be incidental — much like one recollects to friends how breakfast burned or the missed train crashed. Diary entries, letters, and newspaper articles are superb sources for creating narrative accounts. When David Emerson "remembers" how his Continental soldier character David McCaffrey survived four days without supplies by making soup boiled down from a tallow candle and shoe leather, it conjures up a much more vivid picture of the trials of a winter encampment than simply stating that many of the soldiers went hungry for days at a time.

Interpreter Bill Barker, who portrays Thomas Jefferson at Colonial Williamsburg, confided that his interpretation was inspired by the natural storytellers in his family: "I remember visiting with my family down South. Many of the older relatives would talk about the Civil War as if it had just happened. These people . . . had a special art of painting a picture in their conversation. . . . That's what I try to keep in mind all the time."[17]

There are many books available on the mechanics of storytelling.[18] Interpreter-storyteller Mike Follin of the Ohio Historical Society urges interpreters to develop their own internal visualization of historical scenes and objects, to incorporate visually loaded words, and to support verbal techniques with nonverbal behavior (such as implying the hot, tiring work of ironing by wiping the forehead). Motions, Follin suggests, can accompany verbal descriptions or substitute for them.[19] Follin also emphasizes the value of eye gaze in interpretive storytelling. He advises direct eye contact when introducing a story; space visualization — looking over the heads of visitors into the distance — when describing a "memory"; and looking directly at a visitor when relating a "recalled" dialogue, as a way of putting one of the listeners into the shoes of one of the characters in the narrative.[20]

Storytelling techniques are stressed at Mystic Seaport Museum. The director of the roleplay program, Glenn Gordinier, is himself a master yarnspinner. Storytelling, says Gordinier, should convey the basic interpretive themes of the museum.[21] At Mystic, this is life at sea and on shore. Bettye Noyes, who plays Mrs. Reynolds, the wife of a sea captain, leans heavily on storytelling in her interpretation, especially when a large crowd is in the Sailor's Reading Room (where much of the roleplaying at Mystic takes place). Bettye's character relates tales as diverse as travels with her husband, meeting a Pacific island king and queen, neighborly gossip, the Centennial celebration, and the agony of missing her children while at sea. These stories — based on real-life incidents — truly personalized the life of a sea captain's wife for me as a visitor. Bettye effectively alternated her yarns with stretches of question-and-answer time.[22]

There are multiple considerations and creative options for transforming factual accounts into interpretive stories. Will a story be described as something that happened to the character directly, or will it be related as a second- or third-hand incident? Or will it be retold verbatim, as is a period joke or jest? Can some facts be recited as dialogue? Should some details be left out, added, or changed for the sake of clarity or to better fit the interests of the character, the program message, or the audience? If elements need to be added, can they be added without distorting history? Are factual details used with balance in mind — enough to season the story with historical veracity without bogging down the flow (or the listeners)? Is the selection appropriate for the audience; will they identify with it? Will they recognize events and terminology?

Ralph Archbold, as character speaker Benjamin Franklin, says it is important to realize what one can and cannot do with different types of audiences. An audience comprised of historical society members and another of salesmen require different strategies and levels of detail: "I don't get into dates but I do get into interesting stories and personalities. A historical society gets 'the full load,' of course, because they enjoy the minutiae, but I would lose other types of audiences with an hour-long 'history lesson.' Both markets are fun, but they are very different — and it's important to keep that in perspective."[23]

How long should a story last? Glenn Gordinier limits them to the thirty-second to three-minute range.[24] In truth, there is no rule of thumb. The key — as with other aspects of interpretation — is to observe the listeners. If interest seems to be wandering — if they look as if they are seeking an escape route — the story is probably too long or not of interest to those particular visitors. A storytelling-based style — though often highly enjoyable — can inhibit verbal interaction. Perhaps visitors have questions they are anxious to ask. It's important, even at the expense of the interpreter's ego, to deal pleasantly with such a situation. Unrelated queries are a sure sign that interest is focused elsewhere. If the interpreter is regaling a group, and most of the group appears interested, an acknowledgment such as "Glad you asked, I'll get back to you in a moment," or a visual signal such as a raised hand and index finger, is a reasonable compromise. Occasionally it may be necessary to interrupt a story to answer a question, then go back to it. By keeping the presentation incidental, a pause to answer a question can seem perfectly natural.

In the technique's favor, stories and anecdotes lift the burden of participation off listeners and are very effective with large groups where a lot of visitor interaction is impractical — or where props and activities are at a minimum. Its greatest benefit: a good storyteller is absolutely absorbing.

Humor is another popular technique cited by interpreters for breaking the ice and enlivening a presentation. When not overdone, it reminds visitors that people of the past also possessed a sense of fun. Studies have revealed that people who can inject humor successfully into their conversation are perceived as more likable, and this in turn enables them to have greater influence on people.[25] Humor is fostered by incongruity — an unexpected conflict or inconsistency between two ideas, or an unexpected resolution to a train of thought. Appreciation (or dislike) of a particular jest or comment depends on the reference point of the listener. Humor can backfire, even if it is "period-correct." Some people find humor in topics that are no longer politically or socially appropriate, such as eighteenth-century opinions on the "nature of women" or nineteenth-century antagonisms toward immigrant groups. Others do not. Interpreters will need their keenest perception skills to gauge the tolerance level of their listeners. Intended or not, if a jest targets a victim with whom listeners identify, the result could be alienation and loss of credibility. If hostility or shock is not a response that one wishes to risk, stick to safe humor, such as an anecdote in which the teller is the butt of the joke.

For many interpreters, humor is a vehicle for attracting and keeping visitor attention. Says Lisa Simon Walbridge: "If you can get the visitors to smile, you have them hooked."[26] Glenn Gordinier, who induces unrestrained laughter with some of his own sailor tales, warns interpreters to avoid the "stand-up comedy act."[27] The authors of *The Interpreter's Guidebook* also advise the subtle touch: "A humorous story or anecdote should arrive unannounced. It should drift in and out of the plot as unobtrusively as Clark Kent, not as flamboyantly as Superman."[28] There are occasions, however, when broad humor is appropriate and welcomed. Some situations or characters naturally invite amusement. Interpreters portraying street performers, puppeteers, fops, and head-reading phrenologists, for instance, are expected to jump on every opportunity to milk laughs from visitors.

Eddie Grogan frequently draws laughter (at himself) when one of his 1836 characters pronounces with certainty that "Henry Clay will be the next president." Grogan notes that this statement in itself is not humorous but a good example of something his character might say. The humor occurs if the listener knows that Martin Van Buren ultimately won the election, or at least that Henry Clay was never president.[29] The statement becomes funny because the character's opinion is at odds with what really happened and because of Grogan's self-assuredness. If the statement is out of the visitor's point of

Historical Diversions' re-creation of an eighteenth-century puppet show, "Blackbeard the Pirate." The antics of the puppeteers are just as funny as those of the puppets. (photo: Stacy Roth)

reference, nothing is really lost — it is simply time to talk more about who Henry Clay "is" — or switch the subject.

Claire Gregoire is pleased that the Old Sturbridge Village staff have been working more humor into their presentations. To Claire, humor debunks the stereotype of the pious New Englander. "We want to show that people [in 1830s New England] had a sense of humor, they did like to be entertained, and that life was not all work and no play."[30] When interpreters revive the works of local contemporary writers and present them in context in the village — in settings such as public readings — visitors can get a sense of the type of humor that Jacksonian-American New Englanders enjoyed. Claire finds that there are some problems inherent in presenting such material. Many references are unfamiliar to twentieth-century visitors, so the meaning of some jests — particularly political ones — go completely over most heads. On the other hand, items that relate to human situations, such as love, jealousy, or foolish behavior, are very well received and understood. Interpreters at Old Sturbridge Village use letters, diaries, and pieces of prose, as well as the musings of writers, as sources for humorous incidents.[31]

Situational humor can also be effective. One of Tom Kelleher's (Old Sturbridge Village) many characters is a self-conscious Irish laborer who does such inappropriate things as barging into ladies' tea parties. Tom, who has portrayed everything from traveling salesmen to ministers, observes from experience that visitors feel more at ease around "lower class" characters rather than pompous ones. Characters such as his poor laborer, he adds, "tend to provide comic relief almost like the more buffoonish characters in Shakespearian plays." [32]

The Plimoth interpreters, who speak in seventeen period dialects from Great Britain, often have a jolly time joking with visitors from England. Those who are particularly proficient at their adopted speech "crank it up" and take advantage of related humor. Stuart Bolton entertained one group of visitors who revealed that they hailed from Hertfordshire even though they spoke Received Standard English. Bolton mentioned surprisedly to one, "You don't sound like a man that comes from those parts. You've spent some time in London." He added that "his own dialect" had been modified while living in London and thought it was a shame how rural folks must modify their speech when in London so as not to be thought bumpkins. The visitors laughed in sympathy, as attitudes concerning fashionable speech continue to be reflected in such prejudices. [33]

Some interpreters favor what Moira Turnan Hannon calls "the guerrilla approach." The guerrilla interpreter surprises visitors with the more unusual or offbeat aspects of an era, like the character at Plimoth who stood in the street and discussed visitors' personality characteristics based on the humoral theory. "A guerrilla interpreter will be the one who tells you an herbal cure for hemorrhoids," adds Moira. [34]

{11}

Body Language and Tone of Voice

Earlier I affirmed that interpreters are responsible for shepherding the first-person encounter. But although interpreters dominate interaction, visitors continually communicate through facial expression and body language. Savvy interpreters evaluate and observe visitors' responses and adjust their tactics for optimum effectiveness. Are visitors comprehending or lost? Enraptured or bored? Comfortable or uncomfortable? Pleased? Offended?

Body language and tone of voice convey much more about attitudes and emotions in face-to-face conversation than do words alone. First-person interpreters can strategically enhance communication charisma with nonverbal messages to optimize content reception, emphasize character traits, and help audiences visualize the unseen. Visitors' faces, bodies, and inflections are bellwethers for shortening, prolonging, or redirecting interaction and measuring effectiveness.[1] Because visitors often refrain from verbalizing their feelings — especially negative ones — knowing how to project and read body language and facial cues are invaluable skills.[2]

Many interpreters pay attention to audience reactions. They look for signs of interest, boredom, tolerance, humor, and cooperation and signals to participate in, continue, or conclude conversations. However, interpreters are frequently so focused on their performance that visitors' signals go unnoticed or unheeded. Obviously, compensating for one "poker face" can distract an interpreter into losing track of an otherwise contented crowd, but overall, awareness of nonverbal signals can make a big difference in the ultimate success of intimate audience presentations.[3]

In the next few pages, we will examine the effects of body language and voice, applying them to both visitors and interpreters. Most of the existing literature on nonverbal communication addresses typical conversation situations, public speaking, and third-person guiding. This overview will focus on selected concepts with special applications for first-person interpretation.

An interpreter chooses behavior to produce a desired effect — much the way a golfer selects clubs or an artist picks colors. Because interpretation is highly individualistic, we can tailor nonverbal characteristics to suit personal style, scenario, character, audience, and educational purpose. Smirking while relating the death of the sheriff, for example, could be out of place if you are his widow but quite appropriate if you just shot him.

BODY LANGUAGE

Body language includes facial expression, eye contact, distance, touch, posture, gesture, and appearance.[4]

Facial Expression

Oh yeah. If you've watched Jack Benny or Johnny Carson — people like that — you know the value of a kind of quizzical look — or a kind of puzzled head-scratching look — or a pregnant pause.

Eddie Grogan

The face is a window on the emotions. It can support or contradict a speaker. By knowing how to use facial expressions, then, it is possible to mask or emphasize true feelings. Facial animation is situation dependent. Generally, the larger the audience, the broader the detail. When addressing small groups of visitors, behaviors and expressions are more intimate in scale, and high emotions are modified.

In usual roleplayer-visitor conversation (that is, not in the midst of an emotional scene), certain facial expressions can help elicit positive (or negative) reactions that can encourage (or impede) visitors' involvement. For example, if one looks interested in visitors' questions — by looking directly at them with a pleasant expression — visitors will feel more confident. Friendly smiling generally makes people more comfortable. Negative looks (frowning, scowling, or rolling eyes) can intimidate listeners. (Those of us who frown when concentrating need to remember this.) A blank face can indicate hostility.[5] Interpreter inhibition and performance jitters, by the way, can create a deadpan expression, which may unintentionally project disdain.[6]

There are six basic emotions that we convey through our faces. They are happiness, surprise, fear, anger, disgust, and sadness. Each registers a particular configuration of changes in the forehead, eyebrows, eyelids, cheeks, nose, lips, and chin. Although there are slight changes from face to face — and different combinations of emotions, such as fearfully surprised or happily surprised — each emotion has its own blueprint or combination of characteristics that disclose feelings, even when we are trying to hide them. Knowing the language of the face enhances interpreter ability to emphasize or mask emotions and anticipate or shape visitor reactions. By observing visitor expressions, an interpreter receives immediate feedback. While the art of reading facial cues is far too complicated to be explained in the space permitted here, the following synopsis of the six key emotions and their characteristics (based on Paul Ekman's fascinating *Unmasking the Face* and Peter Marsh's *Eye to Eye*) provides the basics:

Happiness. Smiling mouth; wrinkles around eyes.

Surprise. Raised, curved eyebrows; open mouth; horizontal wrinkles across forehead (occasionally); eyes wide. There are several types of surprise that differ according to the expression of the mouth. For instance, a surprised forehead combined with a mouth that registers disgust signals doubt or disbelief.

Fear. Brows raised and drawn together; upper eyelids raised and lower eyelids tense, exposing more of the white above the iris; the mouth may be open; the lips are tense and drawn back.

Disgust. Wrinkled nose; raised upper lip; brows lowered; cheeks and lower eyelids raised. Closed lips show contempt. When registering disgusted surprise, the eyebrows remain up.

Anger. Eyes in a penetrating stare, sometimes with tensed lids; brows lowered; lips either pressed tightly together or apart with teeth bared. A wrinkled nose and raised upper lip conveys angry disgust. A raised corner of the mouth can display contempt, and an open mouth can convey surprise in addition to anger.

Sadness. Raised inner corners of eyebrows; mouth downturned or has trembling appearance; raised lower lids occasionally. Sadness can also be combined with other emotions.

Happiness

Surprise

Fear

Disgust

David Emerson models the six basic emotions. (photos: Stacy Roth)

Anger   *Sadness*

Eye Contact

The eyes convince listeners of our confidence or nervousness, our level of friendship or hostility, and our trustworthiness. Those are fairly important qualities. For instance, comfortable eye contact, in many cultures, encourages friendship and familiarity, but avoiding it makes one appear nervous, self-conscious, or untrustworthy. Too much staring, on the other hand, can convey hostility.[7]

Gaze is intricately connected with language. Speakers vary gaze to show pauses and breaks in conversation, to emphasize words or thoughts, to indicate where to look or to signal a turn to speak, and to check for feedback and signals that encourage us to keep the interpretive ball bouncing. People frequently avert their eyes while formulating what they are about to say next. A receiver's gaze can indicate attention and willingness to listen, a desire to continue conversation, a reaction to content, concentration, or attempts to avoid informational or emotional overload.[8] There are special gaze techniques for inducing visitors to see objects that are not physically present (stare off into the distance over listeners' heads) and for placing visitors in imaginary roles (gaze directly at the intended person).[9]

How much eye contact is sufficient or proper? According to Peter Marsh, in a one-on-one conversation the speaker looks directly into the eyes of the listener on an intermittent basis for less than half the time he or she is speaking, but no single glance should last more than one second, otherwise the listener will feel uncomfortable. The listener, on the other hand, looks at the speaker's face three-quarters of the time in glances lasting from one to seven seconds — if he or she is interested.[10] The issue is complicated by culture and gender. The Japanese and other Asians, for example, do not regard eye contact as important to communication as do most Westerners, and Native Americans consider sustained eye contact a sign of disrespect.[11] As for gender phenomena, researchers found that women listeners generally spend more time focusing on the face of a speaker than do men, but that they will avert their gaze if they perceive that a male is staring at them.[12]

When one person addresses a small gathering — a likely situation for an interpreter — Eugene E. White advises speakers to look at each person several times, because most people like to believe that the speaker is aware of their presence.[13] I have observed that the most personable interpreters look at many different visitors in a group, rather than at just one or two, even if one person is asking most of the questions. Plimoth interpreter Larry Erickson suggests that brief eye contact with visitors who enter a room while an earlier conversation is in progress makes newcomers feel welcomed into the conversation and more likely to be comfortable joining in.[14]

The gaze patterns of listeners in an interpretive setting differ from those of typical conversation because visitors are often surrounded by objects and activities that divert visual attention from the speaker. Paul Risk suggests that recognizing the difference between natural gaze breaks and those that occur for no apparent reason is the key to assessing how well interpretation is received. For instance, visitors commonly look aside to reflect after a thought-provoking comment or question or divert their eyes to an object under discussion. However, if gaze wanders to places other than where directed, attention may be waning.[15] The ultimate signal that visitors have run the course of their attention span is repeated gazing — at their watches. That is when Eddie Grogan stops in his tracks and says, "Whoa! Are you folks pressed for time?"[16]

Many interpreters zero in on visitors' eyes. Jeff Scotland looks for the "eyes to light up" when he hits on a topic of particular interest to visitors.[17] Others watch for a "gleam in the eye" that represents a tolerance for humor or potentially offensive material. The gleam indicates a tacit "go-ahead." It telegraphs unspoken messages such as, "I'm enjoying what you are doing," "I know I made a wisecrack but I can take it as well as give it," or "I have a sense of humor."[18] Glenn Gordinier watches for "the darting eye," which tells him that the visitor would like to move on but may be too polite to walk away. An interpreter, noticing this, can "give [the visitor] the 'out.'"[19]

Distance

In a typical conversation, people place themselves at a distance from the speaker that feels naturally comfortable to them. This comfort zone varies from culture to culture. Southern Europeans and Middle Easterners stand closer together than North Americans when conversing, and North Americans stand closer than Northern Europeans. Distance also depends on level of intimacy, age, and one's ability to hear.

In their book *The Good Guide*, Alison L. Grinder and E. Sue McCoy define four regions of space (for North American culture):

1. intimate: under 18 inches; used with lovers, close friends and relatives, and children;
2. personal: 18 to 30 inches (close personal) and 2½ to 4 feet (far personal); used with persons we know well;
3. social: 4 to 12 feet; used for formal or business communications; and
4. public: 12 feet or more; used with strangers.[20]

Most interaction between third-person tour guides and visitors takes place in the third zone.[21] Much first-person interpretation is in the third zone, too. However, demonstrations and cramped logistics draw (or force) visitors into the second zone or even the intimate zone. Children, untainted by the un-

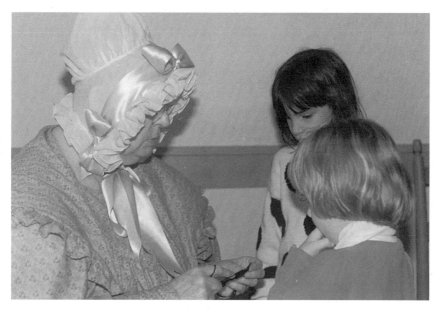

Two little girls sidle up to a grandmotherly Conner Prairie interpreter. (photo: Stacy Roth)

written rules of social distancing, move into the close personal and intimate zones as interpreters encourage them to handle or examine objects. Gitta Paans, a Plimoth interpreter acknowledged by colleagues as a natural with children, feels more at ease transcending personal space with children than with adults.[22]

When interaction is visitor paced, people choose their own distance or comfort zone in relation to the interpreter. Frequently they cautiously (or politely) allow extra distance between themselves and the character, if space permits. Interpreters who invite visitors to move closer reassure their public and appear friendlier.

In crowded conditions visitors are in the close personal and intimate zones of other visitors. Many accept this as part of playing tourist, even if they find it uncomfortable. In crowded situations individuals establish personal space by standing with arms in, looking away from others, and avoiding physical contact with strangers. We can increase visitors' comfort by adjusting interpretive spaces or shifting positions to maximize visibility. For instance, if crowds are expected, it is possible to create distance between interpreters and visitors by placing objects as "obstacles" in such a way that the speaker cannot be crowded by a row of people who block the vision of others, by speaking up clearly so that all can hear, and by using broader gestures.

Touch

Interpersonal touching, in many cultures, is reserved for intimate relationships except for certain circumstances, such as shaking hands, congratulating someone with pats on the back or arm, aiding someone in an emergency, and working with children. The touching that occurs in an interpretive setting usually involves engaging a visitor in a hands-on activity. Touching an adult anywhere other than on the hands, the arms, or the hair is usually considered intimate, pushy, or invasive.[23] Selected characters (dancing master, phrenologist) have more license due to the nature of their roles. But visitors can be touchy about touching in our suspicious and litigious society. Male interpreters, especially, must be increasingly wary about physical contact with children. Innocent actions can be transformed into career-jeopardizing complaints by manipulative children and over-reacting parents.

Interpreters also suffer their share of handling by visitors, such as the ones who examine clothing details or hug them while posing for a photographic souvenir.[24] While such acts bother some, it is part of the job, and it is important to keep one's face from registering a disapproving or disgusted look. So go ahead and smile.

Posture

The way we bear our bodies relates important characteristics about us. In public speaking situations, standing with "good" posture — head up and back straight — strengthens the authority and self-assuredness of the speaker and inspires the listener's confidence. Slumping the shoulders, bowing the head, folding the arms, deflating the chest, slouching, leaning, or jiggling are all seen as negative traits that signal qualities such as laziness, nervousness, depression, and untrustworthiness. Optimal public speaking traits, however, are not necessarily the aim of roleplaying, where characterization is important and credibility is judged differently.

The posture of people of the past was different from our own, owing to factors such as the wearing of stays and corsets, class-based habits, and fashion. The walk of a post-Restoration upper-class male, for instance, would be considered quite effeminate by today's standards. Accurate period clothing, especially proper undergarments, can help modern interpreters attain historical posture. Taking the time to "psyche up" into a role can also prompt appropriate bearing. Pat Baker, who crafts the period attire of the interpreters at Plimoth Plantation, can tell whether people are in or out of character even if she cannot hear them, because their posture (and other movements) changes visibly when they assume their roles.[25] A good character interpreter will adopt a stance reflecting class, sex, personality, and scenario circumstances. Posture changes with context. For instance, a servant might address a master in a humbled pose, behave cockily to a fellow servant, and strike yet another attitude with visitors, depending on their role or perceived station.

Gesture

Gestures support the spoken word. It's almost impossible to talk without them. Purposeful movement can show dynamism and enthusiasm, provide emphasis, and work to maintain listeners' attention. Descriptive movements help audiences picture unseen objects and settings. Unnecessary and indecisive movements, on the other hand, diffuse meaning, distract concentration, or strike the listener as aggressive.[26]

Certain gestures convey universally known messages. For example, speakers stab the air with an index finger to emphasize important concepts. The display of open or upward palms helps project a message. A pincer movement of the fingers (as if holding a marble between index finger and thumb) draws attention to a precise point. A palms-facing-with-spread-fingers pose transmits an intricacy or delicacy of subject matter. An upward motion of the hands screams excitement; downward warns, "take it easy — don't get upset."[27] Some gestures are more abstract than the ones mentioned above. Their meaning can vary drastically from one culture to another. The commonly benign goodbye wave (palm out, fingers waving up and down), for instance, is a gross insult to Greeks and Nigerians.[28] The cultural aspects of gestures will be covered in greater detail in the next chapter.

The entire body is an instrument that can attract or repel. A nodding head, for instance, in most cultures, confers agreement. Open arms, placed asymmetrically, appear friendlier than if crossed abreast or held straight at the sides.[29] Hands on hips, traditionally the stance of a fishwife, make the speaker seem larger and more aggressive.[30] Thus friendly movements draw people closer and aggressive movements keep them at a distance.

As Mrs. Reynolds, the sea captain's wife, Bettye Noyes enjoys accenting interpretation with gestures to purposefully reinforce her stories and to display intimacy and openness of character. She enumerates points by counting on her fingertips and liberally adopts a palms-open-fingers-spread stance. She leans forward when listening to questions and when sharing "confidential" insights.[31] Her gestures, combined with generous eye contact and well-developed material, gives Bettye a command over audiences that draws them in and enables them to suspend disbelief.

Tom Kelleher (Old Sturbridge Village), who occasionally plays the flamboyant actor Edwin Forrest and the lively Reverend Burchard (the latter made

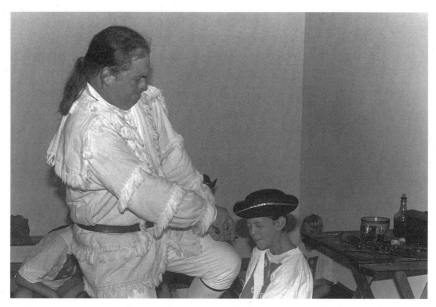

Combining pantomime, reproduction tools, and a few grunts and groans, David Emerson convinces a young friend to imagine how a primitive tooth extraction felt. (photo: Stacy Roth, courtesy Old Barracks Museum)

a name for himself by walking across the tops of church pews), assigns idio-syncratic gestures in the character development phase. "Forrest and Burch-ard were noted for exhibitionistic acts," says Tom, but he also fleshes out the personalities of his not-so-flamboyant roles with revealing little "habits." His Irish laborer character, for example, fingers his hat as a sign of self-consciousness.[32]

Pantomimed gestures can enhance spoken description. Glenn Gordinier actually "hoists a rope" during his sea tales.[33] David Emerson "bites off a chaw of tobacco" when describing a swap with an enemy soldier.

Improvisational theater games are a good way to practice body movements and evaluate how gestures transmit to others. Exercises in which participants rely on the body to communicate are effective for honing skills. Activities such as those in which players take turns striking poses that illustrate emotions, substitute gibberish for dialogue, or ask each other to plug up their ears and guess what a scene is about are perfect for creating awareness of physical communication.[34]

Appearance
If she's wearing a habit, I try not to talk about Catholics.
David Emerson

Each of us makes an impression before ever saying a word. We size up visitors all the time, anticipating behavior from their age, clothing, and demeanor. What do they think of interpreters, disguised as we are in the threads of an-other time? Many writers have stressed the importance of historically accurate costuming and accoutrements for first-person interpreters. But for many rea-sons — including tight budgets and/or lack of skilled construction personnel — compromises are made. Items such as shoes and eyeglasses are commonly a sticking point when assembling a fully accurate kit.

Ken Yellis suggests that when visitors identify bogus details, interpreter credibility is downgraded and visitors launch into a frame of mind to find other inaccuracies.[35] Certainly this is true of visitors who are historical re-enactors, buffs, or other interpreters. Most visitors, though, lack the height-ened awareness to recognize the difference between authentic period detailing and less-than-perfect substitutions. They can, however, spot wild anachro-nisms such as sneakers and wristwatches and will call attention to them.

One 1981 research study implied that the mania for authentic details is a symptom of interpreter mindset and far less important for the general pub-lic.[36] However, since 1981 there has been a significant growth in the living his-tory movement, with its attendant newsletter advice columns, historic dress experts, public workshops, pattern sourcebooks, and pattern availability, as well as an explosion of ready-made clothing and accoutrement businesses. Motion pictures, too, have paid increasing attention to garbing actors and actresses in the most accurate styles. Is everybody going to care? Probably not. But it seems like a lot more people care now than did fifteen years ago.

Realistically, the appearance of the interpreters, their information base, their techniques, and — for living history sites — their environment all affect the first-person experience. Sartorial perfection is laudable and reinforces academic credence, and its minute details can be springboards to important educational concepts; but it is not the linchpin on which successful interpretation hangs.

Glenn Gordinier raises another concern relating to appearance: the interpreter whose imposing size, shaggy beard, and/or shabby clothes threaten or frighten visitors. The "sailors" at Mystic often fall into this category. Likewise, roleplayers who are extremely well dressed can be intimidating or seem unapproachable. Gordinier advises that these interpreters should adopt a broad style, addressing crowds rather than individuals.[37] Imposing people can compensate by adopting subtle body language that encourages conversation (such as the eyebrow flash) and use hooks that invite participation.

VOICE

Speak softly of tragedy. Speak loudly of outrage.
B. J. Pryor

My characters are LOUD!!!
William Kashatus III

Madame Tussaud and Miss [Clara] Barton, when disgruntled or angry,
would never raise their voices — rather, lower them.
Sarah Grant Reid

The voice, like movement, should support what an interpreter says. Effective speakers know that a voice which possesses moderate tone and volume, clarity, audibility, fluidity (rather than hesitation or stuttering), sincerity, animation, and varied pitch and pace is considered the most pleasant and easiest to listen to.[38] A first-person interpreter must balance the need to speak well in public with the demands of his or her character. These needs change from audience to audience, character to character, and visitor to visitor.

Bettye Noyes of Mystic Seaport Museum is always conscious of how her voice affects visitors. She is attuned to the presence of background noises and

Bettye Noyes of Mystic Seaport Museum and Jeremy Fried of Colonial Williamsburg effectively combine eye contact, gaze, body movement, posture, and hand gestures. (photos: Edward Baker [Bettye Noyes] and Stacy Roth [Jeremy Fried])

other distractions that prompt her to project her voice as necessary. Outdoors, she uses a "stage voice" — louder and broadly directed — to imply that a conversation will take place for the visitors' benefit.[39]

Bil Orland (Plimoth) has one voice for visitors and another for addressing fellow interpreters. Bil retains polite speaking tones when addressing visitors, reserving his angry or sarcastic inflections for interaction with other interpreters. By doing so, he restricts aggressive behavior to a "performance" context, so that it is never directed at visitors.[40] Larry Erickson softens his voice when speaking to children, compensating for his tall, burly, bearded appearance, but with adults he raises it to indicate his character's certainty over an issue.[41] B. J. Pryor (Colonial Williamsburg) manipulates his voice to emphasize emotions and to highlight important concepts. Pryor speaks softly "to encourage careful listening," raising his volume as the heart of the matter under discussion is reached.[42]

Another facet of voice is dialect. Many interpreters develop period and regional dialects to heighten realism. Dialect enthusiasts must not only sustain their exotic speech pattern and rhythm but must be conscious of listener comprehension. Even if a dialect is perfectly executed, visitors may not be able to understand a single word, or they might have to struggle to decipher it. Unless another interpreter is playing "translator" for effect, modification is necessary. Interpreters at Plimoth Plantation tone down their dialects for foreign visitors and children, especially, and for others who appear to have difficulty.[43]

Visitors, of course, use tonal cues, too, but because interpreters do most of the talking, most communication from the visitor is nonverbal. When visitors ask a question or make a comment, their tone of voice indicates interest, surprise, skepticism, or insult (for example). Rick Jenkinson, a potter at Old Sturbridge Village, who frequently interprets to children, mentioned a preference for reading visitors' vocal rather than physical or facial cues. Jenkinson aims to excite children about his craft, so he feeds off the level of enthusiasm in their young voices.[44]

Interpreters who are involved in sight-demanding activity, such as needlework, chopping wood, or pottery, may at times need to rely on the visitor's tone of voice as their main source of feedback. Problems occur when interpreters focus on their activities to the exclusion of visitors. It is endemic when craftsmen are on a mandated production schedule, but it also happens during cooking (or other activities) that once initiated, depend on timing and attention. The optimum solution is to add a second interpreter whose primary responsibility is to talk, but this is not often a realistic option. The communication-conscious demonstrator will look intermittently at visitors as opportunity permits, acknowledge arrivals with a glance, and pause whenever possible to engage in sustained conversation.[45]

To summarize, nonverbal communication enables interpreters to amplify the spoken word, galvanize attention, improve content reception, add character dimension, and monitor effectiveness. Awareness and mastery of these skills is no easy task, but when incorporated, they provide interpreters with an extra edge that will ultimately improve the visitor experience.

{IV}

Roleplay and Relevance

Shaping Interpretation for Different Audiences

{12}

Interpreting to Adults, Families, Seniors, and Foreign Visitors

Who are the ideal audiences for first-person interpretation? It would be overly optimistic to claim that the genre succeeds with everyone. In general, the audiences best served by it are age nine or older, speak the same language as the interpreters, and are free from severe mental impairments. Young children lack the sense of historical time and informational background to take full advantage of it, as do many mentally impaired people. Those who have difficulty understanding the language spoken by roleplayers lose meaning and nuance unless they are accompanied by a skilled translator. Such obstacles are not unique to first-person. However, interpreters can and do make historical character interpretation work for those who do not fit the ideal profile. The next three chapters explore how interpreters have adapted first-person to suit diverse audiences, both ideal and challenging: adults, families, senior citizens, and foreign visitors (Chapter 12); preschoolers, primary and secondary school-aged children, and middle teens (Chapter 13); and disadvantaged and special-needs visitors (Chapter 14).[1] Chapter 12 also addresses creative methods for orienting visitors who encounter first-person unexpectedly, those who fail to catch on, and those who purposefully antagonize interpreters.

Familiarity with the learning styles, motivations, age level capabilities, and social characteristics of visitor subgroups can help first-person interpreters craft meaningful and enjoyable experiences for diverse audiences. Interpreters forearmed with basic cognitive and sociological models can anticipate techniques that are likely to work and avoid those that alienate or fail to communicate effectively.[2]

An adult visitor gleefully assists the author in illustrating the proper way to hold a teacup.
(photo: Stacia Partin, courtesy William Trent House)

ADULTS

Adults are impossible to categorize with a blanket assessment, other than to attest to their diversity. They approach first-person programs from many motivations and backgrounds. They often seek educational experiences as a form of entertainment and frequently consider a visit to a historic site or an encounter with a living history presentation in that light. As learners, they enjoy leisure events that build on prior knowledge and personal interests.

Because they commonly attend interpretation programs voluntarily, adults frequently display more interest and enthusiasm than the schoolchild on a class trip or the family member who is dragged along unwillingly.[3] Adults appreciate the depth of knowledge, storytelling abilities, and other skills of good interpreters. A one-on-one conversation on a favorite subject can absorb adults for long periods of time. The art of "verbal prospecting" (suggesting a palette of topics and watching for the one that piques the interest of the visitor), is one of the key techniques that interpreters use to establish links to the unpredictable and varied backgrounds of adults.

Adults also respond enthusiastically to humor, especially the type of remarks that fly over children's heads and appeal to the shared experiences of roleplayer and visitor. Husband-wife relations, battle-of-the-sexes stories, and lawyer and doctor barbs all bring sparkles of delight to the eyes of mature listeners. Frequent are the chuckles of personal identification when Conner Prairie's Dr. Campbell (Eddie Grogan) complains that his wife made him spend so much money on their new French wallpaper.[4]

Every interpreter knows that children love to touch objects and try out activities, but adults enjoy hands-on participation too. At one summer festival, while portraying a character en route to a distant city, satchel of spare clothing in tow, I encouraged those curious about my eighteenth-century attire to try on the spares — stays, gown, and panniers included. Two adults were among those who were game. I inquired what they thought of my clothes in comparison to the ones "they arrived in." One woman remarked that she felt more graceful, while another marveled, "Boy, I wouldn't want to wear this all day long. How did they put up with it?" Each expressed joyful appreciation for the chance to "play dress-up."

FAMILIES

Families are a significant part of the audience at historic sites, museums, and other venues where roleplaying is a feature. Family leisure and learning theorists have discovered that parents plan weekend and summer outings to foster social interaction among family members. Educational value is often an important part of the decision but plays a secondary role. John H. Falk and Lynn D. Dierking, authors of *The Museum Experience*, maintain that family experiences in museums are shaped by the personal interests of individual family members, the nature of interaction among themselves, and their physical relationship with the site environment.[5]

Family group visitors have special needs and expectations. Marilyn G. Hood reports that criteria valued by family-centered visitors are different from those prized by frequent museum attenders and the staffs themselves. Hood warns that because family visitors are primarily interested in social interaction, active participation, and entertainment, their desires can clash with those of staff, who can be more interested in providing educational opportunities laden with content.[6] "Information overload" is a common result when this is the case.

What are the implications of these findings for first-person interpreters? A preference for interaction and entertainment bodes well for roleplaying. Hood's analysis of Indianapolis-area residents' willingness to visit a new addition to Conner Prairie revealed that many family survey respondents preferred living history sites to traditional museums as potential outing desti-

Interaction between family members is an important part of a visit to a historic site.
(photo: Stacy Roth)

nations.[7] "Entertainment," by the way, does not automatically demean the presentation of history. While the word can conjure up a Hollywood revue, it also means "an activity that holds attention" — certainly a goal of good interpretation.

One of the advantages of living history programs is their ability to adapt to individual and group interests. But as site audiences become increasingly heterogeneous in composition, ethnicity, race, educational background, and class, interpreters will be challenged to offer experiences that families will appreciate, while keeping to their educational mandates. Interpreters must develop new ways of stimulating family interaction. Techniques that not only shift between subjects that appeal to children, to parents, and to grandparents but stimulate child-adult interaction will capture the loyalty of family visitors. Clever interpreters do this by discussing subjects that concern both parents and children and by addressing the perspectives of each. A conversation on schooling, for instance, might touch on a typical day's activities for the child and the factors that affect a parent's decision to enroll a child in school. Interpreters can encourage parents and children to participate together in an activity or jointly solve a problem. They can select stories that have universal appeal and evoke emotions: childhood memories, sagas of heroism, suspenseful stories, and tales with a moral. Interpreters may linger on certain points if the interest is there; families do not need to be flooded with information.

Many parents are content when their children are productively engaged and enjoying themselves. However, one of the highest compliments an interpreter can receive is "He/She kept the kids riveted and was interesting to us, too."

There are many ways that parents, children, and interpreters interact. Some family groups listen passively to interpreters, perhaps because they are uncertain about what to do or are anxious that they may say the wrong thing. It is especially important to make such families feel comfortable by indicating that questions are welcome, including obvious clues that one is in character, eliminating the need for responses if they are at a loss for words, and providing examples of appropriate questions. For instance:

> "Good day to ya, folks. I've got fine quality merchandise at reasonable prices for ladies and gentlemen and young'uns. If anything on my shelves strikes your fancy, why you just go ahead and ask me about it and I'll fetch it down for your examination." Pause; follow visitor interest or, if no verbal response, pull a novel item off the shelf and explain its use. Answer questions or, if family doesn't respond verbally but is obviously interested, take all burden for interaction off the family by highlighting other objects or launching into a story. "I was just thinking about what I plan to do on the Glorious Fourth — the birthday of our great nation." [8]

Moira Turnan Hannon and Effie Cummings, Plimoth Plantation interpreters with a natural affinity for young children and families, sweep children into an activity such as stirring pottage or grinding corn. While the children are absorbed in the physical task, the Pilgrim goodwives explain to parents what the children are doing, describing the food itself in a little more detail. Hannon and Cummings like to ask children what they think of the work and if they help their parents with a task like this at home, questions that encourage children to compare new experiences with familiar ones.

Caroline Roberts (Maggie Wright, servant) of Upper Canada Village likes to play parents and children off each other as she describes the advantages to both of putting children out to service. Then the kids get an earful of all of the work that is involved for scanty pay. All of a sudden, getting away from Mom and Dad doesn't seem all that attractive. [9]

Parents who are comfortable in museum settings often play the contextualist with their children, suggest questions to ask, and explore the answers along with their children: "Look Johnny, there is the sea captain, where do you think he has been on his voyages? Shall we ask him? Go ahead, ask him. . . . He said that he sailed out of Nantucket. We were there last summer. Do you remember what it was like?" Others ask questions through their children: "Johnny, ask him what kind of whales he catches when he is out at sea."

Seniors are another group that poses special challenges for first-person interpreters, but many of the problems interpreters used to have with older visitors are on the wane. When first-person was new, older visitors took a while to catch on to it. They were surprised by alterations in interpretation at their favorite sites and frequently reacted negatively — or with confusion — to new methods. That is changing. Seniors today are one of the fastest growing visitor groups, and their number will continue to mushroom as the baby-boom generation joins their ranks. Many retirees who visit parks, museums, and historic sites are full of energy, healthy, well-educated, well-traveled, and financially secure.[10] A good portion have seen first-person programs through the years and are not surprised when they encounter them.

There is not much data available on older visitors and their perceptions of first-person interpretation; however, several themes emerged from interpreter responses. Seniors often travel with friends or organized tour groups. Consequently, interacting with fellow visitors is a major part of their experience, as much as, if not more than, the site or program they are viewing. In the autumn of full lives, seniors have memories that are rekindled by conversations with interpreters. "They love to reminisce," chuckles Eddie Grogan.[11] Sociable interpreters realize this and encourage their contributions — even if it is sometimes difficult to wrestle the spotlight back from them once they start. Ophelia Wellington of Freetown Village (Indianapolis, Ind.) greets seniors fondly, as if they are old personal friends, inviting casual intimacy.[12] Certain topics, too, are bound to get the old juices flowing: military service, farm life, one-room schoolhouses, and manners that were more formal.

Older visitors take special enjoyment in fraternizing with older interpreters. They appreciate the perspective of "one of their own." Peter Cazaly, who portrays Nicholas Hart, the gentlemanly printer at Upper Canada Village, enjoys his "stardom" among retired visitors; the women flirt outrageously with him.[13]

Awareness of seniors' physical comfort earns their gratitude. Even when they are healthy and full of energy, their sight, hearing, and stamina may be diminished. A clear, audible interpreter will spare them the awkwardness of asking for repetition. A place to rest is always welcomed. A long drive or bus trip can be wearing; interpreters should take special care to watch out for fatigue and accommodate it, if possible. Caroline Roberts of Upper Canada Village arranges seating in places conducive to conversation — and near the warm stove when the weather is cold and damp.[14] It is always worth the extra effort to ask seniors if they would care to sit down, since they may not realize that they are welcome to.

Asian visitors at Colonial Williamsburg. (photo: Stacy Roth)

FOREIGN VISITORS

Edward T. Hall and William Foote Whyte observed what so many interpreters, first- and third-person alike, confess: "If you cannot speak a man's language you are terribly handicapped at communicating with him." [15]

Foreign and ethnic-minority visitors present special challenges for the first-person interpreter. Not only are messages filtered through an interpersonal context but a cultural one as well. [16] While this topic is far too broad to cover in a few paragraphs, I have highlighted interpreters' current strategies for accommodating world travelers, immigrants, and visitors whose native tongue is not that of the interpreter.

When visitors do not understand the interpreter's words, meaningful discussion is well nigh impossible. When no verbal communication can take place, interpreters make the best of a bad situation by smiling, displaying friendly body language, engaging in demonstration, making music, pointing out objects of interest, and willingly posing for photographs.

Multilingual interpreters have an advantage. They may shift into visitors' native tongues or seek a common second language. Several staff at Upper Canada Village are comfortable with two or three languages, among them English, French, German, Spanish, and Dutch. Sarah Grant Reid (who portrays Madame Tussaud, Clara Barton, and Josephine Bonaparte) is an internationalist and a fluent speaker of French and German. She presents entirely in those languages upon request. Some interpreters at Plimoth have learned Dutch — primarily to add more realism to their seventeenth-century Congregation of Saints characters (many of whom lived in Holland for over a dozen years) — and find that it benefits their frequent Dutch visitors. I observed Lisa Simon Walbridge deftly shifting between Dutch and English for a mixed audience of Dutch and American visitors. She alternated between the two tongues, capitalizing on bilingualism as an entrée to her character's travels and translating all of the questions and answers so that everyone could undersand them.

Statistics show that foreign visitation and immigration to the United States is increasing. The largest immigrant and temporary resident populations are Asian and Hispanic,[17] groups to whom the concept of first-person may be surprising and potentially confusing. Of those two nationalities, Asian tourists are a more common sight at large living history museums where first-person is a component. Unfortunately, very few first-person interpreters in the West are fluent in Japanese or Korean.

What happens when foreign language abilities are not part of the knowledge base of an interpreter's character? Should one "cheat" by conversing in another tongue? For the sake of providing a tolerable experience for foreign visitors, it may be best to do so, especially in a one-on-one environment. When other visitors are present, it is likely that they will be sympathetic, as long as they are not kept out of the conversation for too long.

Many foreign visitors speak English. Others commonly travel in groups with a guide or interpreter. When reasonable communication can be effected, the following strategies improve comprehension and make the experience pleasant for our national guests:

Be friendly. A smile is a smile in every language.

Maximize understandability by speaking slowly and clearly, avoiding slang and idiomatic expressions.

If possible, touch on topics that relate to the visitors' country or nationality. For instance, Eddie Grogan discusses his memories of the Marquis de Lafayette's visit to the United States in the 1820s with French visitors or shares remarks about Simon Bolivar with South American visitors. Such efforts demonstrate an interest in foreign visitors' cultures and increase the odds of starting from references within the visitors' experience.[18]

Provide opportunities for visitors to compare their memories with those being described or demonstrated. Foreign visitors are sometimes familiar with many of our historical crafts and agricultural techniques. They readily contribute tips or cultural comparisons based on their own skills or recollections of families and neighbors. Interpreters can occasionally discover revealing "tricks of the trade" that way. In the military hospital display at the Old Barracks Museum, the surgeon's "blistering glass" has prompted European visitors' descriptions of its firsthand application.

When dispensing humor, remember to keep a twinkle in the eye and be wary of crossing the line into insult. John Lowe (Colonial Williamsburg) enjoys teasing some of his foreign visitors. He joyfully welcomes Japanese tour groups, beaming, "How wonderful it is to meet an Indian delegation." They appreciate the hospitable greeting and howl at his error.[19] Peter Cazaly chooses irony, chiding his French visitors about the instability of the French government in 1866 and warning them about the "Prussian menace."[20]

Familiarity with the cultural characteristics of foreign visitor groups extends goodwill and helps prevent embarrassment. Scholarly studies on intercultural communication and works on conducting business abroad are good sources of information. The latter, aimed at executives and salespeople to help them avoid international faux pas, are available in the business sections of major book dealers.[21] The suggestions below are selected from both types of resources. Keep in mind that many of the tips are generalizations. Some people who appear "foreign" have assimilated into the host culture; others prefer to "do as the Romans do" when on the road.

Avoid gestures that are offensive in visitors' nonverbal vocabulary. Certain innocent U.S. gestures are unintentionally insulting to other cultures. The "bye-bye" wave (palm out, fingers flapping up and down) enrages a Greek. Stroking a cheek to gather thoughts means "thin and ill" to many Europeans. The common signal of approval made by forming a circle with thumb and forefinger pantomimes a bodily orifice to some Mediterranean visitors and "zero" (that is, "dunce") to French, Spanish, and Belgian visitors. "Thumbs up" is rude to Australians. A Briton reacts to the gesture illustrating the number two — two fingers in a "V" with nails out (as in "two burgers, please") — with the same ire that a Yank expends when faced with a defiant raised middle finger. Middle Easterners will take offense if beckoned with an index finger.[22]

Japanese tourists place importance on maintaining face and presenting a polite demeanor. They avoid forthright individual thought and action. Questions that single out one person from the group might cause discomfort, and a difficult hands-on activity unsuccessfully executed could precipitate embarrassment.[23]

WHAT DO YOU DO WHEN THEY DON'T CATCH ON?

Uninitiated visitors need time to adjust to first-person. They may be caught off guard by their first introduction, uncertain how to respond or interact. A few folks never quite figure it out. The best defense against confusion is a thorough orientation. However, in reality, many visitors inadvertently miss orientations, skip them, aren't paying close attention, or are in situations where advance warning is catch-as-catch-can (such as street festivals and Colonial Williamsburg's admission-free streets and shops). A problem? No. Skilled interpreters should be adept at gracefully orienting unsuspecting individuals — without dropping character or alienating anyone.

Unprepared visitors demonstrate several predictable behaviors. They initiate a conversation, ask a question, or respond to a greeting by discussing subject matter that is outside a program's historical context. Most adult visitors catch on after a few exchanges with the interpreters. A very few just don't get it, no matter how many hints are thrown their way. Another minority refuses to play along and persists with anachronistic or antagonistic comments. How should an interpreter behave with these latter situations? Opinions vary.

One school of thought contends that visitors' desires should override the presentation format. Interpreters who subscribe to this view do not feel obliged to stay in character or limit conversation to a given date. Those at the opposite extreme believe that breaking character destroys historical mood, compromises a presentation, and confuses visitors even further. Such interpreters almost never drop out of role. In betwixt are those who prefer to stay in character if possible, but occasionally make exceptions. Staffing, resources, and typical visitor composition ultimately affect policies for coping with confused or obstinate individuals. It is important, however, for programs with multiple interpretive stations to establish a sitewide approach. Otherwise, the rules keep changing, and visitors don't know what to expect from one interpreter to the next.

Tom Sanders of Fort Snelling recommends that first-person players break character and switch into third-person if they perceive difficulties, contending that "visitors cannot experience the past if they can't understand it or feel that the interpreters are rude or evasive." He developed the my time/your time approach, in which characters have a timeless quality that permits them to know and compare past with present, as an alternative for accommodating young children, senior citizens, foreign visitors, and the mentally impaired.[24]

Ken Yellis argues that falling in and out of character disorients: "It may not be just the purist living historian who is likely to be confused when role players break character and then *slip back in*. Suppose, for example, a visitor's weak sense of time prompted the out-of-period question that led the interpreter to break period. Is the visitor's sense of time strengthened by alternating responses . . . out of the same speaker?"[25]

Yellis believes that maintaining character helps develop further the sense of "then-ness" and "now-ness." He reasons that while visitors have paid to utilize staff, they have intended to do so within the context of a program. It is the responsibility of the organizers to provide a quality program that will offer the visitor a satisfying experience.[26]

Tom Vance supports interpreter insistence on remaining in character but admits that there may be times when a serious or sincere question can justify a step out of role. "Indiscriminate role-breaking," he cautions, "can destroy the illusion being created by other interpreters or for other visit[or]s, and lessen the impact of the whole purpose of a first-person program."[27] George Chapman, who shares this outlook, related an incident that happened to him when he was an interpreter at Plimoth Plantation in the early 1980s, when first-person was still in its infancy.

Sometimes [breaking character] is all one can do to relieve a very stressful time for the visitor. An example: One day in Hopkins House [the simulated home of Pilgrim Stephen Hopkins] I observed a man sit down on a bench in the corner and hold his head in his hands, obviously deeply disturbed. When the house had emptied he still sat in that position. I went to him and asked if there was anything I could do for him. He burst out "I have been here for 3 hours and haven't had a single question answered that I have asked. This is the worst museum I have ever visited." Looking quickly out the doors and windows to see we were not about to be interrupted, I questioned him . . . and discovered that he asked questions in a manner that most interpreters could not answer directly. So I said "You need to know that there are rules to playing our game. Questions must [be] phrased so we can answer them." I then taught him how. 2 hours later I saw him coming from the bottom of the street past Hopkins. I asked "Sir, did you solve that problem you told me about?" He replied "I sure did. You know this is the best museum I have ever visited."[28]

The decision to step out of role is complicated when just one person in a group seems confused. Nearby visitors frequently volunteer to straighten out the perplexed person. If not, skilled interpreters have found ways of responding to anachronistic statements and questions in ways that reorient visitors by feeding them direct hints, often incorporating clever puns. Date and current event references are one of the most common techniques, such as Glenn Gordinier's example: "This is, after all, the year of our Centennial, 1876." [29] Visitors who claim a Mayflower passenger is their ancestor often receive puzzled replies, such as, "What a scandal! He isn't even married yet!" If visitors still fail to catch on — and it is extremely rare when they don't — most interpreters behave politely to the confused person but perform to the majority who understand, rather than exasperate everyone with continued attempts to educate one visitor.

In the early days of first-person interpretation, many roleplayers replied to "unanswerable" questions with a perplexed "I don't know what you mean." This was one of the prime frustrations of visitors. Over the years, interpreters discovered that their feigned puzzlement must indicate the specific concepts foreign to their characters and include clues that illustrate historical ways of thinking. They have developed responses to anachronistic questions that are not rude or evasive and in many cases actually provide answers.

Frequently visitors ask reasonable questions that are phrased with terminology or ideas unrecognizable to past cultures. Interpreters can "translate" many of these. Stuart Bolton, who was portraying Edward Winslow on the day I spoke with him at Plimoth Plantation, converts questions that are not sensible to a seventeenth-century person into ones that are: "If you mean [rephrased question], then [appropriate answer]." Carson Hudson (Colonial Williamsburg and Living History Associates) prompts visitors to explain or rephrase questions when there is an educational opportunity created by doing so. At other times, Hudson notes, it makes more sense to "cheat a little bit" and answer the question.[30] To a desperate "Where is the bathroom?" for instance, many interpreters spare visitors the torture of pretending not to know what a bathroom is by simply indicating that the place the person seeks is "beyond the gates of the town," then pointing them in the necessary direction.

Occasionally questions that do not push character fidelity too far afield can be answered by prognosticating. In this example, the setting is a Revolutionary War camp in July or August 1780, weeks before Benedict Arnold's West Point debacle and the hanging of conspirator Maj. John André.

> Visitor: So, what do you think of that traitor Benedict Arnold? And that other fellow that was involved with him, "Robert" André, was it? What ever happened to him?

Officer: Arnold, a traitor? As far as I know, he's in command of West
Point. Wouldn't be surprised if he tried something treasonous after that
misconduct in Philadelphia and a near court-martial, plus that Tory
wife of his. Is he planning mischief with "John" André, that scribbler of
plays? If he is, and our boys bag him, hanging would be in order.

Sometimes interpreters bend the rules a bit when alone with one or two
people. When David Emerson is playing a fictional character and a visitor
asks, "Where can I purchase clothes like the ones you are wearing?" he tells
them, "From a tailor named ———" (giving the name of the person or estab-
lishment who actually made the garment), then offers to write down the address. Some interpreters discreetly step aside with visitors to accommodate
this type of request or have offered to meet them outside the confines of the
first-person area at an appointed time.

Once when I was portraying a Quaker at the time of the American Revolution at a community festival, I had been chatting in character with one
woman for a good quarter-hour when she asked me how Quakerism changed
from the eighteenth century to the twentieth and requested the titles of a few
relevant books. I asked if she "desired an answer, even if it meant stepping out
of the past." She said yes, so I obliged, mentioning that if other visitors walked
up, I would shift back into character and resume our discussion once they left.

The availability of noncostumed, clearly identifiable third-person interpreters who can answer nonperiod questions — either in the interpretive area
or just outside it — eliminates the agony of turning aside earnest postperiod
questions. Greeters, such as the Visitor Services personnel at the gangway of
Mayflower II, alert visitors to program parameters and offer to answer questions that are beyond the scope of those on the ship. Alternatively, guides who
escort visitors through first-person areas can accommodate queries and help
newcomers communicate with roleplayers. The employment of additional
third-person interpreters will depend, of course, on the sophistication of the
first-person program and its resources. If such staffing exists, it is a reasonable
compromise to explain that an answer is "beyond me," or some other suitable
phrase, and suggest that they inquire "to the person over there with the shield
on his cap," "at the stall with the blue roof," or whatever gets the message
across.

One frequent intrusion into our reconstructed pasts is the camera- or
video-wielding visitor. Drawing attention to anachronistic photographic devices is a useless waste of time, so most experienced interpreters have figured
out a way to accommodate shutterbugs with as little disruption as possible.
Mystic Seaport Museum, in fact, encourages its interpreters to welcome photo

opportunities because the visitors enjoy them.[31] At sites that pre-date the invention of the camera, interpreters respond to "Mind if I take your picture?" with comments such as, "Well, if you must," "As long as it doesn't hurt," or "I don't know what you are talking about but go ahead anyway." There are still some who jest that the visitor must be a witch or an inventor, but most savvy interpreters have dropped that from their repertoire. It's too corny.

Some visitors are rude or bothersome. These folks, while rare, can be unpleasant and annoying to interpreters and other visitors alike. Some intentionally goad interpreters by badgering them with twentieth-centuryisms such as "Do you know what a McDonald's is?" or "Do you drive a car?" or by zeroing in on anachronisms. Some ask rude, sexually charged questions or try to pick fights. Some are perversely playful and want to test how well interpreters can stick to their character. The meaner sort, like vandals, take pleasure in destroying an illusion or somehow feel superior if they succeed in finding errors and embarrassing or disrupting others.

There is no consensus on how to handle problematic adults. Some interpreters tune them out; others reprimand them or usher them out with a comment such as, "I'm too busy for this kind of chat"; and some will continue to be congenial — in character — until the offending visitor finally leaves. A few defend themselves with humor or sarcastic putdowns. It is not unusual for fellow visitors to put spoilsports in their place.

Most unintentionally irritating visitor wisecracks are best met with a like sense of humor. Chris Hall, who occasionally plays John Billington at Plimoth Plantation, replied to a man who announced his profession as computer programmer, "Oh you make pewter! We certainly could use some of that around here." Unavoidable anachronisms should be tossed off with a smile, too. I once witnessed an interpreter answer a visitor who pointed heavenward at a skywriting airplane and asked, "What's that?" Peering up suspiciously, the interpreter said, "It must be French." David Emerson related an incident that happened to him as Stephen Hopkins at Plimoth. He had just finished telling a visitor that the sound of church bells was what his character missed most about his home in England. No sooner had the words left his mouth, when the local congregation's bells began to peal. Without missing a beat, he smiled and added, "Sometimes, when I think of them bells, it is as if I can almost hear them."

{13}

Interpreting to Children

I feel the most comfortable with children because, in my opinion, children are sort of like characters themselves. They will say anything and ask anything that is on their minds.
Larry Earl, Colonial Williamsburg

The importance of effective interpretation for children cannot be underestimated. Most of us who are fascinated by the past can recall a childhood mentor or specific incident that set our imaginations on fire. Every time we interpret to young people, we, too, have the opportunity to ignite that spark or to fan the flames. Conversely, boring or uninspired interpretation can repel a child, perhaps indefinitely, from further investigation of our most beloved topics. With the alternative diversions of the electronic age multiplying exponentially, we bear a serious responsibility for keeping history alive into the future. Forgive me for belaboring the pyro-metaphor, but we can either pass the torch or drop it in a puddle!

Interpreters cannot guarantee what young audiences will learn; the absorption of knowledge is too individualistic. But smart interpretive choices can help learning happen when we know what to expect from visitors at different stages in their growth and match appropriate techniques. Freeman Tilden, the quintessential lifelong interpreter, emphasized that children's interpretation should not be a diluted version of adult programming but should be fundamentally different.[1] To spark children's imaginations we must develop strategies that start from within young cognitive and social experiences, add a healthy dose of excitement, and lead them into new territory. Because first-person interpretation allows children to discover new people, objects, atti-

133

Lisa Simon Walbridge (Plimoth Plantation) and friends. (courtesy Plimoth Plantation)

tudes, activities, dress, and technology in the context of everyday life, it has powerful potential for meaningful learning.[2]

Children are introduced to first-person via trips to historic sites and museums with their class or with parents, or by visits to their classrooms by character interpreters. Not always the best audiences, their attendance is frequently involuntary, their concentration is easily distracted, their attention spans are often short, and many view anything labeled "educational" by their elders in the same category as cauliflower and liver.

What do we want children to gain from their encounters with roleplayers? There is no single answer, but I feel that first-person adventures should exercise children's senses and critical thinking skills and embrace their love of play. Many programs are designed with specific educational goals in mind. For example, when the students attending the "Matter of Choice" program at the Old Barracks Museum return to their classroom, staff hope students will recognize that the decision to become a patriot, loyalist, or neutral during the American Revolution was complicated and often based on personal circumstances. To balance intellectual activity with physical participation and exposure to visual stimuli, students are also sworn into the Continental Army by a rousing recruiting officer and introduced to the material culture of an army hospital.

In some programs, interpretation is more open ended and flows with the interests of the children. Or it does a bit of both, focusing on a few themes but diverging down individualized paths of conversation. At Plimoth Plantation, students break into small groups to wander at will and/or perform specific tasks defined by their teachers. Alternatively, school visitors to Plimoth attend an education enhancement program, where they are prepared with background by staff educators, who lead them around the village, suggest questions to ask the Pilgrims, and encourage comparisons. Children's visits are much more meaningful if participants are exposed to related subjects beforehand, either through teachers' lesson plans, through pre-visit materials supplied by the site or school performer, by discussing what they expect to see with parents, by reading a book, or by viewing a video.

Authorities agree that interpretation for children is improved by applying established learning theories such as those developed by Jean Piaget, Jerome Bruner, Howard Gardner, Kieran Egan, and Robert Selman.[3] At least three writers have examined the application of educational theory on the field of interpretation. Donald Ecroyd, communications specialist, Temple University professor of speech, and communications instructor for the National Park Service, advocated Piaget's cognitive framework. He suggested types of stories, games, and humor that are appropriate at each developmental level; described the linguistic, speaking, and listening abilities of each age cluster; and suggested methods of discipline for each stage.[4]

Gary E. Machlis, in an article with Donald R. Field titled "Getting Connected: An Approach To Children's Interpretation," and in another work with Maureen McDonough, *Children's Interpretation: A Discovery Book for Interpreters*, prescribes three criteria for reaching young visitors: understanding the developmental phases of childhood growth with its opportunities and limitations at various social and chronological stages; recognizing the importance of group life on children and realizing its impact on interpretation; and employing the three keys to any program that involves children: action and activity, a sense of fantasy and imagination, and instruction that connects with children's experience.[5]

Brendan Smith, an interpreter at Plimoth Plantation and an M.A. candidate at the State University of New York (Oneonta), conducted a case study examining how the theories of Piaget, Bruner, Egan, and Gardner compared with the field experiences of his first-person coworkers. Smith divided childhood development into four categories: early elementary (ages 5 to 8), elementary (ages 8 to 12), junior high (ages 12 to 15), and high school (ages 15 to 18).[6] While stressing that cognitive models do not alone prepare an interpreter for the field, he concluded that established theories do provide insights that can improve interpreter effectiveness. He identified four strategies by which first-person interpreters could apply learning theories to their craft: involve students actively, tell stories, direct the interpretation to the students' own experience, and vary interpretive methods.[7]

Models of cognitive development are valuable guidelines when preparing programs for specific age levels, but interpreters should allow for some latitude. Theorists occasionally contradict one another. Interpreters, too, may discover that some of their own winning techniques do not always coincide with established models. Obviously, if a technique really succeeds, keep with it. If it doesn't, educational models can help pinpoint weaknesses or inspire new strategies.

A thumbnail sketch of several theories follows below:

Swiss psychologist Jean Piaget (1896–1980) is well known for his pioneering work on the development of analytical reasoning and cognition from birth through adolescence. At Piaget's "sensorimotor" stage (birth to 2 years), children negotiate their environment by sensing rather than thinking. At the next level, "preoperational" (ages 2 to 7), children are egocentric, can compare likenesses and differences, but generally do not engage in abstract thought. They can respond to events but do not ponder their meaning. Their sense of cause and effect is not well developed, and they still relate to the world primarily through sensory experiences. The senses continue to dominate perception in the "concrete-operational" stage (ages 7 to 11), but during the upper years they become less self-centered, can predict consequences that will result from actions, can reflect on relationships, and are able to keep ideas and images in mind for contrast, reflection, and identification. The last of Piaget's stages of childhood, from early adolescence to adulthood, finds young people honing their abilities for mature thought and formal operations. They begin to theorize, see cause and effect, hypothesize, and draw conclusions from observed data.[8]

Subsequent researchers have picked away at Piaget's theories, finding them limited to mathematical-logical intelligence (to the exclusion of other skills) and a Western value orientation. Nevertheless, they remain a staple of countless educators. Piaget provides a logical framework for planning a successful mix of sensory activity, subject focus, and complexity for each age level.

Robert Selman formulated a model of young peoples' social development. Between ages 2 and 7, children are highly egocentric, relating all experiences to themselves. At ages 5 to 9, they become aware that other perspectives exist. From ages 7 to 12, they begin to draw inferences about other peoples' beliefs and actions. By age 10 through age 15, they are able to conceptualize third-party perspectives. After mid-adolescence, they are supposed to understand their own as well as others' societal orientation.[9] Selman's model presents first-person interpreters a scale for selecting the personal voice of anecdotes, stories, and discussion. Young children relate well to imagining themselves in action ("This is what you do if you live here"). As they mature they identify with others who are like them ("This happened to a child just like you"). Eventually they can appreciate experiences that are more abstract, identifying with common emotions or beliefs rather than the age or gender of the subject.

Canadian educator Kieran Egan identified stages in which children from age 5 make sense of life. From 5 through 10 years old, which Egan dubs the "mythic" stage, children are rigid thinkers with a need for precise explanations. Stories with polar oppositions (good/bad, brave/cowardly, right/wrong) appeal to their desire to label and categorize. From ages 10 to 15, they enter a "romantic" stage. According to Egan, "History is best understood at this stage as a kind of mosaic of bright elements — anecdotes, facts, dramatic events."[10] His writings on early adolescent behavior highlight this group's overriding interest in the bizarre, the adventurous, the rebellious, and the extraordinary. In the philosophical stage, from ages 15 through 20, teens and young adults come to the realization that their lives are fixed by their place in the world and that they are not as free to go beyond limits as they once thought. In the last stage, "ironic," from age 20 through adulthood, individuals learn that generalizations cannot fit a complex world.[11] Egan's classification offers interpreters insight into the value of skillful storytelling, suggesting how to select subject matter that will appeal to listeners of a specific age.

In the 1960s psychologist-educator Jerome Bruner developed a model social studies curriculum that embraced a behavioral rather than a fact-based approach, stressing information gathering and inquiry to develop understanding of the past and its application to the future. His curriculum, "Man: a Course of Study," centered around language, toolmaking, social organization, child rearing, and representations of worldview — all of the elements that can be re-created so vividly in a living history site such as Plimoth Plantation. Bruner maintains that inquiry-based coursework is more readily understood and trains students in methods of investigation that are adaptable later.[12] Bruner's theories remind interpreters that history is not simply a story to be told or historical activities to re-create for their own sake, but a way of using inquiry about the past as a model for looking toward the future. Charging students to find out, for example, the skills and beliefs they must acquire to survive successfully in Plimoth Plantation in 1627 has a more personally meaningful focus than simply asking, "How did the Pilgrims live at Plimoth?"

Ronald Vukelich collated existing theories of children's perceptions of historical time. His study provides a year-by-year breakdown of the vocabulary of historical, clock, and calendar time recognized by children ages 4 through 16.[13] According to Vukelich's chronology, children discover broad time language (for example, before and after) around the age of 5 or 6, acquire clock and calendar time at age 6 or 7, know major holidays and gain a general sense of past and present at ages 8 and 9, and recognize periods or eras of historical time around age 9 or 10. Not until age 12 do most children begin to internalize adult time concepts, and not until 14 do they recognize differences within parts of past centuries. Although children vary from this chronology, it is invaluable for selecting and describing suitable historical topics for young audiences. Most 8-year-olds, for instance, would be out of their depth attending a program on the causes of the French and Indian War. One on colonial trades, less time-specific and related to the more familiar concept of "work," is a better match for their emerging sense of the past.

In the 1980s Howard Gardner pioneered a new, pluralistic approach to the way people learn. His theory of multiple intelligences suggests that each individual's learning style is shaped by linguistic, logical-mathematical, spatial, musical, and bodily kinesthetic tendencies, plus two types of "personal intelligences": interpersonal and intrapersonal. Everyone has varying degrees of talent in each of these categories:[14]

> People with dominant *linguistic intelligence* use words precisely and evocatively and have a well-developed sense of rhythm and tone. A poet, for example, has dominant linguistic intelligence.

> *Logical-mathematical intelligence* is the ability to reason logically and manipulate mathematical problems.

> People with well-developed *spatial intelligence* have exceptional skills for creating mental models of multidimensional worlds and can operate and maneuver using that model. Sailors, sculptors, surgeons, and painters possess these skills.

Individuals with *musical intelligence* have the ability to play and make music and discriminate between sounds.

Bodily *kinesthetic intelligence* is the talent to solve problems or make products using one's body. Domestic crafts, artistic crafts, and dancing represent activities of those so gifted.

The remaining two intelligences describe the way individuals understand and work with others:

People with *interpersonal intelligence* notice others' behavior, moods, motivations, temperament, and intentions, and can act effectively upon that knowledge. Interpersonal learners work well in collaborative situations. Skilled teachers, convincing salespeople, therapists, and political leaders, for instance, often possess highly developed interpersonal intelligence.

Individuals with *intrapersonal intelligence* understand themselves well and capitalize on inner directedness. They commonly have realistic views of themselves, focus on inward feelings and dreams, follow their instincts, can work alone and pursue their own interests, and enjoy being original.

If variety is the spice of life, it is also the spice of interpretation. Gardner's theories of multiple intelligences underscore the importance of multiple approaches for stirring the imaginations of children (as well as adults). Interpreters frequently personify Gardner's categories. Logical-mathematical interpreters can explain complicated politics, religion, and economics; warbling interpreters love to sing period songs; spatial and bodily kinesthetic interpreters gravitate to craft and domestic activities; linguistic interpreters excel in dialects and storytelling; interpersonal interpreters enthusiastically encourage everybody's participation; and the intrapersonal interpreter can grip an audience with a monologue that stirs the emotions. Interpreters who can incorporate several styles and techniques, such as storytelling, singing, guided inquiry and discovery, demonstration, hands-on experience, and/or explanation, are likely to catch the largest number of little fish in their net.

Many writers have stressed the importance of incorporating familiar concepts as a launching point for further discovery. One way of predicting subject exposure is to look at local and state school curricula and to talk with teachers. Advance reconnaissance enables interpreters to forecast what children may know about key themes and related subjects. For example, if students meet a colonial housewife and the interpreter knows that the local fourth grade is studying state geography, regional ecology, and nutrition, she could incorporate demonstration and/or discussion of local plants, the seasonality of family diet, and the crucial timing of planting, harvesting, and mucking the garden into her program.

In the next few pages we will look at the characteristics of typical child cognition and behavior at five levels: preschool (ages 3 to 5), primary school (ages 5 to 8), elementary school (ages 8 to 12), junior high (ages 12 to 15), and high school (ages 15 to 18). I will suggest appropriate techniques and provide illustrations of interpreters' favorite ways of working with children.

PRESCHOOL (AGES 3 TO 5)

Obviously, the preschooler is not the ideal audience for first-person interpretation. Preschool classes rarely elect to visit or be visited by first-person characters from the past. Their understanding of the world is derived from sensory perceptions. They focus on broad details such as color, size, and shape, overlooking the unfamiliar. They assume that happenings or objects observed together are related, and they cannot conceive that their perceptions are incorrect. And of course they have no concrete sense of historical time. However, preschoolers are commonly part of family visits, so interpreters should be prepared for them.

Those of us who have worked with preschoolers know that these little ones play "pretend" at the drop of a hat, can do some comparing and classifying, and enjoy surprises and games. Their dependence on the senses requires action, exciting visual experiences, and activity. However, their short attention spans and egocentric lack of patience require ongoing involvement and organized presentation. Activities in which everyone participates at the same time avoid squabbles over turn-taking, and stories that include repetitive elements and phrases that are chanted as a group maintain attention while reinforcing key concepts.[15] Another tip on averting chaos with groups, offered by Brendan Smith, is to limit children's activity choices.[16] If asked whether they want to sing a song, grind corn, or feed chickens, they say yes to everything and can't decide what they want to do. Just pick a task and assign participants.

When performing a first-person character in a festival or site situation where there are families with very young children, I always keep a few tricks on hand. One is a group of three spoons made from three different substances: wood, horn, and pewter. I bring out the three spoons and ask the little ones if they know what I am holding. "Spoons," they shout. "Yes, they are spoons, but are they all alike, or are they different? What are they made of?" The children usually answer "wood, metal, and plastic." I hold up the horned spoon. "A lot of children tell me they think it is something called 'plastic,' but I don't know what 'plastic' is. What else could it be made of? I will give you a clue." I hold the horn spoon at the side of my head like a cow's horn and make a mooing sound. We then talk about how cows have horns and examine the spoon up close. "Can you see through it? Can you see through the others?" With a group of three or fewer, the spoons get passed around, and I encourage them to think about what it would feel like to sip from the spoons (without putting them in our mouths, of course). We make scooping, lifting, and sipping motions. I ask them if they remember the names of all the spoon materials. They frequently forget the word "horn," so we play a game. "Is it wood, metal, and — soap?" "NOOOOOOOOO!" they all giggle and scream. We try again with another silly substitution. If "horn" is completely forgotten, I have them repeat the names of the trio a few more times.

PRIMARY SCHOOL (AGES 5 TO 8)

Children at this age are emerging from the self-centered world of the toddler and are acquiring and internalizing new information at an astounding rate while continuing to learn primarily through their senses. Around age seven, classification skills, ordering, internal manipulations of concrete data, and inductive thinking begin to develop. Their perspective preserves its polarity: people, actions, and issues are right or wrong, good or bad. Gradually they realize that others think differently from themselves.

For first-person interpretation, this is a borderline audience. Most children under age eight recognize seasons, months, and times of day but do not grasp historical time, so their frame of reference is limited. For instance, students in the first, second, and third grades who have experienced holidays with their class or family can recognize the Pilgrims, George Washington, and Abraham Lincoln, but because the past is not firmly differentiated from the present in their minds, they often believe that characters are "real" — not a person dressed up and acting like someone from long ago. Their questions are earnest and they take answers seriously. Steve Gulick, the Quaker freelance interpreter who uses the character of antislavery crusader John Woolman to explore social issues and matters of conscience, remarks that children from kindergarten through third grade are willing to talk uninhibitedly about their feelings in

Tom Kelleher mesmerizes a young mixed-age trio by demonstrating how a bucket is made. (photo: Stacy Roth)

open discussion.[17] So a well-targeted program can be very satisfying for both interpreter and audience.

Practitioners of first-person interpretation have developed strategies for successfully engaging younger children. First-person can be made more understandable to primary (and elementary) schoolers by incorporating techniques of third-person interpretation: questioning and discussing, comparing and classifying, participating in hands-on activity, image-filled storytelling, and encouraging kids to imagine what life would have been like for historical children. The key is to focus on topics in which children have related experience or can see in front of them, include demonstration or activity whenever possible, and add an excited or enthusiastic edge to the interpretive voice. Avoid topics that lack common links for comprehension. Interpreters will quickly lose listener attention by introducing too many abstract concepts; there is novelty aplenty in the costumes, activities, and demonstrations. Watch out for vocabulary adults take for granted but children may not understand. Unfamiliar terms can be decoded as messages one never intended. ("What? That man was born in *whales*?") If an advanced word is important, explain it in appropriate, comprehendible terms.

Mutually recognizable ideas make graduated complexity easier to introduce. When a seven-year-old asked David Emerson as Pilgrim Stephen Hopkins if Pilgrims are friendly with Indians, David responded, "There's no simple answer to that question. It's yes sometimes and no sometimes. Think of it this way: Is everyone that you know your friend? Are there some people that you like better than others? That is the way it is with us and the Indians." He followed with anecdotes illustrating incidents of both friendship and hostility.

Encouraging young visitors to contrast the past with their own experiences without resorting to out-of-period references is one of the greatest challenges of first-person. What does one say to children that only know television, equal rights, the supermarket, and automobiles to imagine a world without them? Interpreters who strictly maintain their historical perspective talk around the obstacles by personalizing questions but avoiding outright modernisms. For instance, an interpreter might describe the dinner items on the hearth and inquire whether or not the children eat such foods "at their own home." When children respond with modern ideas or terminology — for example, "We buy all of our meat at the *supermarket*" — interpreters can respond by admitting puzzlement over an unfamiliar term (although some interpreters prefer not to repeat the modern term itself) and by focusing attention on historical concepts: "We go to the market in town sometimes, but I've never heard it called a supermarket. The market has butchers' stalls where meats can be bought, as well as many other goods, like iron pots and laces and things from far away. But we raise our meats here on the farm. Quite a bit more work, wouldn't you say?"

Parents and teachers, familiar with specific episodes in their charges' lives, frequently help with comparisons: "Remember yesterday, when we went to the store, all of the meat was wrapped in little plastic packages? They didn't have that back then."

Some interpreters prefer my time/your time and ghost interpretation with this age group because it is simpler to explain the difference between past and present using children's contemporary vocabulary. These techniques have been discussed in earlier chapters. When designing programs for 5- to 8-year-olds, first-person is not my method of choice unless the characters and subject matter are unquestionably familiar.

Cynthia Andes and Dan Bassuk creatively tailor first-person for this age group. Andes incorporates first-person as one component of an otherwise third-person presentation, and Bassuk adopts the first-person character of Abraham Lincoln for his unique storytelling sessions. Andes introduces children to Col. Edwin Drake and his discovery of oil at Drake Well Museum (Titusville, Pa.). Her program opens with a brief character monologue in which Andes portrays Drake's mother. She invites the children to step back in time with her to 150 years earlier, when the entrepreneur was a little boy. An imaginary Edwin disturbs her clothesline, prompting his mother to recount a

Cynthia Andes, "Edwin Drake," and friend. (courtesy Cynthia Andes)

series of other escapades highlighting the youth's inquisitiveness and his eventual discovery of oil, the substance that would "light up the whole world." The scenario, says Andes, encourages youngsters to identify with Drake. After her brief monologue she leaves the character and segues into a third-person show-and-tell on the history of oil, uncovering from her laundry basket items that illustrate the history of lighting. A coloring/activity book about life on a Pennsylvania oil lease is available in advance of the program.[18]

Bassuk, an Abraham Lincoln buff, former literature professor, and independent school performer, appears almost exclusively for primary school-age children. Bassuk's Lincoln is accompanied by life-size dolls representing Mrs. Lincoln and sons Willie and Tad, a small library of children's books, try-on clothing, and a slide show. The meat of Bassuk's program is storytelling, with original tales based on factual material. This Lincoln avoids discussing the politics and tactics of the Civil War, catering instead to his listeners' interests and experiences. They hear how Tad "freed" his pet turkey or why Lincoln grew his beard. Bassuk aims to show children "that Lincoln is a loving, sharing, honest man who enjoys children and stories, and wants to share them with kids."[19]

This is the age group that makes the most out of school visits from historical characters and class trips to historic sites. In these years children develop their sense of historical time as well as the ability to relate to abstract ideas (such as the philosophy of a religious movement or the concept of agricultural cycles).[20] By age ten they can match dates to important events and begin to recognize eras of history (for example, the Colonial period), replacing the vague younger notions of "a long time ago."[21] Although they still tend to think in terms of black and white, they develop understanding of others' perspectives (including historical "others"), can think subjectively about their own behavior, and discover that people have different values, outlooks, and feelings. Cognitively, they can retain identities and objects in the mind's eye, anticipate consequences, process complicated sentences, and employ deductive reasoning. They absolutely revel in stories that are full of gore, excitement, rebelliousness, and fantasy.[22] They love to laugh and have a good time, and they adore "secrets." But they are a tough audience. If an interpreter cannot capture their interest and imagination, they will make their boredom known by talking, yawning, looking droopy, and acting obstreperously.

One of Stanley Kugel's fifth-grade boys ponders the effectiveness of a neck stock for keeping one's head despite a blow from an enemy. (photo: Stanley Kugel)

One of the biggest challenges with this age group is balancing the type of discussion, narrative, and activity that we know they like with other information that we think they should be exposed to. Kieran Egan astutely observes that early adolescents are far more interested in exciting, bizarre, and extreme stories than they are in the familiar and the status quo. To stir the imagination of adolescents, Egan recommends selecting lessons that "deal with the outer limits of reality and the extremes of experience" and "put students in touch with the boundaries, the limits, the context of the material they are dealing with."[23] How do we reconcile the routine lives of common people of the past when faced with that? He suggests that teachers (interpreters, in our case) emphasize the transcendent, pugnacious, and heroic even in the most mundane objects and lifestyles. Working in our favor is the foreignness of the past, where something as tedious as plucking a chicken seems exotic to modern children. As an eighteenth-century Loyalist, I could never sway the opinions of adolescents by "upholding the status quo of the old regime," so instead, I "rebel against the rebellion."

As Thomas Jefferson, Bill Barker of Colonial Williamsburg invites listeners to look anew at the lowly clothespin, which he exalts as a recent invention and prized souvenir of his recent trip to France. Larry Earl, who plays Jefferson's slave Jupiter, introduces his own perspective on the object: "It makes the work of slave laundresses much easier. They don't have to lay the linens out all over the hedges anymore."[24]

It doesn't require a genius to figure out that one of the quickest ways to win a child's attention is through hands-on experience. Whether setting type on a printing press, splitting wood, or mucking out stalls, it is all new to them. Purposeful activities are wonderful ways to engage children in concrete learning because the more directly they are involved in a given activity, the greater the likelihood they will remember it.[25] A physical task or craft becomes more meaningful, however, when it is related to other contexts. Why is the activity important? Who benefits from it? What labors or materials preceded it or are associated with it? How would it feel to do the task all day long or every day?

Demonstrations do not always lend themselves to hands-on participation, but that need not limit "minds-on" participation. Children are easily stimulated by questions and like to express their opinions. When put on the spot to show their smarts (or avoid embarrassment), their attention is more focused. Therefore, skilled questioning, in addition to character monologue and demonstrations, can boost learning, increase understanding, and aid retention.

Bonnie Pitman-Gelles identifies four basic questioning strategies for museum education, and to these I have added a fifth:[26]

1. those that test recall of facts;
2. those that require interpretation of facts;
3. those that evaluate or defend the interpretation of facts;
4. those that encourage creative answers that are not necessarily right or wrong;
5. those that compare previous experiences with new ones.

Below are some examples of questioning strategies in a first-person setting, in this case a cooper's shop:

1. *Recalling facts.* Now that I've shown you around my shop, let's see if you would make good apprentices. Can you recall the names and uses of any of these tools?
2. *Putting facts together to solve a problem.* Which of these tools would you use to make a barrel? What do I need to do first?
3. *Evaluating or defending a decision or opinion.* Do you think this job is important in this village? Why? (or Why not?) Which of my neighbors do you think hires my services the most? Why?
4. *Stimulate interest and creativity (no right or wrong answers).* What kinds of objects would you like to make if you were a cooper?
5. *Comparing.* How does this shop compare to the carpenter's shop? Do any of you have a shop at your home? How are the tools in my shop similar or different?

The first-person interpreter must phrase past/present contrast questions carefully. Children often jump to explanations of what they know: objects from the twentieth century. The interpreter must steer the focus to the historical objects and processes in ways that help children themselves identify the differences.

The authors of *A Personal Training Program for Interpreters* recommend asking questions in a sequence that graduates from recall to relationship to application, occasionally backtracking to the previous types of questions to clarify answers.[27] It takes skill to develop good questions. The *Personal Training Program* suggests that interpreters sketch out questioning strategies beforehand, working backward from intended answers.[28]

Another strategy, student roleplay, has been used effectively by classroom teachers at all levels of education since the 1960s. Roleplay helps children develop empathy, use problem-solving skills, improve debating techniques, strengthen research ability, recognize the historical place of class and status, learn interpersonal skills, and discover the effects of chosen behavior.[29] The following are the major components of structured student roleplay:

1. select an issue or situation that will serve as a focus for discussion (for example, a debate, a trial, daily life reenactment, or re-creation of an event);
2. distribute roles, background information, and scenario outline or timetable;
3. guide students in further research and approach to character;
4. initiate the scenario;
5. follow up with a discussion and recap of what students learned and felt from the experience.

Jennifer Hayes and Dorothy Schindel, in their idea-packed book, *Pioneer Journeys: Drama in Museum Education*, describe the creative program at Fraunces Tavern Museum, which encourages children to identify tavern objects in their physical and social context. Classes are issued a pre-visit packet that assigns students role types (such as merchant, sea captain, post rider, tavernkeeper's child, or magician) and splits them into theme groups (business, travel, or politics and government). Children have the opportunity to improvise situations such as placing an order as if they were, for example, a lowly apprentice or an accomplished man of business. Each group also acts out a printed scenario that describes activities but omits the names of the tavern objects that characters would use in their common interaction. The children must recall these from other parts of their class outing and pre-visit study.[30]

Chris Creelman of Old Sturbridge Village supervises roleplaying programs in which groups of schoolchildren portray assigned characters.[31] Chris favors a problem-solving approach, presenting a situation such as deciding whether or not to permit the construction of a new factory in Sturbridge. The children must investigate both sides of the story and apply information they have gathered to reaching a decision. By incorporating an inquiry-based strategy with the teaching of history, not only is learning transformed from a passive to an active endeavor, but students discover that history does not occur on a predetermined path — it is the result of many different factors, including human nature and chance.

When children are encouraged to roleplay, it is an enormous advantage if they have advanced classroom preparation, such as study guides and character sheets, and can research their characters with teacher guidance. Old Sturbridge Village supplies its "Reading and Writing about History" participants with a curriculum unit that introduces students to roleplaying and requires teachers to attend a two-day workshop to model the unit and learn about background resources. The students visit the site twice. On the first visit they gather information and participate in hands-on activities. On the second visit they roleplay.[32]

Even when the children are not roleplaying per se, interpreters can include simple ploys to help children identify with the historical experience by substituting the visiting child for a historical child. "I'm looking for a cabin boy for my ship. You are just about the right age for such employment" or "My stepdaughter, a cheerful girl like yourself . . . " are phrases that help children picture themselves living long ago.

When children have not had advance preparation, interpreters must ferret out gaps and provide important background information. It helps to pause for questions at key concepts, especially at the outset, or ask potentially "theoretical" questions and answer them if the children need more information. For example, "He called me a Tory! Do you know what that implies?" (Pause. Observe response, such as negative head shaking.) "It means that he thinks that my allegiance is to King George and the Parliament; that I am against independence for these colonies."

Young visitors can be overwhelmed by the new and strange experiences they encounter at a living history site. They can also be affected by the presence of their parents, their teachers, or their peers, or by the unfamiliarity of a historical setting. Some may even find the size or appearance of costumed interpreters intimidating.[33] When unruly school groups bound into a site, an intimidating-looking interpreter can be a blessing. But to compensate for distractions, fear, and overexcitement, interpreters may need to allow time for children to adjust. All that initial gabbling that many adults classify as rude behavior is frequently an excited burst of discussion over new sights. A few minutes of observation may actually enhance their capacity to learn.

Eye contact — with as many children as possible — serves several purposes. It signals to young visitors that they, too, are being observed and heightens anticipation as each child wonders who will be looked at next. In addition, it acknowledges their participation and establishes an intimacy that helps children feel included and galvanizes their attention.

Pacing is important. In a novel setting it is easy to succumb to information overload, particularly when too much detail is packed into a presentation. Children like facts, but enumeration should carefully illustrate topics of particular interest, not sound like a recited thesis. Personally I have found that children's recall is better when details are judiciously selected, couched in an anecdotal context, and repeated or reinforced, and when the children's thoughts and opinions are solicited.

Each group of children is different, so interpreters must be flexible. What works well with one does not necessarily succeed with another. Glenn Gordinier advises interpreters to stay alert for clues that indicate interest or boredom. When one technique seems to fall flat, choose another and keep going, but don't keep pushing something that isn't panning out.[34]

JUNIOR HIGH (AGES 12 TO 15) AND
HIGH SCHOOL (AGES 15 TO 18)

Compared with other visitor groups, teenage audiences are infrequent. Their varied schedules and extracurricular demands often make it difficult for arranging day trips to sites, and their independence often absents them from family outings. No doubt about it, teen visitors can test an interpreter's mettle. In class groups they feel very self-conscious, hate to be singled out, find that traditional museums do not relate to their lives, and are reluctant to respond to questions. They can engage in behaviors that are flippant, sarcastic, and downright rude. On the other hand, if an interpreter hits the right note with them, they can be dynamic and intelligent questioners and debaters. As thinkers, many teens can transcend their own perspective to see the perspectives of others. By the time they reach high school, they can examine issues from a

Interpreter Tom Hay guides a junior high school class through eighteenth-century litigation. The teacher and several students play magistrates. (photo: Stacy Roth)

neutral standpoint, recognize causes and relationships, use adult time vocabulary and concepts, and recognize specific historical events and periods.

Considering the self-conscious behaviors of teens, an approach that encourages classes to break into small groups and explore personal interests at their own pace — an alternative at places such as Plimoth Plantation and Colonial Williamsburg — can be more to their taste than a structured program. Whatever the format, interpreters play a key role in setting an atmosphere that will provoke interest or disinterest.

Interpreters who enjoy working with this age group find that teenagers are much more receptive when spoken to in a welcoming, candid, and adult manner.[35] Frequently it takes a few minutes for teenagers to settle into serious discussion because their typical first response is to joke around. Moira Turnan Hannon suggests that if interpreters cheerfully endure silly quips for awhile and show they will not be deterred by them, the quips cease and attention sets in. Moira turns remarks such as, "Oh, you drink beer, can I have some?" into an exploration of why the colonists at Plimoth drink beer, why they constantly run short of supply, and how the goodwives of Plimoth brew it.[36]

Younger teenagers are still attracted to bizarre, heroic, and unusual things. They appreciate stories that shock and surprise them. Thus, image-laden anecdotes about how a shipmate survived getting his boat stove in by a whale and his head pierced by one of the whale's teeth, how mutineers are punished in the army, or how the farmwife foiled the enemy who attempted to raid her larder are all good fodder for this age group.

Kieran Egan marvels at how early adolescents are detail-crazy and that mastering something in exhaustive detail is a powerful learning drive in the typical 10- to 15-year-old.[37] A description of all the grisly tools in the surgeon's bag and what it feels like to be on the patient's end of them, or a scratch and sniff demonstration of herbs and medicinal preparations — with descriptions of diseases and attempted cures — can find them marveling "whoa, cool," and asking welcome and thoughtful questions.

As they mature, older teens seek more meaning in their lives and realize that their place in the world is fraught with limits not recognized at an earlier age. Because they can see two or more perspectives from a neutral standpoint, this is an excellent time to involve students in period conflicts and controversies and solicit opinions on what they would do if faced with similar circumstances. At this level, inquiry, hypothesis, and expansive thinking should be encouraged. Perhaps they know that a conflict under discussion erupted into a war or other rift later. Urge them to think about the subject from the perspective of someone who lives at the same time as the characters. What do they think could be done to prevent disastrous consequences?

In their study of the application of creative thinking techniques with high school students, Byron G. Massialas and Jack Zevin found that critical debate of controversial issues elicited a variety of views from students as they considered differing conclusions and values. Through reasoned argument, the students discovered that judgments cannot be accepted on faith but stand or fall on supporting evidence and implications.[38] Such critical thinking has application far beyond that of the historical issue at hand.

High-school-aged students are often absorbed in predictable themes: the opposite sex, getting through school and moving on to other things, earning a living, and relations with parents. Interpreters capitalize on this by introducing topics that feed into teen interests. William Kashatus appreciates and addresses his teen audiences' concerns over personal values.[39] At Plimoth, interpreters' most frequently discussed topics are expected societal and family roles of young men and women, marriage traditions, and crime and punishment.[40] As for teens' preoccupations with sex and drugs, as long as discussions are not prohibited by site taboos or chaperone request, many interpreters are willing to engage in serious dialogue about such topics. Although conversations often begin on a goofy note, interpreter savvy and subject relevance can inspire real learning.

DISADVANTAGED VISITORS

Machlis and McDonough have observed how the language and life experiences of socioeconomically disadvantaged groups can create significant barriers to effective interpretation of any kind, not just first-person interpretation.[41] Conversely, these groups can inspire us to look for new ways of getting our message across. Flexibility is important, because it may be more difficult to find the commonalities so key to increasing understanding.

Frequently inner-city teachers and group leaders make special efforts to prepare their charges for a visit to a first-person site or a class visit from a historical character. In other instances disadvantaged visitors have very little background that readies them for first-person interpretation or complex historical issues. Underprivileged children may be unfamiliar with topics that privileged students of the same age (and interpreters) take for granted. George Chapman, who worked at Plimoth in the early 1980s and now runs his own freelance interpretation business in California, remembered the surprise of an inner-city teenager discovering how milk comes from a cow.[42] Eddie Grogan recalled an experience he had while playing Prairietown's schoolmaster to a group of teenage girls from a correctional institution. "The schoolmaster's usual routine is to lead all of the 'scholars' in reciting phonetic practice from a blackboard. I thought, 'How is this going to do?' Reading 'be bi biddy bi' off the blackboard? Well, they loved it, and they wanted to do it again. It occurred to me that they were seeing something so different from what they grew up with, that it was like a vacation to them."[43]

It is important to recognize that even if students are well prepared, they will be seeing many of the things they learned about in class (or from books) for the very first time. Interpreters must be flexible enough to adapt on the fly, attempting to ferret out background knowledge and interests, then focusing and building on subjects that will engage attention. A strategy that accommodates the need to explore environments and objects at young visitors' experience level will be time well spent, even at the expense of altering initial program plans.

DISCIPLINE

What do we do with unruly children? Donald Ecroyd offers the following disciplinary suggestions for three age categories: From preschool to age seven, children have an external sense of discipline. Their need for approval of parents and other adults usually holds them in check, and they follow directions without asking for explanations. From ages seven to twelve, discipline is still approval-dependent, but youngsters are now very much aware of their peers. If they sense that peers have more sway than the adult in their midst, they can run amok. Ecroyd suggests that children in this age group should be advised of the rules at the start of a program so that they know what is expected of them. At a historic site this should be part of the orientation, before students meet historical characters. Beyond adolescence, discipline becomes internal to children, who choose their behavior to satisfy the self or out of respect for others. Success with discipline depends on how much respect an interpreter commands.[44] Ecroyd's advice was written with the park ranger interpreter in mind. Commanding respect can sometimes be difficult for characters who are not imposing figures or who play individuals who are low on the social scale.

Hopefully, parents or teachers will help with discipline problems, but in reality, interpreters are often amazed at the failure of chaperones to step in.[45] Interpreters have favorite methods for circumventing and stopping poor behavior. Many "lay down the law" to the children, with accompanying shock and indignity at their awful manners. (This works for imposing interpreters.)

Others patiently remind an excited group of chatterers that no one can be heard if they are all talking at once, or say, "Now it is my turn to talk, you will have your turn in time." Eddie Grogan speaks very softly, so that children must quiet down to hear him. Some interpreters stop talking completely until everyone settles down. Children will frequently shush each other until the group quiets. Cynthia Andes calls on single troublemakers and involves them in demonstrating an activity in front of the rest of the class. When they are truly out of hand or destructive, offenders should be delivered to their leader and asked (or ordered) to leave.

One of the most common problems is the spoilsport who persists in telling interpreters that they are not in the past, they are in the twentieth century. If everyone else has been going along with the program, it can be amusing to encourage classmates to assert that the year is indeed the historical one and the troublemaker is out of his mind. Other tactics include thrusting the annoying child into the middle of a demonstration or firmly staring him down with a few sharp words.

Sarah Grant Reid shared one of her favorite stories about putting a rude junior high student in his place: "At the start of one Junior High program, Miss [Clara] Barton informed a young man that she, not he, had been invited to speak — and she would; he, on the other hand, had been asked to listen, and he would. Needless to say, he did!!" [46]

Following that program, the children had questions for Miss Barton and Ms. Reid. One student asked if Reid had ever considered portraying a man. The student who had been firmly put in his place raised his hand and commented, "You, Miss Barton, would make an excellent General Patton." [47]

I frequently portray working-class characters and hardly look imposing. Yelling and reprimanding, therefore, never work for me. Fortunately the opportunity rarely comes up. First, I don't *expect* children to act like quiet little mice on their field trip. Second, I feed off kids' ebullience and capitalize on it by drawing attention to their excitement and tying it to interpretive themes that include elements of surprise. For example, this greeting, used by a Revolutionary War hospital worker at the Old Barracks Museum, has often redirected the focus of a lively group: "It's good to see some fresh faces around here, but you seem all fired up today! I'd be too if I just joined up with the army and found out that instead of sendin' me off to fight the enemy, they're sendin' me to a hospital for three weeks to catch smallpox on purpose [pause for reaction]. But if you settle down a bit, I'll tell ya what you're in for."

One last note: interpreters should avoid restraining or grabbing unruly children unless it is absolutely necessary. It is frustrating, but today's children are aware that they can create trouble for adults with the "touching" issue.

Interpreters must remember that some children (and their parents) are quick to turn incidents — even those in which youngsters are prevented from hurting themselves, injuring other children, or destroying property — into something quite different. Male interpreters, especially, are susceptible targets. The results can generate negative publicity for sites and endanger interpreters' reputations.

Not many interpreters enjoy disciplining young visitors. Reprimands on a class trip remind me of dents in a car: a few mar the overall effect, even if the car still runs and makes the journey; too many and the car breaks down. That is why it is so important to be familiar with the cognitive and social development of children as they mature and to be prepared with a battery of techniques that actively engage attention and imagination. Interpreting to children is a weighty responsibility that demands a lot of energy if it is to be kept up successfully day after day.

In this chapter, we have seen that elementary school-age children often respond with enthusiasm to first-person interpretation. By identifying strategies (and subjects) that relate to the experiences and behaviors of other age groups, interpreters can also successfully target teen and primary school-age audiences. Freeman Tilden, almost half a century ago, advised us that interpretation for young people must be fundamentally different from that for adults. Likewise, each stage of childhood requires its own special techniques.

{14}

Interpreting to Audiences with Special Needs

In a sense, we are all members of an audience with special needs. We have different learning styles, interests, and ways of processing information. Many of us have minor handicaps or disabilities that affect how we function or perceive information. To be precise, a disability is a clinically defined and identifiable condition; a handicap is a disadvantage — frequently, but not necessarily — caused by a disability. Special-needs visitors are those for whom it is necessary to enhance or modify techniques to improve message reception. They encompass — but are not limited to — people with visual, auditory, mental, or physical handicaps; learning disabilities; and psychological disturbances.

Working with special-needs visitors in first-person embraces basic interpretive philosophy: everyone deserves the interpreter's best efforts to communicate effectively within the confines of the format. By recognizing the characteristics of handicaps and disabilities, interpreters can draw on techniques that best facilitate understanding in those visitors.

Part of Your General Public Is Disabled, an excellent handbook on interpreting to disabled visitors in museums, zoos, and historic houses, describes various disabilities and their symptoms, emergency procedures, and suggestions for making interpretation more enjoyable and meaningful for handicapped visitors.[1] While the text is aimed at third-person museum guiding (hence some of the recommended physical site alterations are incongruous to first-person environments), first-person interpreters can easily incorporate many of these tips into their repertoires and will recognize most of them from practical experience. The following brief overview offers a few strategies that are suitable for first-person interpretation.[2]

Interpreting to people with disabilities or handicaps requires sensitivity, creativity, patience, and common sense. Some travel in groups, such as a class of deaf students, and alert sites to their needs in advance. More commonly they arrive as part of a walk-in visitation and usually do not announce their impairment. Others have minor disabilities and may not even consider themselves handicapped; they may be accustomed to adapting or feel too self-conscious to ask for special services. People with heart ailments or weight problems, for instance, unused to walking outdoor-museum distances, can tire. Or a person on crutches with a sprained ankle may be cheerfully keeping up but showing signs of exhaustion. Is it possible to offer them a place to sit down? Interpreters can do this in character as a simple matter of hospitality. If interpreters do not mention the option, however, it may not occur to visitors that they *can* sit down, and they may not ask.

Here is another example: An interpreter notices a visitor with a hearing aid or spots someone straining to hear (watch for a hand cupping an ear, side of head slightly cocked in speaker's direction, crinkled up nose, and/or squinting). The solution requires mild effort: speak louder; slow down; take care to enunciate clearly, muting a dialect if necessary; and repeat visitors' questions to ensure that everyone hears them.

Many severely and totally deaf visitors read lips. On occasion they are accompanied by a signer. Positioning oneself in light rather than shadow, if possible, improves visibility. Because these visitors must concentrate on the speaker's face or the signer's hands, their experience will be more pleasurable if interpreters pause periodically to give them time to observe activities or look at objects without missing parts of the spoken presentation.

Should a first-person interpreter sign for deaf visitors even though signing would be out of character? That depends on the policy of the program and the availability of other resources, such as a staff or volunteer signer (noncostumed) or special brochures. There are other considerations. Do communication goals outweigh technical constraints? Are the deaf visitors (or their families) the only group in the room or a large part of a small group? Will signing be distracting for others? Even though interpreters who sign or translate are displaying skills beyond the bounds of their characters, it is likely that non-hearing-impaired visitors will be sympathetic to the situation.

Visitors with visual impairments such as blindness, partial blindness, perceptual problems, and bright-to-dim adjustment disorders can have a perfectly enjoyable time with first-person interpreters — especially those who are good storytellers or hands-on types — because they naturally appeal to other senses. Interpreters should also describe details they may take for granted with sighted visitors: the size, shape, color, and/or texture of setting features, period clothing, and featured activities. When possible, offer partially sighted visitors opportunities for close-range exploration. Invoke the senses of touch and smell to their fullest. Encourage personal examination of objects and guide visitors' hands over interesting surfaces. Show off plants and foods with unique and familiar aromas.

Plimoth "Pilgrim" Effie Cummings finds interpreting to disabled visitors a rewarding challenge. She related an especially enjoyable encounter with a blind child: "I told him that I was cooking parsnips and encouraged him to come close and smell them. I needed some more from the garden, so I took the child along with me and let him pull some parsnips out of the earth." [3]

This activity invited the child to discover parsnips in their fullest context. Such opportunities to communicate with touch, smell, sound, and taste make living history sites especially educational for visually handicapped visitors.

Mobility impairments range from a severe loss of motor skills (requiring a wheelchair) to temporary injuries (such as a broken leg) to the slowdown that occurs with old age. Affected visitors appreciate an interpreter's efforts to make sure that they get a chance to see what's going on, either by bringing activities (or objects) closer to them, clearing their view by moving an obstacle, or by asking another visitor to step aside momentarily. Older visitors — and those who look exhausted — may simply need to sit down and would feel much more at ease if invited to do so.

Learning disabilities encompass a variety of symptoms and behaviors. They affect visual, aural, and/or tactile perception interfering with an individual's ability to process information. Those affected may have average or above-average intelligence, but their disability can cause them to exhibit hyperactivity, undermotivation, preoccupation, lack of coordination, or memory disorders.[4] The symptoms of these disabilities are not always readily recognizable; it is easy to mistake those affected as stupid or troublesome. Interpreters who recognize the signs can mediate some of the difficulties by slowing down and patiently clarifying or repeating concepts.

Attention Deficit Disorder (ADD) and Attention Deficit Hyperactive Disorder (ADHD), physiological conditions that result in reduced attention span and agitated behavior, have been receiving increased coverage in the media lately. During a 1991 conference about museum methods for the learning disabled at the Children's Museum of Manhattan, a class of students with attention disorders presented a session on museum experiences they enjoyed versus those they disliked. Living history and science museums — including Plimoth

Plantation and Old Sturbridge Village — topped their list of favorites for several reasons: they appreciated the ability to move about at their own pace without following a guide, and they liked the variety of "new" things and activities to look at. One child was even fascinated by the interpreters' different dialects at Plimoth.

The secret to holding the attention of persons affected with ADD or ADHD is to vary techniques during presentations, not unlike interpreting to the typical school group. Visual, tonal, and topical variety contribute to maintained interest. Alternate between anecdotes, demonstrations, circulating objects, and inquiry and discussion. Shift position occasionally and be expressive with the face and body. Competing noise such as clanking machinery, background music, or crying children can adversely affect the ability of a person with ADD or ADHD to concentrate. It may not be possible to eliminate such distractions, but if it is, it will make a difference.

Mentally retarded people can also enjoy the stimulating hands-on environment of living history sites or the unique experience of meeting a historical character. The severity of impairments differs among individuals. The majority (89 percent) are only mildly retarded and do not have physical characteristics that set them apart from everyone else.[5] The first rule of thumb for the first-person interpreter is to reassess those visitors who seem to ask "stupid" or unrelated questions or fail to catch on to the program. Some of them may, in fact, be slightly retarded. They deserve a kinder and gentler response rather than a dismissal. To better reach this audience, interpreters can simplify subject matter, avoid abstract principles, and express ideas in brief, easily understandable "chunks."[6] Retarded individuals respond positively to enthusiasm, so a ready smile and genuine interest fosters pleasant interaction. For severely retarded visitors, direct sensory experiences are more successful than a lot of talk. Can they stir the beans, pet the animals, or help with a simple chore?

Other individuals that require special care are sufferers of mental disorders. The National Alliance for the Mentally Ill describes mental illness as "a group of disorders causing severe disturbances in thinking, feeling, and relating."[7] Examples include schizophrenia, depression, manic depression, and phobias. Afflictions can be isolated incidents brought on by traumatic events, periodic flare-ups, or chronic. Attacks range from mild to severe. The vast majority do not exhibit outward abnormal behavior, but those who do may seem lethargic, hyperactive, unable to concentrate, or fearful. They might display uncontrollable movements, engage in ritualistic behavior, appear rude, or talk to themselves. Of course, individuals who are not mentally ill are capable of demonstrating such traits, too. When interpreters recognize behaviors that suggest mental disorders are the cause, interpretation need not be altered — except for one key consideration: mentally ill people frequently lack confidence. Avoid remarks that puncture self-esteem and difficult hands-on activities that can frustrate participants. Remember your first try at the drop spindle? Do not pressure those who prefer to sit out participatory activities. Respond to pronounced symptomatic behavior firmly but not rudely; remind someone confessing delusions or asking unrelated questions that it is not the appropriate time or place to discuss such things.[8]

Awareness and sensitivity are crucial when interpreting for audiences with special needs, but recognizing and accommodating handicaps and disabilities have residual benefits. Remember Effie Cummings, the blind child, and the parsnips? Concentrating on the aroma of the potherb and its texture in the earth could be enjoyably effective with sighted visitors. Shifting one's position to maximize the light aids lip readers, but it also improves visibility for all. So concern for the handicapped visitors not only enhances their experiences, but everyone's.

{15}

Interpreting Special Situations
Conflict, Controversy, and Heightened Emotion

Communication leads sometimes to cooperation and sometimes to conflict.
S. I. Hayakawa, Language in Thought and Action

Conflict and controversy are facts of life. Discord and disagreement create momentous events, drive relationships, and split neighbors and nations. Theater and film capitalize on conflict; it is an essential element in social drama.[1] Therefore, as museums and other sponsors aspire to become more socially relevant and realistic, shouldn't they include argument, emotion, and strife as an integral part of the past?[2]

Kate Stover, in her 1988 M.A. thesis on the interpretation of conflict and controversy in living history museums, reported that a few sites were making inroads. She concluded that today's audiences appreciate realism over nostalgia and suggested that museums increase representation of such topics.[3] In the years since Stover's thesis, interpretive programs have aggressively expanded their boundaries, but not without a few border wars along the way. Many now re-create community discord, domestic arguments, and political confrontations and portray slavery, bigotry, religious dissent, bastardy, and other issues traditionally avoided for their potential to offend. Certainly, the freedom to discuss just about any subject with a visitor is one of the greatest pedagogical advances of the past decade.

Interpreting controversy requires careful advance planning. First and foremost, sensitive material should be meaningful within the purpose of a program and complement sponsors' larger missions. What is the intended message and why should audiences learn about it? What attitudes do we want to change — and why? What public response is anticipated? What repercussions

Re-creating the auction of a slave. How will modern audiences react to historical realities now considered offensive? (courtesy Colonial Williamsburg Foundation)

might result? Should ethnic, religious, descendant, or partisan organizations be invited to contribute to the planning process? (Engaging their knowledge and support ahead of time is far more convenient than facing objections later.)

Second, museums (and independents, too) should analyze their image and their audience before acting. They must assess the value of shaking complacent audiences who are more accustomed to idyllic pasts.[4] Institutions that would rather avoid public backlash may want to leave well enough alone. However, any agency of informal education that ranks its research and interpretation on a par with academic standards should consider it a duty to verify its claims by challenging outdated perceptions.

Third, how shall presentation be structured? Will it be automatically incorporated into existing interpretation? Deployed via scenario? Offered with a third-person commentator? Unveiled as a play? Shall it include opportunities for discussion between audiences and first-person characters and/or third-person "contextualists"?

Fourth, interpreters and supporting sponsors must be well prepared with their facts. What type of research, training, and rehearsal are necessary to provide interpreters and other staff with comprehensive background and foster confidence in the program's execution?

Fifth, there are concerns over story line, perspective, and dramatic scale.

Which characters introduce the conflict? Will it be resolved? If so, how? Should it peak with a climactic incident or simmer unconcluded? How many sides of an argument will audiences see? Will individuals with opposing viewpoints actually confront one another? How intense will emotions become? Are there incidents or behaviors better left to description rather than re-creation?

Sixth, how will sponsors or creators prepare their spectators and, later, manage public response and reaction? What special orientation is necessary? Is it possible for all visitors to receive it? What accommodations will be made when children are present? Is there a need for closure or visitor group discussion? How will interpreters respond on the spot to viewers who are emotionally overcome, or those who are upset or angry? Wayne Williams and Ed Schultz observe that interpretive presentations that focus on themes of loss and grief often precipitate strong emotional responses. They suggest that interpreters must have the poise and ability to act appropriately and that visitors need adequate time to process and discuss their feelings.[5]

What sort of orientation will prevent onlookers from confusing the opinions of characters with those of the interpreters who are espousing them, or assuming that such opinions are an official view of museums or sponsors? Public misconception is not limited to first-person interpretation but has dogged third-person programs and gallery exhibits as well. Its troublesome effects were witnessed by Ann Hayward of the Alberta legislature's Visitor Services division.[6] Hayward concludes that confusion stems from a lack of historical understanding by visitors who do not realize that history is an interpretation of the past that changes over time as ongoing scholarship shapes new assumptions. The other problem, she concedes, is that historical context is frequently at odds with modern "political correctness"; politicians and lobby groups who pressure museums to censor "offensive" exhibits cannot fathom institutions' purposes for calling attention to outmoded behavior and practices.

At least two living history practitioners have addressed misconception issues: Nancy Webster of the Friends Historical Association and Ian Bell of Black Creek Pioneer Village. Webster identified problems that can arise between program planners and religious denominations when a historic site plans to interpret the latter's philosophy. Webster recommends that sites work closely with the denomination in question well in advance, and that they demonstrate a thorough understanding of the sect's philosophy. Denominations, Webster warns, want to feel comfortable about portrayals that reflect negative aspects of their religion.[7]

Ian Bell, in a thoughtful paper on his evolving philosophy on the presentation, editing, or abandonment of historical songs for modern audiences, recognized the difficulties that arise when the utterances of first-person interpreters are confused with modern opinion: "In any form of first-person interpretation, we must be convincing. Unfortunately, oral communication effectively removes a lot of the literary safety valves that we depend on when we are dealing with touchy subjects. Without the aid of quotation marks, italics, and parentheses, the interpreter who mouths unpopular ideas is truly working without a net. He has no way of indicating that 'the thoughts you hear are certainly not mine or those of the historic site.'"[8]

Bell's point is well taken, especially as he urges interpreters to "consider the merits and drawbacks [of] each historical editing job we undertake" because "careless presentations of ugly attitudes can stop the learning process altogether."[9] The operative word is "careless." With care and forethought interpreters and sites are developing ways to fulfill their ethical calling to present realistic history without cavalier offensiveness. Judicious editing of the way we present the controversial historical record and how we frame what we say to our audiences is a crucial, yet imperfect process. It is what makes interpretation different from re-creation. The following pages are filled with strategies and solutions devised by our fellow practitioners.

Thought-provoking interpretation is always subject to opposition, but it usually attracts significant praise, too. Only mediocrity is blissfully ignored. And likely as not, some detractors will be offended at excess and others will rail that the critical eye has not gone far enough. Museums shudder at complaints, even those that are unreasonable and unrepresentative of majority reaction. It is no wonder, when the media are quick to give certain causes a public platform and slant the reporting to support the complainants. While museums ponder why they end up as the "bad guys" every once in awhile and how they can educate the public about their purpose, interpreters have been developing strategies for conveying tough topics without unduly antagonizing visitors.[10]

Despite obstacles, museums and interpreters have been eroding the boundaries of old off-limits subjects by describing, if not re-creating them. Not surprisingly, certain topics and offensive language are still restricted at many sites. At the top of the taboo list are bodily functions, sexuality, violence, sexual deviation, cursing, and anything else that could offend most family audiences, however blurry a guideline that may be. Illness, pregnancy, and death, while not as potentially objectionable as sex and violence, are also underrepresented (but not unrepresented). Several sites have staged funerals (including Plimoth Plantation, Conner Prairie, Old Bethpage Village, and Old Sturbridge Village). Colonial Williamsburg has portrayed illness and childbearing in selected presentations, and Plimoth has woven illness, pregnancy, and childbirth into

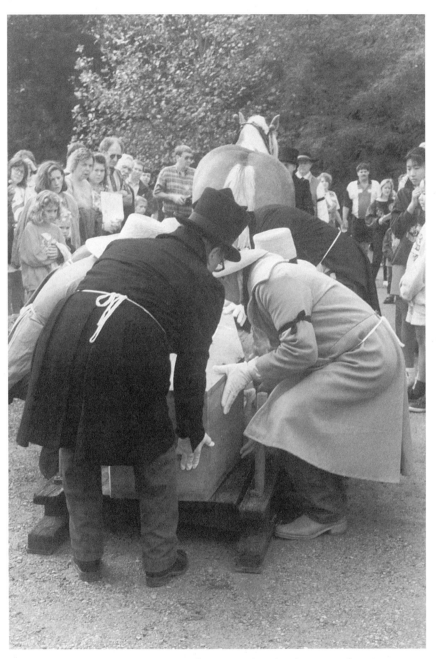

Visitors to Conner Prairie attend a Masonic burial with curious solemnity.
(photo: Stacy Roth)

ongoing interpretation. Snow and others have noted that omission of these topics leads to an incomplete representation of historical reality and compromises the significance of public history in comparison with academic history.[11]

Colonial Williamsburg and Old Sturbridge Village present difficult subjects via "fourth-wall scenes" bracketed by third-person introductions and closure. The fourth-wall method removes visitors from personal involvement in the scene and imitates the performer-spectator relationship of a play.[12] It focuses visitors' attention on specific issues, provides background information that puts the issues in retrospective context, keeps interpretation to a set theme, allows the in-depth presentation of difficult subjects, and gives opportunities for visitors to ask questions at the end. Logistically, fourth-wall scenes require a strategy for convincing audiences to attend at designated times and stay through the conclusion, plus a method for updating or deflecting latecomers.

Alternately, by incorporating sensitive issues into ongoing first-person interpretation, visitor exposure is more thorough; topics are not restricted to scheduled performance times or limited venues. Visitors can converse informally with roleplayers about their positions on the controversy at hand and may, if desired, seek restatement or clarification of complicated points.[13] Depth of discussion is tempered by visitors' interest; when they have heard enough, they say "thanks" and move on.

One of the significant advantages of verbal presentation over text-and-object exhibits is that actual behavior or conditions need not be re-created or posted publicly to interpret them. Private, unpleasant, or repulsive images, such as lovemaking, wife beating, or bear baiting, can be "recalled" by characters as witnessed incident, rumor, or memory. Interpreters determine where, when, how, and to whom taboo subjects are revealed by assessing visitors' interests and speaking within appropriate character boundaries. A responsible interpreter strives for balance between fidelity to history's now-repugnant details and modern sensibilities, and attempts to mollify a visitor who has expressed offense.[14]

Sensitive subjects can be reserved for visitors who probe for more unusual discussions. As Dean MacCannell observed in *The Tourist*, many people are not motivated to see "authentic" views of the culture they are visiting but instead are content with a commercially appealing package. Individuals who desire "native" experiences must make an effort to do so.[15] Surprising as it may seem, it is not uncommon for visitors to ask Pilgrims if they sleep in the nude and what they wear when they are menstruating, to inquire where seafarers relieve themselves, or to question the local clergyman about his views on homosexuals. People really are curious about such things. Thus, the more torrid tidbits of conversation can be reserved as a "reward" for the intrepid museum-goer. The flexibility of casual interpretation allows for interruption of "adult" discussion if others, particularly children, walk into earshot.

Certain topics and attitudes are particularly difficult to act out in first-person. Racism and evangelical religion flow immediately to mind. Racist language, no matter how historically correct, is generally avoided in first-person due to its offensiveness. The chief problem, again, is a matter of blurred communication. One can never be absolutely sure if the interpreter — or the visitor — has a real intellectual investment in politically unacceptable subject matter. There are interpreters and visitors who seriously agree with beliefs that women should be subjugated by men, that ethnic group X is inferior, or that religious creed Y holds the key to the truth. Often the true feelings of interpreters and playful visitors who espouse ideas they do not truly believe are revealed by nonverbal cues that contradict their words. Some interpreters who encounter visitors with bigoted beliefs commonly toss in further pronouncements that underscore that historical supremacist opinions were part of an overall worldview that included other odd or unsavory ideas.

> Interpreter: I have no use for Catholics. The Pope is the Devil incarnate.
> Visitor: I think so, too.
> Interpreter: You're looking unwell. Care to have a purge? A dose of
>   mercury ought to do the trick.

Of course, such techniques brand us with superimposing our own beliefs on historical reality rather than letting the visitor process the information within his own value system — even if it is tempting to do so. Should we heap "raw history" on the public for the sake of historical truth? That is a tough question with no easy answers.

Some sites have introduced prejudice into the composition of their characters. Interpreters at Mystic Seaport Museum, for example, complain disparagingly about Irish immigrants. Pilgrims at Plimoth express hostility toward the French, Spaniards, and others. These ethnic groups are well accepted in the home region of those two sites; the recall of old attitudes does not strike an explosive chord. Even so, interpreters rarely, if ever, loose the type of verbal venom that a person with true hatred espouses; opinions are suggestive rather than blatant. Interpreting prejudice against blacks or Jews — whose legacy as targets still stings — is a much more delicate matter. Upper Canada Village interprets French-English relations and the issues of Fenian terrorism in 1866 but avoids re-creating historical attitudes toward other ethnic cultures. "We are, after all, an agency of government," says interpreter Peter Cazaly, alluding to the state's desire to avoid public misconception.[16]

Some Plimoth staff are hesitant to discuss hard-line anti-Semitism with

Jews or anti-Catholicism with Catholics who identify themselves (either verbally or by their mode of dress).[17] However, some of their coworkers find that these are the very people who are the most interested in such topics. Jewish visitors, for instance, often ask the Pilgrims about the Saints' views on their seventeenth-century ancestors.[18] Such visitor-driven inquiry for taboo information satisfies those who reserve sensitive information as rewards for intrepid tourists.

Dave Cloutier (Old Sturbridge Village) experimented with racism as his minister character and noted an uncomfortable response: "I've occasionally interpreted the historical attitude toward blacks. It really surprises people. They may even find it offensive. They register a flustered, surprised, or tense look or say, 'Oooooh — listen to what he is saying.'"[19]

To Eddie Grogan, it is important to truthfully address historical race relations. However, interpreters must be sensitive to the feelings of minority visitors:

> If blacks bring up the topic [of racial issues] — and some do — I will talk to it from the point of view of my character in the least offensive way possible and still get the message across. . . . I remember once, we were doing a black history program [at Conner Prairie] and I was the schoolmaster, and there was a young black man sitting in the audience. So I singled him out and said, "Son, look, I have nothing against you personally, but if I accepted you as one of my scholars, all the white parents would withdraw their children and the school would shut down. Now tell me what good that would do anyone. Now I'll tell you what. If you are really serious about gettin' yourself an education, what I would do is seek out the Quakers, because they educate people male or female, black or white. That would be your best bet."[20]

Colonial Williamsburg has been struggling to present a more realistic portrayal of African American–white relations since the late 1960s, when the administration began to fill a gaping hole in the story of the town's inhabitants.[21] In 1979 the site planned its first portrayals of slaves and black freemen via scripted monologues in its new first-person interpretation efforts.[22] Rex Ellis, one of those early interpreters and later the director of the African-American Interpretations and Presentations program, recalled the difficulty of finding "actors" willing to play slaves because blacks and whites were equally hesitant to resurrect that part of history.[23]

According to Shomer Zwelling, the research development coordinator at the time, early efforts made both visitors and interpreters uncomfortable. Zwelling discovered to his surprise that some visitors, who at the time were predominantly white, understood when white interpreters were in character, but this was not the case with the black interpreters. Instead, visitors mistakenly assumed that the blacks were employees promoting personal causes. For instance, Rex Ellis's character, preacher Gowan Pamphlet, was occasionally perceived as a "Jesus freak" who worked at Colonial Williamsburg in costume and took every opportunity to spout religion at passersby.[24] Such misunderstanding was the unfortunate result of subtle (or perhaps not-so-subtle) prejudices combined with many white visitors' lack of prior experience in encountering blacks in unfamiliar roles. (In hindsight, it is apparent that the absence of orientation exacerbated the confusion.) The staff modified the presentations by adding out-of-character introductions and conclusions before and after their own monologues, which worked better at the time.[25] Colonial Williamsburg later adopted this technique for living history scenes and events, especially those with potential for controversy. Since the late 1970s and early 1980s, audiences have become much more savvy; "Persons of the Past" are now familiar features on the daily schedule. The occasions when interpreters must introduce themselves or break character have just about disappeared.[26]

Christy Coleman Matthews, the current director of African-American Interpretations and Presentations; Jeremy Fried, the manager of Character Interpretation; and their eager staffs have shifted Colonial Williamsburg onto the cutting edge of interpretation of sensitive and controversial issues, particularly slavery, racism, and black/white relations. Both directors' philosophies stress reliance on solid research and careful balancing of the historical experience by depicting many different behaviors, classes, opinions, backgrounds, occupations, and relationships. Their goal is to illustrate slavery in the lives of eighteenth-century Virginians as a matter-of-fact phenomenon, neither overemphasized nor avoided.[27] Despite their intent, slavery interpretation at Colonial Williamsburg has, on occasion, been sensationalized in the news media and by political pressure groups.

In October 1994 the African-American Interpretations and Presentations and Character Interpretation staffs tested public response to a new, authentic addition to the usual Publick Times auction scenario. They added "slaves" to the many articles of property sold for estate and debt settlements in colonial Virginia. Four slaves would be auctioned off amidst other transactions involving land and goods. Anticipating strong reactions, the staff picked carefully documented cases and scheduled only one showing, on the final day of the three-day Publick Times event. The personal stories involved the sale of a carpenter, the purchase of a laundress by her free black husband, and lastly, the more emotional situation of a husband and wife separated by sale to different masters. The re-creation would be preceded by a third-person orientation and

A protester situates himself in the midst of Colonial Williamsburg's re-creation of an eighteenth-century estate auction that includes the sale of slaves.
(courtesy Colonial Williamsburg Foundation)

followed up with a question-and-answer session, the typical formula for introducing scenarios of an emotionally sensitive nature since 1986.[28] In the week preceding Publick Times, a local newspaper highlighted this new addition to the weekend's programming, and in the next few days media interest snowballed. Although Christy Matthews reviewed the program with the local chapter of the NAACP, who according to Matthews "expressed no opposition," other groups who were unfamiliar with Colonial Williamsburg's track record vocalized their angry concern.[29]

On the day of the scheduled event, staff arrived at the steps of Wetherburn's Tavern (the performance site) to find over 2,000 spectators and a throng of reporters. According to newspaper accounts, 75 percent of the crowd was Caucasian and 25 percent non-Caucasian, a respectable showing of minority attendance by mainstream museum standards. A small band of protesters representing the state chapter of the NAACP, led by its political director Jack Gravely, and the Southern Christian Leadership Conference assembled at the staging area. A handful of college students (mostly white) armed with protest signs also turned out.

The third-person introduction was shouted down by the protesters, who tried to prevent the "auction" from proceeding as scheduled. The interlopers were resoundingly booed by other spectators. The leaders of the demonstration were given an opportunity to address the crowd (and the cameras) with their concerns. Then, two of them sat down in the middle of the performance area and dared the staff to call the police. Christy Matthews made an impassioned plea for the protesters to watch the presentation and praise or condemn it *afterward*. She indicated to them that its purpose is to teach about the evils of slavery and to tell the story of the people who lived through those times. No police were called, and the reenactment proceeded — with the two protesters smack in the middle of it.

When it was over, many spectators were weeping. And Jack Gravely — to his credit and courage — announced that he had changed his mind: "I would be lying if I said I didn't come out with a different view. . . . The presentation was passionate, moving, and educational." [30]

Not everyone was converted. One of the student protesters commented, "It's not showing the true history of what it was like to be a slave. Where is the story of the people who fought back?" He was reminded by interpreter Larry Earl, standing nearby, that this scene was just one of many in an ongoing program.[31] Perhaps the young man was not entirely to blame for his ignorance; reporters described the event so that it certainly sounded like an isolated feature. Its context in Publick Times was never mentioned.

The tenor of protesters' comments, as reported in news stories, indicates that many accused Colonial Williamsburg of showcasing slave auctions for the sake of entertainment. The perception of living history sites as generators of fluff is not helped by well-intended but selectively misleading tidbits such as this one: "The [Colonial Williamsburg] foundation, which operates the restored area, has been accused in the past of sanitizing history. So 15 years ago, the foundation embarked on portrayals of many delicate topics, including an examination of romances between planters and slaves." [32]

To Colonial Williamsburg's credit, Robert Wilburn, president of the Colonial Williamsburg Foundation, and Vice-President of Education D. Stephen "Steve" Elliott supported their staff and refused to placate a judgmental, underinformed vocal minority by aborting a worthwhile program. They struck a blow for intellectual freedom not only in their own programming but for museums everywhere. Judging from visitor response to the auction and public opinion collected in evaluations, visitors are increasingly accepting of the live dramatization of slavery and other serious issues. Comments such as this one from a Colonial Williamsburg visitor are far more usual than negative responses or confusion: "Listening to the slave talk [was most memorable] . . .

because to me she was telling you the way that a human being was treated back then, and it gets me thinking [about] the way it really was back in them days. I never really stopped and thought about it, but listening to her does jar you to think, 'How did they really live like that?' and all, but I guess it was just a way of life. They didn't know any better, so that's what it was." [33]

Coincident with the emergence of controversy and taboo, interpersonal conflict, emotional realism, and the darker sides of human nature are increasingly visible ingredients of interpretation. Audiences are accustomed to such issues on screen and stage and are distanced from it by their passive role. Knocking down the fourth wall can activate personal or cultural aversions to emotional display.[34] Have you ever noticed how many people instinctively create space between themselves and strangers engaged in an argument, a passionate embrace, or intense laughter in a public place, while others strain to see what's going on? If the former type do not realize that interpreters' "negative" behavior is intentional, they react by avoiding the source or becoming upset. Roleplay conflict, then, must simulate real emotions and attitudes while incorporating techniques that pique interest rather than activating an automatic distancing response. Visitors confident that a conflict scene is for their benefit will flock to see what the fuss is all about.

Confusion is common in real-life conflict. Several people talk at once, and emotions are heightened; they say things they do not truly mean and make threats they will never act on. Arguments can stretch on for hours without resolution. In a roleplay situation, confrontation must be focused and organized. Additionally, interpreters must send verbal and nonverbal signals that invite audiences to become voyeurs. "Asides" addressed directly to spectators, such as, "Did you hear what he said?" tell visitors they are not intruding.

Roleplayed disagreements must be resolved before boredom sets in or before the conflict produces such a level of discomfort that everyone leaves. Incidents should lead either to reconciliation, compromise, postponement, or schism and departure. Emotional peaks require decompression. Conflict, of course, does not always burst into emotional debate. Sometimes it's quite civil. The natural speaking voice, body language, tone of voice, and silent pauses are equally effective for expressing contrast of opinion, passive aggression, or emotional upset. Antagonists need not appear together; in some cases their pairing may be historically unlikely. For instance, the "Strangers" of the Pilgrim Village confine their criticisms of the religion of the "Saints" to their own homes.[35] The combination of an extremist and a neutral is a much less combustible pairing for reasoned discussion.

Conflict acted out in noncontiguous formats should be thoughtfully coordinated for balance. How will visitors hear all sides of an argument, including the views not portrayed? How can the opinions of "social inferiors" be communicated in the presence of their "betters" and illustrate the constraints of social pressures? There are many creative ways of addressing these challenges, such as confidential asides or speaking for others, but interpreters must think holistically, know each others' characters well, and brainstorm together to achieve complete and complex solutions.

Emotion can powerfully personalize an era for visitors. This is where first-person shines. For example, a widow's tale of the death of her soldier husband says more about the consequences of war than a page of casualty statistics. The skilled presentation of emotion creates empathy and fosters understanding. Emphasis on emotional characterization and intensity is highly individualized among interpreters. Often it is a matter of establishing the right balance with the audience of the moment in a given situation. Glenn Gordinier (Mystic Seaport Museum) feels that sometimes it is necessary to act a little "larger than life": "Your character can be something of a 'character' as long as the visitors are not made to feel uncomfortable and we don't stretch our historical integrity." [36]

Some interpreters are more animated than others. Jeff Scotland (Plimoth Plantation) considers range — the ability to shift from natural to exaggerated (and points in between) — beneficial. [37] Each interpreter, each site, will find approaches that are right for presenters, venues, and audiences. Mystic Seaport Museum's Sailor's Reading Room, which is strong on atmosphere but sparse on props and is staffed by a lone interpreter, requires a more animated performance than does a site with lots of people and activities. Plimoth, on the other hand, is so rich in period detail and activity that low-key interpretation encourages visitors to divide their attention between characters and environment. A solo interpreter whose presentation is predominantly verbal and is performed for large audiences has to develop strong dramatic and emotional presence to hold audience interest for an extended period of time.

Bettye Noyes (Mystic Seaport Museum) effectively reveals a range of emotions in her character, Mrs. Reynolds, the wife of a sea captain. She is so convincing — emotional, yet in such an incidental and natural way — that I quite forgot I was watching an interpreter at work. Noyes selects stories that touch the heart and capture the imagination of her audiences. When I visited with "Mrs. Reynolds," she recalled the time she was at sea with her husband and received a letter about a sick child. She spoke of the helplessness she felt, not knowing whether her child was alive or dead. Noyes convincingly "remembered" the distress — and later happiness — when Mrs. Reynolds learned of her child's recovery. My eyes were moist by the end, and so were those of other visitors.

Audiences had very little trouble identifying with Mrs. Reynolds's emotional story. The feelings generated over concern for the safety of one's family is a theme that touches many. But other historical emotional experiences can present challenges, particularly when the focus is religion. Fiery warnings about salvation, the bestowing of blessings, or a description of Christ revealing himself touch some but make most modern audiences uncomfortable.[38] Jeff Scotland remarked on the zealousness of the Pilgrims concerning their faith and how Plimoth's interpreters were sensitive to the need for tempering the topic for modern audiences: "We can't interpret religion with emotions that would be true to our characters because it would turn most people off."[39]

What if proselytizing is an important function of a denomination, character, or event? Richard Pickering, research associate at Plimoth, suggests that interpreters camouflage evangelicalism by working religious views into other areas of interpretation, rather than forthrightly discussing doctrine.[40] Some living history sites manage the problem by advertising sermons as special events at a set time and by including third-person introductions. B. J. Pryor's sermons as Reverend Henley at Bruton Parish Church (Colonial Williamsburg) are occasionally offered with a third-person contextualist who explains why Henley's sermons were controversial to the inhabitants of eighteenth-century Williamsburg. Pryor observes that the introduction is crucial to visitor comprehension. Without it, many visitors leave in the middle, and those who stay have little to say. With it, many sit for the entire sermon and ply the reverend with questions afterward.[41] Likewise, Old Sturbridge Village provides a modern introduction to features such as the fire-and-brimstone walk-on-the-tops-of-the-pews exhortations of Tom Kelleher's Reverend Burchard. Even so, a few visitors still mistake the program for a real sermon with a bona fide minister. Kelleher has been offered his own pulpit on more than one occasion.

Another area of controversy and conflict is the portrayal of negative personality traits such as crabbiness, bombasticity, hostility, anger, loneliness, clumsiness, and untrustworthiness, but it can be a lot of fun for those who enjoy "villain" and "character" roles. Some interpreters adopt a Jekyll-and-Hyde approach, confining their barbed-edged comments to fellow interpreters and a civil tongue to visitors. Peter Cazaly (Upper Canada Village), for example, speaks to printer-editor Nicholas Hart's shop employees in a curt, authoritarian, and condescending tone but strikes a formal but gracious demeanor for visitors.[42]

Maverick interpreters confront visitors with a less-than-polite manner, but it is a very special interpreter who can pull it off successfully. Something unspoken — a flash of the brows, a glint in the eye, or the suggestion of a grin — must quietly telegraph playfulness. Chris Hall, who occasionally plays outcast John Billington at Plimoth, is one of the best examples of an interpreter who can be rude and charming at the same time. No matter how gross his dialogue, a twinkle in his eye betrays his likability. Hall's coworker Larry Erickson feels safer displaying the cantankerous side of his characters in front of a crowd, in a situation that bears resemblance to a dramatic performance. Larry, a big fellow well over six feet tall, fears that lone visitors might assume he is picking a fight.[43]

When playing someone with negative traits, interpreting the reasons behind the behavior puts such characterization in perspective for the visitor. John Kemp, director of interpretation at Plimoth, suggests that angry and hostile characters attempt to create an empathetic ally out of the visitor by describing their circumstances and perhaps asking listeners to picture themselves in the same situation.[44] Very few people have a tougher time gaining sympathy from U.S. students than do those who portray Loyalists from the era of the American Revolution. I have experimented with many strategies for presenting the views of these beleaguered "friends of government": adopting the stridency of Dame Edith Evans in *Tom Jones*; stating my best reasonable defense in an assertive way or in a passive-aggressive and questioning way; and by portraying a frightened victim. Donna Evans (Old Barracks Museum) has been through a similar odyssey with her Loyalist character. Both of us found that the less vehement the character — and the more anecdotal the evidence — the more converts we win over to our viewpoint. Donna usually includes a typical Loyalist complaint that children can immediately identify with: "How would you like it if someone came into your house and took your things and destroyed them? Wouldn't you want to see them punished? (Most of the children nod in agreement.) Well, that's just what those men up in Boston did with the tea, and that is just what the rebels around here have been doing to those of us who do not believe in going along with their cause."

One day a ten-year-old girl came up to Donna at the end of the program. "Are you a Loyalist?" she asked. Donna said, "Yes." "Aren't all Loyalists bad?" questioned the young visitor. "Well, do I seem like a bad person to you?" replied Donna. "No, but I'm confused. We always heard that the Loyalists were the bad guys; I guess it was more complicated than that."[45]

Christy Coleman Matthews (Colonial Williamsburg) combines a sensitive topic — slavery — with an angry and uncommunicative character, Cate, one of Benjamin Powell's house slaves. Cate rarely speaks unless spoken to, and when she does, she can be curt and direct. She shows irritation with some questions, particularly those in which visitors euphemistically refer to Cate as a "servant." The word is "slaves," she starkly reminds them.[46] Cate's behavior

Creating sympathy for the enemy at the Old Barracks Museum: Donna Evans as a war-weary Loyalist, Jeff Macechak as a Hessian captive, and Doug Winterich as a bored Royal Provincial prisoner of war (photos: Stacy Roth, courtesy Old Barracks Museum)

is Matthews's vision of the thoughts an indignant eighteenth-century slave would tell people if afforded the opportunity. Cate's smoldering temper and stark responses commonly create audience discomfort, precisely the reaction that Matthews wants to elicit. As Christy told a CBS News "Sunday Morning" reporter, "You will feel *something* when you leave. You may not remember everything I said, but you will remember everything you felt." [47]

There is a danger that visitors will have the impression that Matthews is simply a crabby employee. So other characters strategically reinforce the notion that everyone expects the worst behavior from Cate. One of the Powells, for example, chides Cate for being so churlish and warns visitors to "mind themselves" because Cate "can be grumpy." Scenarios featuring Cate can be effective, however discomforting. Modern visitors are programmed to expect that a slave must be angry. She doesn't have to explain herself. In the character's favor, Matthews's Cate is only one of many first-person interpreters and costumed personnel that audiences meet on their visit to Williamsburg. She provides a memorable contrast but doesn't unbalance the rest of the experience. As much as they are shaken up by Cate, visitors are surprised or perplexed when they encounter a slave character who is relatively content. Visitors commonly believe that slaves who are not miserable constitute fake history. Such are the challenges of assailing audiences' preconceptions. The staff at Colonial Williamsburg assert that character variety illustrates that the lives of the people — both black and white — of eighteenth-century Virginia were not all, well, black and white.

The presentation of controversy, taboo, and interpersonal conflict does indeed add depth to interpretation and visitors' understanding of the past. Ideally, visitors are more receptive to first-person interpretation when they are not threatened and uncomfortable. However, the judicious inclusion of characters such as Cate and events such as slave auctions have an important impact on visitors. Experimentation with "radical" programming is crucial to the growth of interpretation, but in a sense it is like cayenne pepper. Some people love it in large doses and some people abhor it. For the rest, a liberal dash now and then adds tang and wakes up the senses. Too much creates an unpalatable dish. Overemphasis on angst can be just as distorted as its opposite. The key to successful presentation of conflict is thorough preparation, and balance.

In 1991 I embarked on a quest to develop a set of principles that defined effective first-person interpretation. Initially, as a graduate student in a museum studies track, I visited, observed, and interviewed staff at Plimoth Plantation, Old Sturbridge Village, and Mystic Seaport Museum. The results were self-published as *Communicating in First-Person: Perspectives on Interpreter/Visitor Interaction*. When the University of North Carolina Press offered the opportunity for formal publication, I felt a need to broaden the scope of the earlier study. I added more sites, interviewed and consulted independent interpreters, and vastly expanded the sections incorporating visitor behavior, educational theory, comparisons with theater, and the analysis of controversial issues. As my field of observation widened, the idea of a fixed set of "rules" took on greater complexity. However, several significant themes emerged. A few relate to the role of first-person interpretation in late twentieth-century life and into the future. Others reflect the purpose, goals, and foundations for creating and supporting roleplay programs and address the communication context of the first-person experience.

First-person interpretation stands today at an important crossroads. With more than two decades of maturation, its leading practitioners have developed the research, material trappings, and techniques to establish it as a popular creative leisure learning method for the next century. It is low tech, yet highly interactive, a perfect escape from the wired world of computers and television. It stimulates the imagination and the senses. It brings the abstract concepts of formal study to life. It creates an emotional and personal involvement with the past unlike that of television or films because it is unpredictable. It talks back. Asks questions. Surprises listeners with something they never knew before. Relates to personal interests. Adapts to young and old. It might even encourage a trip to the library.

Roleplay does have application to modern concerns. Educators and psychologists have known this for years. Because the intent of interpretation is ultimately to affect listeners' perceptions of the past and the people who went before us — not to convince them to think like a historical person — it can change the way that visitors think about themselves and the modern world.

Tim Breen, in his *Imagining the Past*, illustrated how each generation teaches history in accordance with purposes reflecting contemporary perspective. In the late nineteenth century and the first half of the twentieth, histories abounded with tales of the heroism and self-sacrifice of the founding fathers (and occasionally mothers). Anecdotes emphasized acts of bravery and praised values such as honesty, the willingness to work hard, and other characteristics that conformed to Anglo-American ideals. Authors and educators hoped that such stories would help Americanize the waves of eastern and southern European immigrants relocating to the United States.

Today museum professionals pride themselves on the evenhandedness of their programming, earnestly interpreting a variety of race-, class-, and gender-based perspectives. Countless colleagues have proclaimed their mission to show the past without bias, to reveal "the truth" via democratic process. Such beliefs, while well intended, must be tempered with the recognition that we, too, are influenced by our own worldview and sense of propriety. This book has discussed countless ways interpreters modify historical reality. Reality is often strange, unpleasant, smelly, and offensive. Historical opinions, in comparison with our own, can be infuriating. Interpreters found that such characteristics — faithfully re-created — alienated and angered visitors, obscuring other worthwhile messages about the past.

Today the desire for interracial and international harmony is a prominent theme in our society and, subsequently, throughout the mass media. Virtually all educators and public leaders support a broad agenda of cooperation, toleration, and peaceful conflict resolution. Popular science fiction television series such as "Star Trek: The Next Generation" and "Deep Space Nine" promote these principles, as do shows in "historical" settings, such as "Dr. Quinn, Medicine Woman." And so do living history museums. In the past decade, for example, programs interpreting slavery have increased in number, an advance itself made possible by the popularity of Alex Haley's *Roots*. Such depictions expose visitors to the hard life and plight of people who were held as slaves. To offset outright resentment of the slave owners, portrayals stop short of worst-case abuses, and orientation segments ask us to consider the worldview of the times. The effects are often immediate. "How awful to live as a slave!" "How could one group of people possibly treat another group of human beings like that!" "We can't let that happen again!" Would a hard-line bigot be moved? Perhaps not. But many others are. One interpretive program — along with countless other repetitions of similar messages throughout popular and educational media — works to produce and reflect broad social change. Interpreters and program planners should not feel guilty when they discover they operate from a bias — it cannot be avoided — but acknowledge and use it to achieve the best possible social and cognitive effect on their audiences. The terms "educational purpose" and "institutional mission" create less anxiety, but both are inspired by contemporary philosophies. Knowing this, however, helps us focus our objectives, understand our selectivity, and maximize the message.

In the musical *1776!* when a fellow representative motions to postpone indefinitely the discussion on American independence, Stephen Hopkins, congressman from Rhode Island, exclaims, "I never seen, heard, nor smelled an issue that was so dangerous it couldn't be talked about. Hell yes, I'm for debatin' anything."[1] Likewise, interpretation that incorporates controversial issues, interpersonal conflict, and former taboos promotes public understanding of the past and helps dispel what we now consider nostalgic "myths" and outdated "educational propaganda." (I am smiling as I write this, anticipating the sentiments of historian-educators in the 2090s.) Open discussion of earlier taboo subjects and controversial issues is one of living history's most meaningful achievements. However, interpreters and sponsors bear a responsibility to their audiences to provide orientation and, if necessary, opportunities for closure, clarification, and processing emotions. When orientation is casual or not possible, perceptive discretion and balance should guide interpretation.

I have avoided fixed prescriptions for first-person interpretation in the preceding chapters. There are many options for animating the people of the past. Although there were many common principles among the interpreters observed in this study, exceptions abounded. Even oft-avoided methods — such as hostile or insulting character behavior — found an appropriate outlet or underscored important messages. On two issues, opinions diverged widely: the influence of theatrical conventions and the appropriate situations for breaking character. Ultimately, each site and each interpreter will find strategies that work best for them based on individual circumstances.

Perhaps some readers opened *Past into Present* because they wondered, "Does first-person interpretation work?" Well, first-person succeeds or fails as does any other media, be it storytelling, exhibits, theater, films, or books. If a presentation has a message worth communicating, if it relates to its intended audience, if it stimulates thought and wonder, and if it magnetizes rather than repels, it will be successful. The basics of effective interpretation, spelled out so well by Freeman Tilden almost half a century ago, are still rock solid. Perhaps because Tilden spoke plainly it is easy to assume that interpretation is a simple matter. It isn't.

The interface between an institution and its visitors is what makes or breaks a program, no matter how well conceived or thoroughly researched. A historic site or museum with poor interpreters is like a telephone conversation with a faulty connection. The intended message becomes garbled. The overall effect at sites such as Plimoth Plantation or Conner Prairie, which have worked ceaselessly to achieve the right atmosphere and level of detail, can be significantly dulled by staff who are uninformative, irritating, boring, callous, unobservant, lifeless, or oblivious to the needs of the visitor.

Does first-person work? Yes, if it is done right. It is more demanding of staff than other types of interpretation. To be academically accurate it requires historical and technical competence. It demands thorough research, training, character development and authentic detailing. Communication, informal education, and performance skills are crucial to maximize effectiveness. Ideally, interpreters should like people and enjoy helping them explore the past; be perceptive to audience moods, motivations, and interests; and have a natural resourcefulness in developing and choosing methods that improve listeners' understanding. Interpreters must be proactive. Interaction should seduce rather than burden visitors. Techniques such as ice breakers, hooks, thought linking, demonstrations, storytelling, questioning strategies, and direct participation provoke minds-on involvement and make for satisfying and pleasurable experiences.

After two decades of development, first-person still has plenty of room for creative growth and experimentation. The variety of presentation approaches discussed earlier, such as ghost interpretation, red T-shirting, visitor role assignments, and the addition of contextualists are current examples. I expect there are many other variations and that the future will herald more.

Writers such as Pearce, Moscardo, Hood, Falk, and Dierking have underscored the crucial role that visitors play in leisure heritage experiences. Audiences are diverse. Social context, background knowledge and interests, age, gender, and personal motivation create variations in the nature of each interpretive encounter. Interpreters who have the ability to read visitors, link into what excites them, and lead them to higher levels of understanding are first-person's best ambassadors. But more than popularity is at stake. As heritage educators, we have assumed the responsibility of transferring the stories of those who went before us from our generation to the next. As the electronic age propels us into exciting new territory, flooding our lives with information and rapid change, we risk a collective forgetfulness of the past. First-person is a force that keeps history from becoming abstract. It transforms the past into the present — and into the future.

Glossary

actor: For purposes of this book, someone with dramatic or theatrical training who is accustomed to performing in plays or films, usually using a script.

animation: Canadian term for costumed living history interpretation.

breaking the ice: Innocuous conversation during an initial encounter between visitors and an interpreter. Its purpose is to encourage visitors' comfort and open communication.

character interpretation: Another term for first-person interpretation.[1]

character speaker: Sarah Grant Reid's term for a first-person monologue influenced by public speaking techniques.

composite character: Fictional first-person character based on actual people, primary accounts, and demographic data.

contextualist: A third-person interpreter who provides an introduction and possibly other commentary in conjunction with a first-person program.[2]

first-hand interpretation: The author's definition of third-person interpretation that incorporates a personal perspective, but little or no characterization. Often used by craft, trade, or foodways interpreters, who describe how they themselves experience historical activities.

first-person interpretation: The act of portraying a person from the past (real or composite). For purposes of this book, the standard form is one in which the interpreters refer to the past in the present tense; employ a combination of techniques including storytelling, demonstration, question and answer, and discussion; encourage verbal interaction from the audience; and avoid breaking character.

fourth wall: A presentation that does not offer visitors an opportunity to question or interrupt interpreters' dialogue while a scene is in progress.

ghost interpretation: A first-person character who travels into the present. The interpreter may acknowledge the present.

guided first-person: Program in which third-person guides escort visitors to (or between) first-person locations. See also *red T-shirting*.

historical character interpretation: Broad term referring to the act of playing a person from the past. Can also refer to a part in a play.

hooks: Gambits intended to spur visitors' interest and/or reaction.

improvisation: Working without a script.

interactive historical character interpretation or interactive historical roleplay: Descriptive term for the standard form of *first-person interpretation*.

interpreter: One who translates material culture and human or natural phenomenon to the public in a meaningful, provocative, and interesting way. The term is usually applied to those who work in historic sites, parks, natural areas, zoos, etc.

interpretive impetus: An almost evangelical "calling" to interpret personal interests to others.

live interpretation: Another term for "living history interpretation" or "costumed interpretation." Turns up in U.K. sources.

living history site (or museum): A setting that replicates parts of a historical environment as a featured exhibit area. Can include historic houses, farms, villages, factories, encampments, battlefields, etc.

mixed interpretive medium: Interpretation that combines more than one method of interpretation. For example, a third-person guide who acts as a mediator between visitors and first-person interpreters, or a first-person program that closes with a third-person question-and-answer session.

museum theater: A play, scene, monologue, or first-person interpretation performed in a traditional gallery environment or a museum auditorium. The popularity of museum theater is growing in science, art, and children's museums; some have special platforms and auditoriums devoted to it.

my time/your time approach: A first-person character who understands and acknowledges the present and may make comparisons between various time periods.[3]

persona: Another term for "historical character." Commonly used by members of the Society for Creative Anachronism and many reenactors. I prefer to invoke the word only when referring to characters' personality traits.

red T-shirting: Term coined by Andrew Robertshaw of the Historical Reenactment Workshop. Refers to distinctively dressed third-person interpreters who act as visitor liaisons. They introduce the concept of first-person to visitors, provide background information, offer suggestions for interacting, and engage characters.[4] See also *guided first-person*.

reenactment: The restaging of a historical or prototypical event. Also, common term for battle reenactments and other reenactor activities.

reenactor: Those who engage in historical simulations for personal enjoyment. Some reenactors have a strong interpretive impetus and/or an affinity for first-person. Many interpreters are active reenactors.

role acting: A hybrid of first- and third-person interpretation in which interpreters adopt a historical personality à la first-person but respond beyond its bounds when prompted by out-of-period and personal questions.

scenario: Outlined or semiscripted sequence of dialogue and/or events that adds structure to a first-person presentation.

self-introduced roleplay: First-person interpretation introduced (and/or followed up) in third-person by the same interpreter.

theme park: What most people in the U.S. museum community think of as an entertainment-based, commercial amusement park, along the lines of Disneyland or Wild West City. Outside the United States, living history museums are also included in the definition.

third-person interpretation: Informative, often interactive talks and demonstrations by interpreters who may be dressed in period attire but do not assume character roles.

thought linking: The process of flowing logically from one topic to another, building conversation in a nonscripted roleplay situation.

verbal prospecting: Promoting several subjects likely to pique visitors' curiosity, combined with attention to visitors' verbal and nonverbal cues indicating interest.[5]

worldview: A cultural mindset that affects the way a person functions within his or her society. Historical worldview is the basis for developing appropriate character responses. Pioneered as an important part of interpreter training at Plimoth Plantation.

The Ultimate Character Development List
A Guide for the Gung-ho Interpreter

The purpose of this outline, based on the five-spheres concept presented in Chapter 6, is to stimulate expansive thinking when researching and building a historical character. Slavish adherence is not the intent of this list. Individual program goals and character focus determine and shape research priorities. Instead, it suggests angles for developing self-defining anecdotal "memories" and personal viewpoints.

If the length appears daunting, don't panic. Peruse and choose. Add to it. It is not imperative to know everything about everything to do first-person. However, amassing a repertoire of factual background and meaningful anecdotes prepares interpreters for unusual audience questions and adds the depth necessary for believability and fidelity. Start by working with subjects that visitors are likely to ask about and that relate to central program themes.

Looseleaf notebooks or file folders help organize collected research notes, illustrations, bibliographies, extracts, references, photocopies, and articles. Feel free to use the headings below for archiving documentation, augmenting and subdividing as necessary.

PERSONAL SPHERE

Includes what characters know about themselves, the unique characteristics that set one apart from neighbors, and family traits that define kinship and shape worldview.

Name and Name History
> Is there a story behind your name? For instance, was your given name the same as an ancestor's? A relative's?
> Does your surname have a traceable origin?
> Do you like/dislike your name? How has that affected your life?

Birthdate
> What day/month/year were you born?
> What other remarkable events happened that day, month, or year?

Birthplace
> Where was your character born?
> Are there any special stories affecting the circumstances of the birthplace?
> If the birthplace became home, see *Residence(s) and Habitation*.

Immediate Household and/or Family
> Other members: Who are they and what is their relation to you?
> Recommended: Genealogy chart, character profiles (personal sphere information) of relations and other members of the household.

Family/household/estate status: Are you the oldest? Youngest? Senior officer? Servant?

Family/group commonalities: Does the family/group have standout characteristics — occupational, geographical, personality, customary? (Examples: soldiers in the same regiment, redheads, generations of same occupation, etc.)

Differences from family/group: What differentiates you from your family or group? (For example, are you the studious one, the tall one, the oddball?)

Extended kinship network: Who are they and how do you interact with them? What does membership in that family mean to others? For example, if you are one of the Kennedys, people make certain assumptions about your wealth, political beliefs, etc.

Residence(s) and Habitation
What do/did your dwelling places look like? Interior? Exterior? Outbuildings? Are memories associated with particular spaces or buildings? What technologies (construction, domestic, plumbing, lighting, heat, etc.) were in place? Should you know the dwelling's history?

Your Education
Where and how were you educated? Do you know the rudiments of subjects you would have studied? What features, buildings, people, and events stand out from education-related memories?

Literacy
Do you read, write, and/or cipher? If so, do you know period hand, accounting methods, what is available to you for reading matter? Do you read anything on a regular basis (for example, Bible, almanacs, newspapers, books on a certain subject, society proceedings, etc.)?

Personal Belongings
If you do not have a ready-made inventory, you may want to assemble one. What do your possessions look like, and how are they used? Do any of them have special associations, unique features, or stories?

Personal Health
What is your state of health? What diseases have you suffered? How have those conditions been treated? How does your health affect your personality? Your work?

Personal Habits
These can range from taking a cup of coffee every morning to enjoying an "air bath," using Sen-Sen, or picking your teeth after supper. Think of daily or

seasonal routines, singular habits, peculiarities, things that irritate your spouse, etc.

Travels

Where have you been? Are there standout landmarks, events, or people that you recall from your travels? How do you get from one place to the other? How does the concept of travel apply to your character? Do you enjoy traveling or loathe it?

Past Residences

See *Residence(s) and Habitation*, above.

Important Personal Events

These will vary from person to person and can include marriage(s), birth of loved ones, death of loved ones, apprenticeship, attaining status or honors, experience in military service, and/or local and world events that had an impact on your character.

Social Skills

Are there particular skills for which you are noted or notorious? Do you possess an ability to charm or the cunning to sell a man his own shoes? Are you the perfect hostess? Where/how did you acquire such skills? Do you have recipes handed down from grandmother? (See also *Local Social Skills* under *Local Sphere*.)

Dialect and Speech Patterns

Dialect and speech help emphasize place of origin and class status, highlighting the foreignness of the past and the character. Does your speech resemble or differ from that of your neighbors? What problems or amusements does that cause? Are there unique regional or ethnic words and phrases that authenticate your origins?

LOCAL SPHERE

Local sphere knowledge is what your character shares with others. If your character has traveled, you may have more than one local sphere.

Your Neighborhood and Its Features

Your character should have a mental map of local roads, shops, landmarks, features, terrain, etc.

Local geography: What are the local features, such as landmarks, markets, rivers, landscape appearance, roads, etc.? What is the local climate? What are the local agricultural conditions? Manufacturing sites?

Local events past and present: What are the standout events in the history of your town? How was it founded and settled? What local political battles are going on? What scandals, heroes, boundary disputes, battles, etc., occurred in the past, recent past, and present? Which of these events would your character be likely to know?

Local economy: What is the monetary system, and how does the local economy function? What are the local cash crops and industries? How are business transactions negotiated? Do you travel to other towns to do business?

Local Social Skills

Include here customary talents that are common to your station, status, and class. Are you fair at swordplay? Can you make a proper cup of tea? Are you involved in local charitable societies or other groups? Do you attend a club? You should be able to discuss or demonstrate at least a few rudiments of your character's social competencies.

Common knowledge/survival tactics: What skills do you need to negotiate your world? How does your character avoid getting beaten up in an alleyway, cheated in the marketplace, having a pocket picked? Where do you, for example, "shun the pike"? How do you snag a front seat at the opera? Find a fence for stolen goods?

Health and Illness

What are your basic beliefs about health and illness? What is the general health of the area? Any recent epidemics? What do people do when epidemics strike? What sort of treatment is available at the local level? What are local childbirth practices like? What do you believe will keep you healthy?

Dialect and Speech Customs

What does the local speech sound like? What unusual words or phrases do you use? (If you hail from an area other than your local residence, see *Personal Sphere*.) What words have different meanings in the twentieth century, and how are you going to convey their historical meanings to visitors?

Religion

Are you religious, irreligious, or in the middle? Do you know the basic philosophy of the religion? Its rituals? Practices? How does it affect worldview? How does it affect daily life? Do you belong to a minority or a majority, and how does that affect the way you relate to others?

How much do you know of other religions, and what are your attitudes toward them?

Customs

What are the local customs of your region? How are they celebrated? Who are they celebrated with? Are there seasonal customs? Weekly or monthly customs? What traditions are associated with family events such as births, weddings, and deaths?

Holidays

How do you celebrate them? What foods, customs, activities, objects, and people are associated with them?

Local Lore and Jests

What stories and legends are well known in the area? What types of jokes are common?

Amusements and Pastimes

Do you take part in — or disdain — popular amusements? Do you know the rules to games or the words to popular songs? Are you up on the latest fads? What do you do when you are not working?

Neighbors

Who are your neighbors? What do you think about them? Do you have any stories to impart about them?

Weights and Measures

How do you weigh and measure liquid and dry goods? Can you convert weights and measures into other equivalent amounts? Can you describe them in other terms that a visitor will understand? How are weights and measures used in daily life? For example, how many barrels of pork, pipes of wine, or bushels of wheat are you likely to keep on hand?

Foodways

What are the favorite local dishes, and how are they prepared? Are there seasonal and holiday favorites? What do you drink, and where does it come from? How do food preparation and eating affect your day?

Local Agriculture

What cash and home-use crops are grown in the area? What rituals are associated with the agricultural year? What are the local agricultural practices, particularly the special ones (such as a cranberry harvest, the use of a local marl pit, etc.)?

Local Flora and Fauna

What animals and plants are commonly found? Which are unique to the area? Which ones do you use? How?

Weather

What is the climate at various times of the year? Are there rainy seasons, dry spells, etc.? Do you know local weather lore?

Local Material Culture

What are the common architecture and building styles of the area? Are there objects or styles that are unique to the area, such as furniture, sailing craft, pottery material, etc.? What locally available raw materials are incorporated into products?

Local Laws

What laws affect your life and daily business? Can you vote, own property, or run for office? What happens to you if you break the law?

Local Travel Modes and Conditions

How do you get from one place to the other? What roads would you take to get from your home to other points? What are the conditions of the road at specific times of the year?

OCCUPATIONAL SPHERE

This includes traditional occupations that are a main source of income, a partial occupation (such as dairying or midwifery), avid interests (such as botany or astronomy), and/or other work that may not be a direct source of income but may absorb a great deal of the character's time, such as housewifery and child rearing.

Occupation(s)

What is your occupation or trade, its practices, tools, processes, economic or agricultural cycles, association details (for example, unions, guilds, or professional memberships), occupational traits, and terminology? How much do you make? What are standard prices and rates for goods or services that you buy or sell? How does the occupation relate to other occupations? Where do your materials come from, and how do you get them? How does occupational terminology affect everyday speech? Is your occupation practiced by a few or by many? How does this affect your relationship with others in your community?

Domestic Duties and Skills

What are the typical daily, weekly, seasonal, and annual skills that your character would need to know? What special skills do you have? How is your routine affected by other elements in the local and personal spheres, such as ethnicity, local agriculture, religion, upbringing, social class, the occupation of your spouse, the makeup of your family or household unit, etc.?

Unique Skills or Talents

Are you the local source of jests, the woman whom everyone comes to for remedies, an avid needleworker, an amateur botanist, etc.?

STATIONAL SPHERE

Characteristics and habits related to class, including social competencies, cultivated skills (such as dancing, poaching, charm, social ritual, or courtesies), dress and accoutrements, dining habits, etc.

Customs of Dress

What garments are typical of your station? What garments set you apart from betters and inferiors? How does the quality, construction, color, and material of your clothing compare with that of others?

Dining Habits

What do you eat? How and where do you dine? What manners do you use? What rituals are associated with dining? What vessels and accoutrements do you use? Do you dine out? Where?

Property and Possessions

What are your land and estate holdings? What do they mean to you? Which of your possessions are "status quo" for your class? Which are unusual?

Friends and Enemies

Whom do you cultivate as part of your circle? Why? Whom do you avoid, and why?

Betters and Inferiors

Who are your betters and how do you show deference to them? Who are your inferiors and how do you treat them? What is your relationship to your own class?

Economy

What is the place of your class in the economy? How much power (or lack thereof) do you have over your personal economy? The local economy? The national economy? How do your actions affect the economy of others and other classes? See *Occupational Sphere*, above.

Influence

Whose ear do you have? Whose ear would you like to have? What can you achieve because of your station? What must you do to win influence? What do you do to others if they reject you?

Social Skills

See *Local Social Skills* under *Local Sphere*.

WIDER SPHERE

Knowledge of these will depend on character, social class, education, location, occupation, etc. The higher up the social ladder, the more likely a character would know about events in the following categories:

> World events, past
> World events, present
> Well-known figures, past
> Well-known figures, present
> Inventions and scientific/philosophical developments

World geography
The arts
Music
Dance
Literature
World economy
Law and/or medicine.

Participants

Information gathering for this work occurred in two major blocks of time: in 1991, when this study began as a master's project at the University of Pennsylvania, and in 1994, when the work was updated and expanded for publication.

The following people were interviewed or observed during research trips. The interviews occurred singly, in groups, and casually in conversation.

At Mystic Seaport Museum, Mystic, Conn., April 17, 1991: Glenn Gordinier, Bettye Noyes.

At Old Sturbridge Village, Sturbridge, Mass., April 18–19, 1991: Margaret Piatt, Chris Creelman, Claire Gregoire, Betty Frew, Rick Jenkinson, David Cloutier, Nancy Caouette, Jean Solaroli, Tom Kelleher, Bob Olson.

At Plimoth Plantation, Plymouth, Mass., April 20–22, 1991: Jeff Scotland, Rudy Palenstyn, John Kemp, Steve Ewald, Norbert Palenstyn, Larry Erickson, Jill Costa, Gitta Paans, Bertie Palenstyn, Effie Cummings, Bil Orland, Bill Podzon, Scott Atwood, Karen Atwood, Martha Sulya, Dave Walbridge, Lisa (Simon) Walbridge, David Emerson, Anne Lane, Pat Baker, Lisa Whalen, Stuart Bolton, Kim Longmore-Pontz, Tom Gerhardt, Gary Farias, Brendan Smith, Kathleen Curtin, Pret Woodburn, Rick Currier, Moira Turnan-Hannon, Kathleen Wall, Paula Marcoux, Hank Roach, Regina Scotland, Rita Hutchinson, Jon Lane, Chris Hall, Ron Rathier.

At Colonial Williamsburg, Va., July 28–30, 1994: Jeremy Fried, Bill Barker, Larry Earl, Eran Owens, B. J. Pryor, Thomas Hay, Jack Flintom, John Greenman, Don Coleman, Donald Kline, Ryan Fletcher, Steven Holloway, Susannah Badgett, Carson Hudson, John F. Lowe, Wayne Moss, Clip Carson, Susan Berquist, Kristen Spivey.

Additional questionnaires were filled out by B. J. Pryor, September 1, 1994, and Carson Hudson, November 1994.

Christy Coleman Matthews was interviewed by telephone on August 28, 1994, and April 24, 1995.

At Conner Prairie, Fishers, Ind., September 23–24, 1994: Observation only; staff scheduling did not permit interviews. One interpreter, Eddie Grogan, returned a questionnaire.

At Freetown Village, Indianapolis, Ind., September 23, 1994: Observation only of Khabir Shareef, Deanna Brewster, Linda Johnson, Ophelia Umar Wellington.

Ophelia Wellington, director of Freetown Village, also returned a questionnaire.

The interpreters of Upper Canada Village, Morrisburg, Ontario, responded by questionnaire, October 1994: Jean Jeacle, Peter Cazaly, Patrick Coyne, Caroline Roberts, Heather Froats.

The following independent interpreters returned questionnaires: Cynthia Andes, Titusville, Pa., August 17, 1994; Dan Bassuk, Neshanic, N.J., September 1994; George Chapman, Pasadena, Calif., October 30, 1994; Mark Geisser, Westfield, N.J., November 15, 1994; Steve Gulick, Philadelphia, Pa., December 14, 1994; William Kashatus III, Philadelphia, Pa., August 1994; Sarah Grant Reid, Dallas, Tex., September 6, 1994; Robert L. Spaeth, Sauk Rapids, Minn., August 1994.

I would also like to thank the following interpreters whose casual conversations were noted in the text: Eric Ferguson, Fort Snelling, Minn.; Donna Evans and Larry Schmidt, Old Barracks Museum, Trenton, N.J.; Tom Winslow, Morristown National Historical Park, Morristown, N.J.; Ralph Archbold, Ben Franklin's Colonial Connection, Philadelphia, Pa.; Richard Pickering, Plimoth Plantation.

Please forgive any omissions.

Selected Sites Featuring
First-Person Interpretation

The public sites listed here feature first-person interpretation as part of their daily or weekly programming. The list was compiled mainly from sources I became acquainted with in the process of writing *Past into Present*. I have yet to visit some of these sites, museums, and villages, so the information below is, in part, based on ·data from brochures, the Internet, leads from colleagues, and telephone conversations. (Special thanks go to Jim Powers, Jack Gardner, Harry Needham, Christopher Geist, and William Lawrence for their suggestions.) I have made every effort to check that this information is up to date as of October 1997. Some of these sites are only open in peak seasons and may close one or more days per week, so please call ahead when planning a visit.

There are many more sites with first-person programs, and countless other locations that sponsor roleplay-enhanced special events and occasional first-person scenarios, reenactments, and character appearances. This list will be expanded and maintained in conjunction with the Association for Living Historical Farms and Agricultural Museums' First-Person Interpreters' Professional Network working committee on that organization's page on the World Wide Web (www.alhfam.org). Readers are welcome to send information on additional first-person programs to the author at P.O. Box 421, Burlington, NJ 08016.

Baltimore City Life Museums (temporarily closed)
800 East Lombard St.
Baltimore, MD 21202
(410) 396-8395
Baltimore City Life Museums is a cluster of sites in the Jonestown section of the city. The 1840 House, the reconstructed row house of Irish immigrant and wheelwright John Hutchinson, offered an evolving menu of open-ended dramatic scenes featuring the Hutchinson family, their friends, their African American servants, and other historical characters. The programs addressed racial relations, urban issues, economic struggles, health and illness, and domestic life. Other sites, including the exhibition galleries, the H. L. Mencken House, the Rembrandt Peale Museum, and the Charles Carroll Mansion have also augmented collections and tours with both scripted performance and spontaneous first-person interpretation.

Barkerville Historic Town
P.O. Box 19
Barkerville, British Columbia, Canada V0K 1B0
(250) 994-3302 or (250) 994-3332
Barkerville is a restored mining community encompassing over 140 structures and two towns, Barkerville and Richfield. Its growth was spurred by the discovery of gold in 1862,

and it continued as a living community until 1958. At the local game guide's home a roleplayer portraying a houseguest is in the year 1900, but most of the characters interpret the years around the town's 1870 heyday. First-person interpreters are an ongoing feature of Richfield's courthouse, where visitors meet local figure Judge Begbie. Gold miners, dance hall girls, laundresses, gamblers, and merchants are among the characters encountered on Barkerville's streets and in selected site exhibits. Schoolchildren participate in activities such as a court trial, panning for gold, household chores, and carpentry.

Canadian Museum of Civilization
100 Laurier St.
Hull, Quebec, Canada J8X 4H2
(819) 776-7000
The museum has its own resident theater company, Dramamuse, which develops and presents live interpretation programs that accent the museum's collections and galleries. The company has a repertoire of short plays, sketches, and spontaneous characters who mingle and converse with visitors. The museum's Canada Hall exhibition gallery has life-size reconstructions of various historical environments. Visitors to the hall encounter characters such as a Basque whaler, an innkeeper from eighteenth-century New France, a voyageur, a shanty cook, shop merchants, or a Victorian maid.

Cincinnati History Museum
1301 Western Ave.
Cincinnati, OH 45203
(800) 733-2077 or (513) 287-7000
The Cincinnati History Museum has five indoor gallery environments that incorporate interactive first-person interpreters. They are a 1770 Native American village; an 1828 flatboat; a 1791 hunter's camp; a World War II homefront exhibit that features a full kitchen, living room, and train station; and a re-creation of downtown Cincinnati's public landing in 1859. The last includes the *Queen of the West* steamboat and a row of shops such as a millinery, a pork merchant, a coffeehouse, and a drugstore. Visitors may meet, for example, trader John Anderson in the 1770 village, flatboat passengers Johann and Henrietta Utz, Irish coffeehouse owner Hannah Finn, or steamboat captain Richard Wade at their corresponding exhibits. At minimum, three first-person interpreters are on the floor each afternoon and on weekends. School groups may request morning roleplay programs in advance.

Colonial Williamsburg
Williamsburg, VA 23187-1776
(800) HISTORY [447-8679]
This restored eighteenth-century Virginia capital is the largest and most famous of the living history institutions. Dozens of tours, event re-creations, character interpretations, dramatic events, trade demonstrations, concerts, lectures, and other special programs are presented daily. The lives and times of colonial Virginians, from slaves and servants to the political elite, are portrayed in a variety of first-person formats, includ-

ing interactive conversation, introduced scenarios, re-creations, limited participatory drama, dramatic scenes, and full-scale theatricals. The more spontaneous, interactive interpretive programs are identified with the phrase "A Person of the Past" in the weekly *Visitor's Companion*.

Conner Prairie
13400 Allisonville Road
Fishers, IN 46038-4499
(800) 866-1836 or (317) 776-6000
Conner Prairie commemorates the life and times of William Conner, who established a trading post in central Indiana and became a prominent citizen and political figure. At the site's re-created Prairietown, first-person interpreters portray fictional composite townspeople typical of those who lived in the region in 1836. Characters include a weaver's family, a doctor's family, an innkeeper's family, a household of potters, a schoolmaster, a storekeeper, a Revolutionary War veteran, and others up and down the social ladder. Most of the daily interpretation is casual and conversational. Occasional special scenarios, including a Fourth of July celebration and a funeral, provide additional interpretive context.

Fort Delaware State Park
45 Clinton St.
Delaware City, DE 19706
(302) 834-7941
Fort Delaware, one of several sites in the park system, is a restored Civil War Confederate prison located on Pea Patch Island, accessible only by ferry. The site is staffed by interpreters portraying Union battery officer Captain Stanislaus Mlotkowski, Confederate prisoner Captain Leon Jastremski, Julia Jefferson (a New Castle resident who aided prisoners), and various other characters, such as soldiers, a blacksmith, and a laundress.

Fortress Louisbourg National Historic Site
P.O. Box 160
Louisbourg, Nova Scotia, Canada B0A 1M0
(902) 733-2630 or (902) 733-2280
Two major invasions in 1745 and 1758 crippled the French military presence at Cape Breton Island's Fortress Louisbourg. But in 1744 (the site's focus year) the walled town was a thriving seaport and center of French trade and military strength. In 1961 the government of Canada began an impressive reconstruction of the walled fortress and many of its shops, streets, and yards. Each summer more than 100 interpreters portray the full range of Louisbourg's inhabitants, from fishermen, soldiers, bakers, servants, musicians, and street vendors to the leisured upper classes. A working environment of more than three dozen structures adds to the realism. The first-person program is supported by modern theme centers, exhibits, restaurants, and other public services.

Fort Snelling
Minneapolis, MN 55111
(612) 726-1171
Fort Snelling, constructed between 1819 and 1825 and named after its first commander, Colonel Joseph Snelling, was an army outpost and frontier trade station at the intersection of the Minnesota and Mississippi Rivers. The fort was a hub of frontier activity in 1827, the year portrayed in first-person at the site, and visitors can meet Colonel Snelling and his family, soldiers of the Fifth Regiment, traders, natives, servants, merchants, tradespeople, and travelers of various origins and ethnicities. Special event scenarios include an Independence Day celebration, the arrival of keelboatmen, and a fur trade rendezvous.

Freetown Village
P.O. Box 1041
Indianapolis, IN 46206
(317) 631-1870
Freetown Village depicts the lives of free black Indianapolis citizens in 1870. Though still seeking a permanent site, the organization animates an exhibit at the Indiana State Museum in Indianapolis and offers outreach programs and special events such as dinners, weddings, and holiday celebrations. Characters include a barber and his seamstress wife, a blacksmith's family, a lawyer, a preacher, a root woman (healer), a peddler, a teacher, and a laborer.

George Ranch Historical Park
10215 FM 762
Richmond, TX 77469
(281) 545-9212 or (281) 343-1218
George Ranch Historical Park museum complex includes the 1830s stock farm (a precursor of the ranch) of Henry Jones (and family), the Victorian home of banker/cattleman J. H. P. Davis, and a working 1930s cattle ranch built by Mamie Davis and her husband Albert P. George. First-person is the main form of interpretation at the stock farm site. Roleplayers portray Henry and Nancy Jones and their relatives and neighbors in 1830, usually while performing appropriate daily activities. The Davis and George households are occasionally roleplayed in vignettes and for special events, the former in 1896 and the latter in 1938. Each October the complex holds a Market Days festival evoking the wild trading days of 1820s colonial Texas.

Historic St. Mary's City
St. Mary's City, MD 20686
(800) SMC-1634 or (301) 862-0990
HSMC is the re-created first capital of Maryland, established by Governor Leonard Calvert in 1634. Live interpretation, however, focuses on the latter end of the seventeenth century. The site features a town center (the Governor's Field area), which in-

cludes a reconstructed 1676 statehouse and 1670s ordinary, a re-created 1660s tobacco plantation and Woodland Indian hamlet, and a replica of the *Maryland Dove*, a 1680s coastal trading vessel. Interpreters at the plantation portray the Godiah Spray family and servants in 1661; those in the Governor's Field area and on the *Maryland Dove* are in 1685. Special weekend events center on special themes such as a militia muster, seventeenth-century agriculture, domestic skills, and trades.

Knott's Berry Farm
8020 South Beach Blvd.
Buena Park, CA 90620
(714) 827-1776 or (714) 220-5244 (educational programs reservations)
Knott's Berry Farm is an enormous theme park, complete with a ghost town, a Native American presentation area, rides, and a "Peanuts"-themed Camp Snoopy. It also boasts a complete reproduction of Philadelphia's Independence Hall, where the Declaration of Independence was debated and proclaimed. From Monday through Friday, walk-in visitors and prescheduled tour groups can meet with Benjamin Franklin or Patrick Henry (portrayed alternately by the same interpreter, Gene Collins). Despite the glamour of the surroundings, Collins is reported to present convincing, museum-caliber interpretation.

Lincoln Log Cabin State Historic Site
R.R. #1, Box 172A
Lerna, IL 62440
(217) 345-6489
Interpreters at the re-created home and farm of Abraham Lincoln's parents, Thomas and Sarah Bush Lincoln, and the restored home and farm of progressive farmer Stephen Sargent portray the Lincoln family and their neighbors in 1845. First-person programming is available daily during the summer and on weekends during spring and fall. Special events include a Sunday religious service, a wedding, and a visit by Abraham Lincoln as a young lawyer.

Museum of the Moving Image
South Bank Arts Centre
Waterloo, London, SE1 8XT
0171 401 2636
MOMI's exhibits trace the history of animation, film, and television from its roots to the present. "Actor guides" with appropriate historical dress and demeanor are attached to selected galleries.

Mystic Seaport Museum
Mystic, CT 06355
(860) 572-0711
Mystic Seaport Museum houses seventeen acres of galleries, ships, boats, and restored and re-created maritime buildings and exhibits. The seaport's roleplayers are featured several times per day at selected interpretive sites, including the Sailor's Reading Room. Characters include a female doctor, a whaling captain's wife, sea captains, whalers, and

sailors. Storytelling is the primary roleplaying technique, employed very successfully. Mystic also has an active museum theater program.

Norlands Living History Center
290 Norlands Road
Livermore, ME 04253
(207) 897-2236 or (207) 897-4366
Although the Norlands was owned by the Washburn political dynasty, the living history focus of this working farm and schoolhouse site is the daily lives of the rural Pray and Waters families and their neighbors. Norlands offers a unique three-day, live-in roleplay program aimed at teachers and others who want to "rough it" in 1870. Participants are assigned roles — which do not necessarily correspond to their age or gender — and maintain those roles throughout a chore-filled weekend.

Ohio Historical Village
1982 Velma Ave.
Columbus, OH 43211
(614) 287-2300
Ohio Historical Village, administered and located next to the Ohio Historical Center, is a completely re-created Ohio village at the time of the American Civil War. Structures in the village include a hotel, a general store, a print shop, a schoolhouse, a doctor's house, a black freeman's house, a tinsmith's, a Soldier's Aid Society office, and a farmhouse. On most weekends visitors are likely to walk into events such as a temperance meeting or a literary society meeting, or meet conversation-inclined first-person characters. A unique feature of first-person at the village is their choice to rotate the focus year annually. One year it is 1861, the next 1862, and so forth.

Old Barracks Museum
Barrack Street
Trenton, NJ 08608
(609) 396-1776
The Old Barracks, originally constructed during the French and Indian War, is restored to its appearance during the American Revolution, when it was utilized as a military hospital. First-person programs about the differences between patriots and Loyalists, the activities of the hospital, and the December 1776 battle of Trenton between General Washington's troops and occupying Hessians are offered to schoolchildren and other groups by advance registration.

Old Cowtown Museum
1871 Slim Park Dr.
Wichita, KS 67203
(316) 264-0671
Old Cowtown's approximately three dozen relocated structures re-create two blocks of time in Wichita's Anglo-American settlement. Its earliest days, 1865 to 1869, are reflected in the settlement agent's house, a settler's cabin, and the Episcopal church. The rest of the site depicts Wichita in the 1870s, including a business district full of store-

fronts, a railroad depot, and a residential area. First-person — mostly planned scenarios and scripted scenes — is a common feature on weekends, when family visitors might encounter characters such as a sheriff, a doctor, a housewife, a farmer, or cowboys discussing the cattle trade, gun regulations, and other daily concerns.

Old Fort Wayne (defunct)
Fort Wayne, IN
The restored fort depicted garrison life in "Indian Country" in 1816. The engaging characters of the site's daily first-person program attracted the attention of *Early American Life* magazine in a 1983 article by Merry Neff titled "The Interpreters of Old Fort Wayne." Members of Major John Whistler's family, the family of Indian agent Benjamin Franklin Stickney, and assorted soldiers, traders, and laborers were depicted. The site closed in 1994.

Old Fort William
Vickers Heights Post Office
Thunder Bay, Ontario, Canada PoT 2Zo
(807) 473-2344 (site) or (800) 667-8386 (Thunder Bay Tourism)
Old Fort William is a reconstructed headquarters of the North West Company, established in 1798 near the Kaministiquia River. The settlement became the center of the North American Fur Trade, a rendezvous point for French voyageurs and Ojibway trappers. The interpretive focus year is 1815, the year before North West's takeover by the Hudson Bay Company. Interpreters portray North West's owner William McGillivray, mapmaker David Thompson, and assorted natives, voyageurs, artisans, and company clerks.

Old Sturbridge Village
1 Old Sturbridge Village Road
Sturbridge, MA 01566
(508) 347-3362
OSV is a collection of restored and re-created nineteenth-century homes, farms, trade shops, and town buildings that reproduce the atmosphere of early industrial New England in the 1830s. Selected sites; featured appearances by nineteenth-century personalities such as a magician, an abolitionist, or an actress; and events such as weddings, funerals, and town meetings employ first-person interpretation. At many interpretive stations, individual interpreters have the option of choosing first- or third-person, depending on how they read each visitor group and how visitors enjoy interacting.

Plimoth Plantation
P.O. Box 1620
Plymouth, MA 02362
(508) 746-1622
Plimoth Plantation re-creates the world of English settlers — known to us today as the Pilgrims — and the Wampanoag natives who also inhabit the western side of Cape Cod Bay. At the site's Pilgrim Village, first-person interpreters portray the original inhabitants of Plymouth Colony in a re-creation of the settlement's two main streets, gardens, and fields as they would have appeared in 1627. Three miles away it is always

March 1621 on board a reconstruction of *Mayflower*, the ship that transported the Congregation of Saints and their fellow voyagers, whom they referred to as Strangers, to the New World. Other interpretive features include exhibits, a crafts demonstration center, and a third-person Native American habitation.

Sainte Marie among the Iroquois
P.O. Box 146
Liverpool, NY 13088
(315) 453-6767
Sainte Marie among the Iroquois, formerly known as Sainte Marie de Gannetaha, commemorates the two-year foray of Jesuit missionaries to establish a religious outpost among the Onondaga nation, 1656–58. A reconstructed mission is the background for first-person interpreters who portray actual priests, soldiers, and brothers in 1657, discussing the purpose of the mission, their perceptions of the natives, comparisons between life in Old France and New France, and other aspects of life in the seventeenth century. The mission's brothers also demonstrate and discuss their secular labors, including blacksmithing, carpentry, and other domestic tasks. The Native American viewpoint is interpreted in a separate third-person area, currently under development.

Science Museum of London
Exhibition Road
South Kensington, London SW7 2DD
United Kingdom
0171 938-8008/8080
Museum theater augments the museum's collections and exhibits. Historical personalities such as astronauts, aviators, and shipyard workers add a live dimension to selected galleries.

Sovereign Hill
Ballarat, Victoria 3350
Australia
03 5331 1944
The Victoria Gold Rush of the 1850s is the theme of Sovereign Hill, a re-created mining village and exhibit center. Visitors tour an underground gold mine, visit diggings where they can pan for gold, and wander through a mining encampment, local Chinatown, and reconstructed street of functioning historical shops. Although most of the live interpretation is in third-person, dramatic scenarios between miners, camp followers, and other characters unfold in the streets. Visitors have the opportunity to interact informally with the characters, who linger in the area as each scene concludes.

Upper Canada Village (St. Lawrence Parks Commission)
R.R. #1 (11 Kilometers east of Morrisburg)
Morrisburg, Ontario, Canada K0C 1X0
(613) 543-3704
Upper Canada Village is the resting place of over two dozen buildings that were rescued and relocated from locations now under the waters of the Saint Lawrence Seaway.

These, augmented with several reproduction structures, illustrate the daily life of a typical Ontario community in 1866, the year prior to Canadian confederation. While many trades are depicted in third-person, selected sites are staffed by first-person interpreters portraying a Lutheran pastor, a tavern keeper, a houschold servant, a newspaper editor, and a Methodist Sunday school superintendent who is also the convener of the Total Abstinence Society. The roleplayers also interact as a group in special scenarios such as an Abstinence Society meeting.

Wylie House
307 East 2nd St.
Bloomington, IN 47405
(812) 855-6224

Wylie House (constructed 1835) was the home of Indiana University's first president, Andrew Wylie, and his family. Today the university owns and operates the home as an 1840s historic house museum. Bonnie Williams, the site's curator, offers a "ghost interpretation" portrayal of Wylie's adult daughter Elizabeth. Other characters are available as staffing permits. Visiting groups must request the program in advance.

NOTES

ABBREVIATIONS USED IN THE NOTES

CP: Conner Prairie
CW: Colonial Williamsburg
MSM: Mystic Seaport Museum
NPS: National Park Service
OSV: Old Sturbridge Village
Plimoth: Plimoth Plantation
UCV: Upper Canada Village

INTRODUCTION

1. Jay Anderson, *Time Machines*, 179–93.

2. Yellis, "Real Time," August 24, 1991, 5. A published version appears as "Not Time Machines but Real Time: Living History at Plimoth Plantation."

CHAPTER ONE

1. Jay Anderson, "Living History," 3.

2. The classic work on the ethos of interpretation is Tilden, *Interpreting Our Heritage*. In it Tilden defines the major principles of interpreting history and the environment to the public. Other sources on interpretive philosophy and the history of interpretation include Sharpe, *Interpreting the Environment*; Machlis and Field, *On Interpretation*; Machlis, *Interpretive Views*; Uzzell, *Heritage Interpretation*; Alderson and Low, *Interpretation of Historic Sites*; Regnier, Gross, and Zimmerman, *Interpreter's Guidebook*; Pond, *Professional Guide*; Mackintosh, *Interpretation in the National Park Service*; Cherem, "Professional Interpretor."

3. Tilden, *Interpreting Our Heritage*, 8–9.

4. There are numerous sources on why people visit museums. See Barthel, "Nostalgia for America's Village Past"; Falk and Dierking, *Museum Experience*; Field and Wager, "Visitor Groups and Interpretation in Parks and Other Outdoor Leisure Settings"; Graburn, "Museum and the Visitor Experience"; Ham, "Familiarity and Adaptation"; Hooper-Greenhill, *Museums and Their Visitors*; Kaplan, Bardwell, and Slater, "Museum as Restorative Environment"; *Marriage and Family Review* 13, no. 3/4 (1989) (special issue dedicated to family learning and museums); Littlejohn and Machlis, *Diversity of Visitors to the National Park System*; Machlis and Field, *On Interpretation*; Melton, "Some Behavior Characteristics of Museum Visitors."

5. See Hayes and Schindel, *Pioneer Journeys*; Farmelo, "Drama on the Galleries"; Alsford and Parry, "Interpretive Theatre"; Bicknell and Fisher, "Enlightening or Embarrassing?"; Stillman, "Living History in an Art Museum"; "Museum Theater"; Canadian Museum of Civilization, *Evaluation of the Live Interpretation Program*. The worldwide support and networking group for museum theater professionals is the International Museum Theatre Alliance, c/o Museum of Science, Science Park, Boston, Mass. 02114-1099, telephone 617-589-0449.

6. These two terms are assigned by the author.

7. Jay Anderson, *Living History Sourcebook*, 440. See also Anderson's chronicling of the reenactment movement in pt. 3 of his *Time Machines*.

8. See, for example, Chapman, "Living History Stew," and Knutson, "Recruiting and Interpreting." For articles on site/reenactor collaborations, see Deakin, "Reenactors and History"; Pritchard, "Fort Ross"; Hanson, "Flip Side."

9. For descriptions of Plimoth, CP, and other living history sites, see Gutek and Gutek, *Experiencing America's Past*.

10. Robertshaw, "From Houses into Homes," 18.

11. Term used by Susannah Badgett and B. J. Pryor, CW, group interview, July 28, 1994.

12. For background on OSV's Teacher Training Institute, which prepares teachers to ready their students for programs such as "Farm to Factory," see Gibson-Quigley and Rowden, "Social Change in America." For the experience of Mt. Holyoke students at Plimoth, see Allgore, "Not Going as Tourists," and "Finding History in Day-to-Day Life with the Pilgrims."

13. For practical advice on organizing classroom roleplaying, see Fairclough, *Teacher's Guide to History through Roleplay*; Chiodo and Klausmeier, "'V.T.'"; Hurst and Otis, "Living History in the Classroom"; Keller, "Roleplaying and Simulation in History Classes"; Shannon, "Introducing Simulation and Role Play"; and Van Ments, *Effective Use of Role-Play*.

14. Piatt, "Role Acting," and "Outline of Theatrical Forms," 5.

15. Discussion with Tom Kelleher, April 18, 1991, and Dave Cloutier, April 19, 1991. OSV's smorgasbord approach to interpretation offers third-person at most stations, role acting at others (depending on the proclivities of the interpreter), standard first-person at its Parsonage site, and special programs that combine fourth-wall roleplay with third-person commentary.

16. See Sanders, "Thoughts on Effective Living History," 11–12, 21. Sanders also called this form of interpretation "ghost interpretation," but see the next paragraph for a distinction between the two.

17. Author's conversation with Eric Ferguson, June 1993, Fort Snelling, Minn.

18. Williams, "Playing in the Stream of History."

19. Ibid., 9.

20. Butler, "Historians to Stage Revealing Court Martial."

21. Reid portrays Madame Tussaud, Clara Barton, and Empress Josephine; Spaeth offers a presentation titled "Galileo Speaks Out"; and Kashatus presents Thomas Paine, baseball great Eddie Collins, and George Fox, among others.

CHAPTER TWO

1. I would particularly like to thank Dr. John Kemp of Plimoth for sharing his thoughts on the goals of first-person interpretation.

2. See Vance, "Developing a First Person Program," 180; Jay Anderson, *Time Machines*; Moore, "Folklife Museums."

3. See Bradley Commission, *Building a Curriculum*, 9.

4. See Jay Anderson, *Time Machines*, pt. 2, "Time Bandits: Living History as Research," 85–131; Lowenthal, *Past Is a Foreign Country*, 300; Jay Anderson, "Immaterial

Material Culture"; Callender, "Reliving the Past"; Woods, "Living Historical Farming"; Timothy Green, "Modern Britons Try the Iron Age."

5. Borne out by the Canadian Museum of Civilization's recent *Evaluation of the Live Interpretation Program*, 36, 52. Visitors at first-person programs interacted with one another twice as often as those viewing static exhibits.

6. Cecilia Miller, *Giambattista Vico*, 118. Many thanks to Dr. Gary Machlis of the University of Idaho for introducing me to Vico.

7. Berlin, *Crooked Timber of Humanity*, 64–65.

8. Walsh, *Representation of the Past*, particularly chap. 5, "Simulating the Past," 94–115; Barnes, "Living History"; Fortier, "Moment in Time"; Lowenthal, *Past Is a Foreign Country*; Peterson, "There Is No Living History," 28; Sherfy, "Honesty in Interpreting the Cultural Past"; Glassberg, "Living in the Past"; Hudson, *Museums of Influence*; Levstik, "Living History — Isn't"; Horvath and Bin, "From Reality to Hyperreality"; Richard Handler, "Overpowered by Realism."

9. Advocates of living history/first-person interpretation include Jay Anderson, "Living History," *Time Machines*, and *Living History Sourcebook*; Yellis, "Not Time Machines"; Charles C. Cole, *Active Group Learning*; Lynch, *What Time Is This Place?*, 51–52; Vance, "Developing a First Person Program"; Hurst and Otis, "Living History in the Classroom"; and popular press articles too numerous to mention.

10. Leon and Piatt, "Living History Museums"; Burcaw, "Can History Be Too Lively?"; Schafernich, "On Site Museums."

11. *Time Machines* took the brunt of the criticism, however.

12. Jay Anderson, *Living History Sourcebook*, 446.

13. Glassberg, "Living in the Past."

14. Lowenthal, *Past Is a Foreign Country*. Cf. Ronsheim, "Is the Past Dead?," and Richard Handler, "Overpowered by Realism."

15. Lowenthal, *Past Is a Foreign Country*, 298. See also Stover, "Interpretation of Historical Conflict," 248.

16. See Williams and Schultz, "Dealing with the Disturbing."

17. Alexander, *Museums in Motion*, 201.

18. Fortier, "Dilemmas," 5–6. Fortier's use of the term "first-person interpretation" differs from standard usage and refers more to the type of interpretation described under "role acting."

19. Comments to author by Harry Needham, Chief, Audit and Evaluation, Canadian Museum of Civilization.

20. Ibid.; Fortier, "Moment in Time," 38–40.

21. Yellis, "Real Time," October 1, 1990, 27.

22. Leon and Piatt, "Living History Museums," 89.

23. Sanders, "Thoughts on Effective Living History."

24. Peterson used the term "living history." He is, however, clearly referring to "first-person interpretation" from the context of the article.

25. Peterson, "There Is No Living History."

26. Yellis, "Real Time," all versions.

27. Fortier, "Moment in Time," 37.

28. Walsh, *Representation of the Past*, 102.

29. Vance, "Developing a First Person Program," 162–64; Yellis, "Real Time,"

August 24, 1991, 8, and October 1, 1990, 25–26; Alexander, *Museums in Motion*, 195–96; Leon and Piatt, "Living History Museums," 89.

30. Yellis, "Real Time," October 1, 1990, 16.

31. Krugler, "Keeping the Illusion of Historical Accuracy," 10.

32. Charles C. Cole, *Active Group Learning*, 45.

33. Vance, "Developing a First Person Program."

34. For a rather humorous indictment of modern-day academic historiographic writing, see Schama, "Clio Has a Problem."

35. Baker and Leon, "Old Sturbridge Village Introduces Social Conflict"; Patricia Leigh Brown, "Away from the Big House"; Patterson, "Conner Prairie Refocuses"; Crowley, "Out of the Maine Stream"; Snow, "Theatre of the Pilgrims"; Stover, "Interpretation of Historical Conflict" and "Is It REAL History Yet?"; Roth, "Sense and Sensibility."

36. In CW's 1994 evaluation of how visitors perceived key themes, recall of facts seemed vague at best. Emotional responses — to programs such as the trial of a slave or activities such as participating in a military drill — were far more vivid.

37. Vicki Ann Green, "Oral History of a Field Trip." For similar perspectives on the value of living history environments as educational tools, see also Schlereth, "Historic Museum Village as a Learning Environment"; McQuarie, "'Experiences in History'"; Ahern, "Where History Really Lives"; Joseph J. Ryan, "Early Morning Mist."

38. Conversation with Lawrence Schmidt, former curator of interpretation, January 28, 1995.

39. Korn, "Evaluation of the 'Becoming Americans' Theme," 58–60.

40. Canadian Museum of Civilization, *Evaluation of the Live Interpretation Program*, 53. Thirty percent of respondents attributed interpreter skill (among eight choices from which only one answer could be selected) as the key reason for staying through a complete presentation. Ninety-five percent of all survey respondents said that live interpretation enhanced their visit to the museum.

CHAPTER THREE

1. There are several good overviews of the history of the living history museum movement available, so I will refrain from repeating its full story here. For a general discussion of its development, see Leon and Piatt, "Living History Museums"; Jay Anderson, *Time Machines*; Stover, "Interpretation of Historical Conflict"; and Matelic, "Through the Historical Looking Glass." On the living history farms movement, see Schlebecker and Peterson, *Living Historical Farms Handbook*, and Sharrer, "Hitching History to the Plow."

2. The study of the motivation of people to re-create the past is a fascinating and underexplored subject. See Glassberg, *American Historical Pageantry*; Schechner, *Between Theater and Anthropology*; Turner and Turner, "Performing Ethnography"; Jay Anderson, *Time Machines*.

3. For comment on the new social history, see Greene, "'New History.'" For the implications of new social history in the museum world, see Carson, "Living Museums," and Deetz, "Sense of Another World."

4. Carson, "Living Museums," 23.

5. For more information on the Association for Living Historical Farms and Agri-

cultural Museums, contact Judith M. Sheridan, Secretary-Treasurer, 8774 Route 45 NW, North Bloomfield, OH 44450. The author is the committee chair for the first-person interpreters' subcommittee. ALHFAM's website is www.alhfam.org.

6. Mackintosh, *Interpretation in the National Park Service*, 54.

7. Discussion with Ron Thomson of NPS's Mid-Atlantic Region, April 1991.

8. Ecroyd, *Living History*, 42.

9. See Ecroyd, *Living History*. Freeman Tilden, as early as 1957, advocated reliance on dominant themes and simplicity in interpretation at national parks. See Tilden, *Interpreting Our Heritage*.

10. Conversation with Margaret Piatt at OSV, April 19, 1991; Snow, "Theatre of the Pilgrims," 81–83; letter from Cindy Kupiainen, Publications Editor, CP, to the author, September 28, 1994.

11. Leon and Piatt, "Living History Museums," 87.

12. Baker, "Worldview at Plimoth Plantation," 64; Snow, "Theatre of the Pilgrims," 81–83.

13. Snow, "Theatre of the Pilgrims," 81–83.

14. Deetz, "Link from Object to Person to Concept," 32.

15. Conversation with John Kemp, Plimoth, March 1992.

16. Snow, "Theatre of the Pilgrims." 84.

17. Baker, "Worldview at Plimoth Plantation," 64–65; Kemp, "World View and the Interpreter."

18. Leon and Piatt, "Living History Museums," 87.

19. Yellis, "Real Time," August 24, 1991, 29.

20. Leon and Piatt, "Living History Museums," 87.

21. Yellis, "Real Time," October 1, 1990, 28.

22. For a comprehensive history of the one-person show from the nineteenth century to the present, see Gentile, *Cast of One*.

23. Ibid., 42–43.

24. Holzer, "Disarmingly Abe," 43.

25. Gentile, *Cast of One*, 96–100.

26. Case and Case, *We Called It Culture*, 54.

27. Gentile, *Cast of One*, 119–24.

28. Holbrook, *Mark Twain Tonight!*

29. Jackson, "Analysis of Hal Holbrook's Development and Performance of the Role of Mark Twain."

30. Carnahan, "Time Travelers"; Mandell, "Details, Details, Details"; "Living History."

31. Mimi Handler, "How Do We View the Past?"

32. Lisa Whalen, memo to author, April 20, 1991.

33. Stuart Bolton, Plimoth interpreter, in conversation, April 22, 1991: "We are kinder, gentler, Pilgrims"; conversation with John Kemp, Plimoth, April 20, 1991.

34. Scenarios have been featured at CW, Plimoth, OSV, CP, MSM, Freetown Village (a new African American living history site in Indianapolis, Ind.), Morristown National Historical Park, Independence National Historic Park, the 1840 House (Baltimore, Md.), Pennsbury Manor (Morrisville, Pa.), the Old Barracks Museum (Trenton, N.J.), and even traditional exhibit-oriented sites such as the Historical Society of Penn-

sylvania, the Chicago Historical Society, the National Museum of American History at the Smithsonian, the Canadian Museum of Civilization, and the Walters Art Gallery in Baltimore. This list is, of course, just the tip of the iceberg. See, for instance, Farmelo, "Drama on the Galleries"; "Museum Theater"; and "History Goes on Stage."

35. See, for example, Zwelling, "Social History Hits the Street"; Munley, *Evaluation Study Report*; Historical Society of Pennsylvania, "Partners with the Past"; Baltimore City Life Museums, descriptive brochure for "Steps in Time" (ca. 1988); "When Israel Was in Egypt's Land"; Stillman, "Living History in an Art Museum"; Butler, "Historians to Stage Revealing Court Martial"; Living History Foundation, flyer seeking players for eighteenth-century murder mystery at Carlyle House, Alexandria, Va., 1991; Carmody, "Brandywine Christmas and Beyond."

36. See Stover, "Interpretation of Historical Conflict"; Bordewich, "Williamsburg"; "When Israel Was in Egypt's Land"; Zwelling, "Social History Hits the Street"; Carson, "From the Bottom Up"; Munley, *Evaluation Study Report*; Patterson, "Conner Prairie Refocuses"; Baker and Leon, "Old Sturbridge Village Introduces Social Conflict"; Patricia Leigh Brown, "Away from the Big House"; "Living History"; Mimi Handler, "How Do We View the Past?"; Leon and Piatt, "Living History Museums"; Bell, "Skeletons in the Closet."

37. Quoted in Schimmel, *Just Enough to Make a Story*, 37.

38. Interview with Glenn Gordinier, Director of Interpretation, MSM, April 17, 1991.

CHAPTER FOUR

1. Ecroyd, *Living History*, 43; Vance, "Developing a First Person Program," 178.

2. David Emerson's name will crop up frequently in this book. His career has taken him from CW to Plimoth, where I first met him, to Morristown National Historical Park and the Old Barracks Museum. In 1993 David and I launched History on the Hoof, a freelance company that features four centuries of first- and third-person interpretive programs.

3. Ecroyd, *Living History*, 43.

4. Vance, "Developing a First Person Program," 178.

5. Interview with Dave Cloutier, OSV, April 19, 1991.

6. Yellis, "Not Time Machines" and "Real Time," all versions; Vance, "Developing a First Person Program"; Ecroyd, *Living History*; Fortier, "Dilemmas" and "Thoughts on the Re-creation and Interpretation of Historical Environments"; Alexander, *Museums in Motion*. Only Yellis and Vance are concerned solely with first-person interpretation. The others are more general in their application to all types of living history sites.

7. Yellis, "Real Time," August 24, 1991, 13; Vance, "Developing a First Person Program," 163; *Teaching History at Colonial Williamsburg*.

8. Kay, *Keep It Alive!*, 3; see also Yellis, "Real Time," August 24, 1991, 15; Fortier, "Dilemmas," 9; Fortier, "Thoughts on the Re-creation and Interpretation of Historical Environments," 7.

9. Yellis, "Real Time," August 24, 1991, 18–21.

10. Ibid., 15–17, 24.

11. See Matelic et al., "Research for Interpretation."

12. Ecroyd, *Living History*, 28.

13. For comments on training, see Vance, "Developing a First Person Program," 171–72; Ecroyd, *Living History*, 25; Tramposch, "'Put There a Spark.'"

14. Vance, "Developing a First Person Program," 169; Piatt, "Role Acting"; examination of components from the manuals of Plimoth, Pennsbury Manor, Lincoln Log Cabin, MSM, Historic Fort Wayne, and UCV.

15. Interviews with Claire Gregoire and Betty Frew, OSV, April 18, 1991.

16. These types of exercises are outlined in Piatt and Jones, "Planning Effective Living History Performances," and Piatt, "Role Acting."

17. For examples of these exercises, see Spolin, *Improvisation for the Theater* and *Theatre Games*.

18. Ecroyd, *Living History*, 43.

19. Interview with Chris Creelman, OSV, April 18, 1991.

20. Sarah Grant Reid, questionnaire response, September 1994.

21. Interview with Rick Jenkinson, OSV, April 18, 1991.

22. Eric Olsen, questionnaire response, September 1994.

23. Interview with Dave Cloutier, OSV, April 19, 1991.

CHAPTER FIVE

1. Snow, "Theatre of the Pilgrims"; Schechner, *Between Theater and Anthropology*, 79–92.

2. Schechner, *Between Theater and Anthropology*, 79–92. He also put living history museums in the same category as theme parks such as Disneyland, calling them "pilgrimage centers where performances, goods, services, and ideologies are displayed and exchanged."

3. Constantin Stanislavsky was a Russian actor who pioneered a naturalistic method of characterization, advising actors to study their characters' subconscious and organic reactions to circumstances to create believability and artistic truth from the inside out. Stanislavsky's techniques were further developed by Stella Adler and Lee Strassberg in the United States, where the technique was dubbed "method acting." As an interesting comparison, Bertold Brecht advised the opposite approach to character-building: to construct traits by analyzing story line and asking dialectical questions, creating a persona from the outside in. See Stanislavsky, *Building a Character*; Hodgson and Richards, *Improvisation*, 85–89; Cole and Chinoy, *Actors on Acting*, 484–85.

4. Snow, "Theatre of the Pilgrims," 377. The published version is *Performing the Pilgrims: A Study of Ethnohistorical Role-Playing at Plimoth Plantation*.

5. Schechner, *Between Theater and Anthropology*, 38; Hodgson and Richards, *Improvisation*, 11.

6. Snow and Schechner elaborate on these shared attributes.

7. McCalmon and Moe, *Creating Historical Drama*, 16–20.

8. Ibid., 194–98. The quote is on p. 198.

9. Stone and Edwards, *1776!*, 158. These comments appear in the historical notes and addendum.

10. Mark Giesser, letter to author, November 15, 1994.

11. Cf. Erving Goffman's description of the differences between real and staged activity in *Frame Analysis*, 138–44.

12. Turner and Turner, "Performing Ethnography," 33. Under the guidance of the Turners, anthropology students at the University of Virginia and drama students at New York University created scenes drawn from ethnographic literature. The experiment was meant to connect the students with the cultures they were studying rather than to train them as actors. Even though the instructors felt that the students needed better immersion in background materials, the students were enthusiastic about the results.

13. Gordinier, "Guidelines for Roleplayers."

14. Stover, "Interpretation of Historical Conflict," 243.

15. Interviews with Claire Gregoire and Betty Frew, OSV, April 18, 1991.

CHAPTER SIX

1. Kemp, "World View and the Interpreter," 68.

2. Yellis, "Real Time," August 24, 1991, 18. See also Yellis, "Dying 'Interstate'" and "Not Time Machines"; Kemp, "Worldview and the Interpreter," and Baker, "Worldview at Plimoth Plantation."

3. Yellis, "Real Time," August 24, 1991, 18.

4. Garbarino, *Sociocultural Theory in Anthropology*, 82–83.

5. The framework was inspired by conversations and memo exchanges with my former colleague Charlie Thomforde; a list of folkways systems in Fischer, *Albion's Seed*, 8–9; and a character outline (1988) by the Living History Foundation, P.O. Box 220155, Chantilly, Va. 22022-0155. Living history writer/artist Cathy Johnson has published a sixty-page guide to developing a "persona," titled *Who Was I?* Aimed at recent and potential converts to reenacting, it includes suggestions on how to research character histories, guidelines for choosing reasonably authentic traits, advice on choosing clothing, and lists of library, text, and other resources. Johnson also covered the subject in her recent *Living History: Drawing on the Past*.

6. From a two-page essay titled "First Person Interpretation: Personalizing History," by Gregory L. Manifold, 1984, in the training materials of Historic Fort Wayne.

7. Ecroyd, *Living History*, 30.

8. Interview with Nancy Caouette, OSV, April 18, 1991.

9. Interview with Claire Gregoire, OSV, April 18, 1991.

10. David Emerson, now my partner in the interactive history venture we call History on the Hoof, enjoys finding special details that surprise visitors. The visitors' reaction is reward enough for the effort.

11. Barto, "Teacher as Actor."

12. William Kashatus, III, taped questionnaire response, August 1994.

13. Steve Gulick, questionnaire response, November 1994.

CHAPTER SEVEN

1. Yellis, "Real Time," October 1, 1990, 5.

2. Interview with Dave Cloutier, OSV, April 19, 1991. General sentiments of a number of interpreters at Plimoth.

3. Yellis, "Real Time," October 1, 1990, 5; Kemp, "World View and the Interpreter."

4. Piatt, "How the Grasshopper Sprang from the Soil," 19–21.

5. Yellis, "Real Time," October 1, 1990, 19.

6. Lisa Whalen, memo to author, April 20, 1991.

7. White, *Practical Public Speaking*, 26–27.

8. Tilden, *Interpreting Our Heritage*, 9.

9. Ralph Archbold, telephone conversation with author, November 1994.

10. Carson Hudson, taped questionnaire, November 1994.

11. White, *Practical Public Speaking*, 26–27.

12. See, for example, "Living History"; Mimi Handler, "How Do We View the Past?"; Naylor, "Living History Farms and Museums"; Sussman, "From Williamsburg to Conner Prairie."

13. Dierking, "First-Person Interpretation," 240.

CHAPTER EIGHT

1. See Stephens, "The Visitor"; Machlis and Field, introduction to *On Interpretation*, 1–8. Machlis and Field recommend the use of sociological technique for understanding park visitors and stress the service role of interpretation. P. L. Pearce suggests that those in the tourism industry (including living history sites and museums) integrate the expectations, motives, and values of visitors into assessment and evaluation. See Pearce, *Ulysses Factor*, 25.

2. Some of the more general tourist motivation theories will be discussed in this chapter, while those relating to specific museum audiences will appear in greater depth in following chapters.

3. Piatt, "How the Grasshopper Sprang from the Soil."

4. Falk and Dierking, *Museum Experience*.

5. Moscardo and Pearce, "Historic Theme Parks."

6. Skobalski, "Issues in Open Air Museum Management," 93.

7. Hayward and Jensen, "Enhancing a Sense of the Past."

8. For the concept of regions and region behavior, see Goffman, *Presentation of Self in Everyday Life*, 106–40.

9. Cohen, "Phenomenology of Tourist Experiences."

10. Pearce, *Ulysses Factor*, 27–31.

11. Snow, *Performing the Pilgrims*, 163.

12. See Falk and Dierking, *Museum Experience*, 157.

13. Cf. Pearce, "Tourist-Guide Interaction," 143.

14. Conversation with John Kemp, Plimoth, October 25, 1991.

15. Based on general observation and comments by Peter Ryan, Historical Interpretation Workshop sponsored by the Living History Foundation held at the Landis Valley Museum (Pa.), February 2–3, 1991; Patrick Coyne, UCV, questionnaire response, October 1994; Peter Cazaly, UCV, questionnaire response, October 2, 1994; Eric Olsen, Morristown National Historical Park, questionnaire response, September 1994.

16. Interviews with Glenn Gordinier and Bettye Noyes, MSM, April 17, 1991. Eddie Grogan, CP, taped questionnaire, November 17, 1994, also made a similar comment, albeit for the 1830s.

17. Observation, September 23, 1994.

18. Interview with Larry Earl, CW Department of African American Interpretation and Presentations, Carter's Grove, July 30, 1994.

19. Jean Jeacle, UCV, questionnaire response, October 3, 1994; Ophelia Wellington, Director, Freetown Village, questionnaire response, October 1994.

20. For accounts of the weekend live-ins at Norlands, see Crowley, "Out of the Maine Stream"; Craig, "Retreat into History"; and "Seventy-Two Hours in 1870."

21. Scott Atwood, during group interview at Plimoth, April 22, 1991.

22. Plimoth Plantation, "Plimoth Plantation Welcomes You."

23. Yellis, "Real Time," all versions; comments from Plimoth interpreters at group interviews held on April 20, 22, 1991; Mimi Handler, "How Do We View the Past?"; Sussman, "From Williamsburg to Conner Prairie"; Stover, "Interpretation of Historical Conflict."

CHAPTER NINE

1. See Condon, "When People Talk with People," 45–46.

2. Jeff Scotland, during group interview, Plimoth, April 20, 1991.

3. Interview with Betty Frew, OSV, April 18, 1991. Vance, "Developing a First Person Program," concurs, as do the interpreters at Plimoth (group interview, April 20, 1991).

4. Interview with Moira Turnan Hannon, Plimoth, April 22, 1991.

5. Interview with Betty Frew, OSV, April 18, 1991.

6. See, for instance, Marsh, *Eye to Eye*, 98–99; Grinder and McCoy, *Good Guide*, 131; Goffman, "Facial Engagements."

7. Risk, "On-Site Real-Time Observational Techniques," 125.

8. Interview with Claire Gregoire, OSV, April 19, 1991.

9. Scott Atwood, during group interview, Plimoth, April 22, 1991.

10. Jack Flintom, group interview, CW, July 28, 1994.

11. Susannah Badgett, group interview with CW character interpreters, July 28, 1994.

12. This is not an exact quote from Glenn Gordinier but an approach structured in a fashion similar to other examples.

13. Interview with Glenn Gordinier, MSM, April 17, 1991.

14. Vance, "Developing a First Person Program."

15. Bruneau, "Communicative Silences," 30.

16. Telephone interview with Christy Coleman Matthews, August 28, 1994; CBS "Sunday Morning," segment on the African American history program at CW, airdate February 14, 1993; Durham, "Trips into Black History."

17. Interview with Betty Frew, OSV, April 18, 1991.

18. Silverman, "Our Children Were Shy at First," 7.

19. Conversation with Tom Kelleher, OSV, April 18, 1991.

20. Peter Ryan, Historical Interpretation Workshop, Landis Valley Museum, February 2, 1991.

21. Scott Atwood, during group interview, Plimoth, April 22, 1991.

22. See "breaking the ice," discussed earlier.

23. Jeff Scotland, during group interview, Plimoth, April 20, 1991.

24. Tom Hay, informal conversation, July 28, 1994.

25. Observation, July 29, 1994.

26. Ecroyd, *Living History*, 22.

27. Interview with Nancy Caouette, OSV, April 18, 1991.

28. Silverman, "Our Children Were Shy at First," 7.

29. Conversation with Moira Turnan Hannon, Plimoth, April 22, 1991.

30. Conversation with Lisa Simon Walbridge, Plimoth, April 21, 1991.

31. Observation, April 20, 1991.

32. David Emerson, during group interview at Plimoth, April 20, 1991.

33. Eddie Grogan, CP, taped questionnaire response, November 17, 1994.

34. Ecroyd, *Living History*, 37; Silverman, "Our Children Were Shy at First," 6; numerous interpreters.

35. Comment by several Plimoth interpreters at group interview, April 20, 1991.

36. Sorenson, "Three in One." Ashpaugh worked at CP in the early 1980s and was not on staff when I visited in 1994.

37. Silverman, "Our Children Were Shy at First," 6; see also Gordinier, "Guidelines for Roleplayers."

38. Silverman, "Our Children Were Shy at First," 6.

39. Ibid., 10.

40. Conversation with Jeff Scotland and Lisa Simon Walbridge, Plimoth, April 21, 1991.

41. John Kemp, during Plimoth group interview, April 20, 1991.

42. Group interview at Plimoth, April 22, 1991.

43. Interview with Glenn Gordinier, MSM, April 17, 1991.

44. Group interview at Plimoth, April 22, 1991.

45. Silverman, "Our Children Were Shy at First," 6–10.

46. Group interview at Plimoth, April 20, 1991; Stacy Flora Roth, "Roleplaying at Pennsbury Manor Fair," 1991, Pennsbury Manor training memo; Vance, "Developing a First Person Program," 177.

CHAPTER TEN

1. Observations, April 21, 1991.

2. Observation, April 22, 1991.

3. See also Sanders, "Thoughts on Effective Living History."

4. Moira Turnan Hannon, during conversation with her and Lisa Whalen, Plimoth, April 22, 1991.

5. Conversation with Moira Turnan Hannon and Lisa Whalen, Plimoth, April 22, 1991.

6. Interview with Chris Creelman, OSV, April 18, 1991.

7. Observation, April 20, 1991. Also conversation with David Emerson, September 8, 1991.

8. Observation, April 23, 1991.

9. Comments during Plimoth group interview, April 22, 1991.

10. Eddie Grogan, taped questionnaire response, November 17, 1994.

11. Ibid.

12. B. J. Pryor, questionnaire response, September 1, 1994.

13. John Kemp, during group interview, Plimoth, April 20, 1991.

14. Carson Hudson, taped questionnaire response, November 1994; cf. Ecroyd, *Living History*, 31–37.

15. Sarnoff, *Never Be Nervous Again*, 23.

16. B. J. Pryor, questionnaire response, September 1, 1994.

17. Interview with Bill Barker, CW, July 29, 1994.

18. The most relevant one examined by this author is Breneman and Breneman, *Once upon a Time*. Others include Schimmel, *Just Enough to Make a Story*, and Baker and Green, *Storytelling*.

19. Follin, "Historical Mindset." Follin's article is directed toward both first- and third-person interpreters.

20. Ibid., 101–2.

21. MSM training materials (written by Gordinier).

22. Observation, April 17, 1991.

23. Ralph Archbold, telephone conversation with author, December 1994.

24. Interview with Glenn Gordinier, MSM, April 17, 1991.

25. Marsh, *Eye to Eye*, 112–13.

26. Conversation with Lisa Simon Walbridge, Plimoth, April 22, 1991.

27. Interview with Glenn Gordinier, MSM, April 17, 1991.

28. Regnier, Gross, and Zimmerman, *Interpreter's Guidebook*, 30.

29. Eddie Grogan, taped questionnaire response, November 17, 1994.

30. Interview with Claire Gregoire, OSV, April 18, 1991.

31. Ibid.

32. Conversation with Tom Kelleher, OSV, April 18, 1991.

33. Observations, April 22, 1991.

34. Conversation with Moira Turnan Hannon and Lisa Whalen, Plimoth, April 22, 1991.

CHAPTER ELEVEN

1. See Risk, "On-Site Real-Time Observational Techniques"; Marsh, *Eye to Eye*, 46–47; Mehrabian, "Communication without Words"; Bolton, *People Skills*, 78–86; Follin, "Historical Mindset," 102; Goffman, "Facial Engagements."

2. The definitive book on reading facial expressions is Ekman, *Unmasking the Face*. Ekman defines the causes of emotions, explores their intensity as well as the subtlety of combination and controlled emotions, and provides lots of photographic examples. Marsh, *Eye to Eye*, 80, contains an abbreviated treatment of the subject. Other books offer advice on effective use of body and voice for public speaking, tour guiding, interpersonal communication, and acting. Much of this can be applied to first-person interpretation as well. See Marsh, *Eye to Eye*; White, *Practical Public Speaking*; Grinder and McCoy, *Good Guide*; Pond, *Professional Guide*, particularly chap. 8, "Presentation and Speaking Skills," 124–37; Carnegie, *How to Win Friends*; Bolton, *People Skills*; Sarnoff, *Speech Can Change Your Life*.

3. Risk, "Interpretive Talk," 161.

4. Drawn from Marsh, *Eye to Eye*, 49; White, *Practical Public Speaking*, 312–13; Grinder and McCoy, *Good Guide*, 128–32.

5. Marsh, *Eye to Eye*, 49.

6. White, *Practical Public Speaking*, 297.

7. Grinder and McCoy, *Good Guide*, 131; Marsh, *Eye to Eye*, 49.

8. Beattie, *TALK*, 57. Beattie provides a thorough overview of gaze research to 1983.

9. Follin, "Historical Mindset," 101–2.

10. Marsh, *Eye to Eye*, 72–73.

11. Porter and Samovar, "Basic Principles of Intercultural Communication," 18.

12. Eakins and Eakins, "Sex Differences in Non-Verbal Communication," 298–301.

13. White, *Practical Public Speaking*, 296–97.

14. Larry Erickson, during group interview, Plimoth, April 20, 1991.

15. Risk, "On-Site Real-Time Observational Techniques," 124.

16. Eddie Grogan, taped questionnaire response, November 17, 1994.

17. Jeff Scotland, during group interview, Plimoth, April 20, 1991.

18. Comments of Chris Creelman, OSV, April 18, 1991, and Scott Atwood and Effie Cummings, Plimoth group discussion, April 22, 1991.

19. Interview with Glenn Gordinier, MSM, April 17, 1991.

20. Grinder and McCoy, *Good Guide*, 129.

21. Ibid.

22. Group discussion, Plimoth, April 22, 1991.

23. Cf. Marsh, *Eye to Eye*, 88–89.

24. Mentioned by Karen Atwood, Plimoth group discussion, April 22, 1991, and by Glenn Gordinier and Bettye Noyes, MSM, April 17, 1991.

25. Casual discussion with Pat Baker, Plimoth, April 21, 1991.

26. See White, *Practical Public Speaking*, 299–300; Marsh, *Eye to Eye*, 50–51.

27. Marsh, *Eye to Eye*, 50–51.

28. Axtell, *Do's and Taboos around the World*, 43.

29. Marsh, *Eye to Eye*, 49.

30. Peter Ryan, Historical Interpretation Workshop, Landis Valley Museum, February 2, 1991.

31. Interview with Bettye Noyes, MSM, April 17, 1991.

32. Conversation with Tom Kelleher, OSV, April 18, 1991.

33. Interview with Glenn Gordinier, MSM, April 17, 1991.

34. See Viola Spolin's books, *Improvisation for the Theater* and *Theatre Games*.

35. Yellis, "Real Time," all versions.

36. Hayward and Jensen, "Enhancing a Sense of the Past." According to Hayward and Jensen, interviews with 100 visitors and questionnaires from 49 interpreters revealed that — at least at OSV in 1979 and 1980 — visitors found that interpreters who had "incomplete costumes, lacked enthusiasm, and were not roleplaying" (slightly rephrased) had very little effect on the visitors' "sense of the past." Interpreters, on the other hand, perceived these drawbacks as an interference with a sense of the past. Unfortunately, all three of these factors—which are very different kinds of drawbacks — were lumped into the same question, making it impossible to tell just how much weight the costume issue has for the visitor.

37. Interview with Glenn Gordinier, MSM, April 17, 1991.

38. White, *Practical Public Speaking*, 277–78, 301–13; Grinder and McCoy, *Good Guide*, 122–26; Piatt and Jones, "Planning Effective Living History Performances."

39. Interview with Bettye Noyes, MSM, April 17, 1991.

40. Bil Orland, during group discussion, Plimoth, April 20, 1991.

41. Larry Erickson, during group discussion, Plimoth, April 20, 1991.

42. B. J. Pryor, questionnaire response, September 1, 1994.

43. Comments of John Kemp, Scott Atwood, Steve Ewald, Stuart Bolton, and others, Plimoth, April 20–22, 1991.

44. Interview with Rick Jenkinson, OSV, April 18, 1991.

45. Ecroyd, *Living History*, 20.

CHAPTER TWELVE

1. For overviews of visitor group characteristics, see Grinder and McCoy, *Good Guide*, chap. 6, "Audiences: Who's Listening," 90–116, and Pond, *Professional Guide*.

2. Over the past several decades, museums, historic sites, and even Renaissance festivals and other "entertainments" have become increasingly conscious of their role as informal learning environments. See Peart, "Interpretation in Informal Learning"; Falk and Dierking, *Museum Experience*, xv; Pahl, "Forsooth!" The importance of understanding the social characteristics of visitors has been emphasized by Machlis and Field, editors and contributors to *On Interpretation*.

3. For an assessment of adult learning skills and the application of adult learning theory to humanities program and museum settings, see Charles C. Cole, *Active Group Learning*, particularly 23–24; O'Connell, "Adult Education and the Museum Experience"; and Collins, *Museums, Adults, and the Humanities*, particularly the contributions by Hiemstra, "State of the Art," and Knox, "Basic Components of Adult Programming."

4. Eddie Grogan, taped questionnaire interview, November 17, 1994.

5. See Falk and Dierking, *Museum Experience*; Ham, "Familiarity and Adaptation," 126; Leichter, Hensel, and Larsen, "Families and Museums"; Kropf and Wolins, "How Families Learn"; Silverman, "Johnny Showed Us the Butterflies."

6. Hood, "Leisure Criteria of Family Participation and Non-Participation in Museums."

7. Ibid.

8. Composite example drawn from numerous shopkeeper settings.

9. Caroline Roberts, UCV, questionnaire response, October 1994.

10. Pond, *Professional Guide*, 235.

11. Eddie Grogan, taped questionnaire response, November 17, 1994.

12. Ophelia Wellington, questionnaire response, October 28, 1994.

13. Peter Cazaly, UCV, questionnaire response, October 2, 1994.

14. Caroline Roberts, UCV, questionnaire response, October 1994.

15. Hall and Whyte, "Intercultural Communication," 298.

16. See Porter and Samovar, "Basic Principles of Intercultural Communication," 8.

17. Kabagarama, *Breaking the Ice*, 4–10.

18. Eddie Grogan, taped questionnaire response, November 17, 1994.

19. Group interview, CW, July 28, 1994.

20. Peter Cazaly, UCV, questionnaire response, October 2, 1994.

21. See, for instance, Axtell, *Do's and Taboos around the World*; Samovar and Porter, *Intercultural Communication*; Machlis, Field, and Van Every, "Sociological Look at the Japanese Tourist"; Gramann, Floyd, and Ewert, "Interpretation and Hispanic American Ethnicity"; Kabagarama, *Breaking the Ice*.

22. See Morris et al., *Gestures*, and Axtell, *Do's and Taboos around the World*.

23. Machlis, Field, and Van Every, "Sociological Look at the Japanese Tourist."

24. Sanders, "Thoughts on Effective Living History," 11.

25. Yellis, "Real Time," October 1, 1990, 20.

26. Ibid.

27. Vance, "Developing a First Person Program," 178–79; quote is on 179. Brackets assume a typographical error in the original.

28. George Chapman, questionnaire response, October 30, 1994.

29. Interview with Glenn Gordinier, MSM, April 17, 1991; Vance, "Developing a First Person Program," 179.

30. Carson Hudson, taped questionnaire response, November 1994.

31. Gordinier, "Exhibit Job Description."

CHAPTER THIRTEEN

1. Tilden, *Interpreting Our Heritage*, chap. 7, "For the Younger Mind," 47–54.

2. See also Pitman-Gelles, *Museums, Magic, and Children*, 39–40.

3. Machlis and Field, "Getting Connected"; Grinder and McCoy, *Good Guide*; Ecroyd, *Talking with Young Visitors*; Rayner and Speidel, "Learning Theories and History Museums"; Regnier, Gross, and Zimmerman, *Interpreter's Guidebook*, 82–90; Machlis and McDonough, *Children's Interpretation*.

4. Ecroyd, *Talking with Young Visitors*.

5. Machlis and Field, "Getting Connected"; Machlis and McDonough, *Children's Interpretation*.

6. Smith, "Interpreting to School Children."

7. Ibid., 30.

8. Rayner and Speidel, "Learning Theories and History Museums"; Grinder and McCoy, *Good Guide*, 28–31.

9. Grinder and McCoy, *Good Guide*, 32–34.

10. Kieran Egan, quoted in Rayner and Speidel, "Learning Theories and History Museums," 25.

11. Egan, "Teaching the Romantic Mind" and "Relevance and the Romantic Imagination of Students."

12. Rayner and Speidel, "Learning Theories and History Museums"; Bruner, *Toward a Theory of Instruction*, chap. 4, "Man: A Course of Study," 73–101.

13. Vukelich, "Time Language."

14. Howard Gardner, *Frames of Mind*.

15. Ecroyd, *Talking with Young Visitors*, 36–38.

16. Smith, "Interpreting to School Children," 17.

17. Steve Gulick, questionnaire response, November 1994.

18. Cynthia Andes, questionnaire response, August 17, 1994.

19. Dan Bassuk, questionnaire response, October 3, 1994. Bassuk is also the president of the Society of Lincoln Presenters, which includes over eighty-four other Lincoln interpreters and actors. Their motto: "Now He Belongs to the Stages." See Holzer, "Disarmingly Abe."

20. Pitman-Gelles, *Museums, Magic, and Children*, 49.

21. Vukelich, "Time Language."

22. Rayner and Speidel, "Learning Theories and History Museums"; Grinder and

McCoy, *Good Guide*, 30–34; Ecroyd, *Talking with Young Visitors*, 37–39; Machlis and McDonough, *Children's Interpretation*, 11; Egan, "Teaching the Romantic Mind."

23. Egan, "Teaching the Romantic Mind," 19.

24. Bill Barker, observation, CW, July 28, 1994; interview with Larry Earl, CW, July 30, 1994.

25. Peart, "Interpretation in Informal Learning," 38.

26. Pitman-Gelles, *Museums, Magic, and Children*, 52–53.

27. *Personal Training Program for Interpreters*, 43.

28. Ibid., 54. The *Personal Training Program* provides multiple examples of each type of question and dissects the questioning structure of entire third-person talks.

29. See Fairclough, *Teacher's Guide to History through Roleplay*; Chiodo and Klausmeier, "'V.T.'"; Van Ments, *Effective Use of Role-Play*, 16–30; Keller, "Roleplaying and Simulation in History Classes"; Shannon, "Introducing Simulation and Roleplay," 27–34; Hurst and Otis, "Living History in the Classroom"; Gibson-Quigley and Rowden, "Social Change in America."

30. Hayes and Schindel, *Pioneer Journeys*, 82–97.

31. Interview with Chris Creelman, OSV, April 18, 1991.

32. Application, 1990–91, School Programs at OSV. For examples of lesson plan materials, see Gibson-Quigley and Rowden, "Social Change in America"; Piatt and Schwerdtfeger, "Reading and Writing about History"; Pitman-Gelles, *Museums, Magic, and Children*, 71–74.

33. Plimoth interpreters, April 22, 1991; interview with Glenn Gordinier, MSM, April 17, 1991.

34. Gordinier, "Exhibit Job Description."

35. William Kashatus III, taped questionnaire interview, August 1994; Eddie Grogan, taped questionnaire interview, November 17, 1994; Smith, "Interpreting to School Children," 61–68.

36. Smith, "Interpreting to School Children," 63–64.

37. Egan, "Teaching the Romantic Mind," 21.

38. Massialas and Zevin, *Teaching Creatively*, 241.

39. William Kashatus III, taped questionnaire interview, August 1994.

40. Smith, "Interpreting to School Children," 77–81.

41. Machlis and McDonough, *Children's Interpretation*, 13.

42. George Chapman, questionnaire response, October 30, 1994.

43. Eddie Grogan, taped questionnaire response, November 17, 1994.

44. Ecroyd, *Talking with Young Visitors*, 39–41.

45. Many museums request that school groups require one adult for every ten children and stress the responsibility of the adults in the handling of behavioral problems.

46. Sarah Grant Reid, questionnaire response, September 6, 1994.

47. Ibid.

CHAPTER FOURTEEN

1. Majewski, *Part of Your General Public Is Disabled*.

2. I have omitted any mention of emergency procedures. Emergencies generally require an interpreter to step out of the program and protect the health of the indi-

vidual and those around him or her. For coverage of this topic, I refer the reader to Majewski's book.

3. Effie Cummings, during Plimoth group discussion, April 20, 1991.

4. Majewski, *Part of Your General Public Is Disabled*, 11–13.

5. Ibid., 3. Down's syndrome is frequently identifiable by physical characteristics such as a round flat face, slanted eyes, and a stumpy build. Down's also ranges from mild to severe.

6. Ibid., 3–8.

7. Ibid., 65.

8. Ibid., 65–70.

CHAPTER FIFTEEN

1. Anthropologist Victor Turner states that any social drama consists of four phases: breach, crisis, redressive action, and reintegration or schism. See Snow, "Theatre of the Pilgrims," 16–17.

2. See Vanderstel, "Death, Racism, and Intemperance." Vanderstel suggests it is the ethical responsibility of museums as public educators to communicate real historical processes, including negative ones.

3. Stover, "Interpretation of Historical Conflict," ii; see also her "Is It REAL History Yet?" Of course, not all visitors like or appreciate these innovations. As Leon and Piatt have noted in their chapter on living history museums in *History Museums in the United States*, some visitors still cling to the old or nostalgic views of the past and have no desire to see old myths assailed.

4. For a rather searing indictment on how U.S. history museums and theme parks such as EPCOT influence the public's perception of the past, see Wallace, "Mickey Mouse History" and "Visiting the Past." In "Future of History Museums," Wallace discusses the potential for history museums to help the public develop their historical sensibilities beyond the function of class affirmation chronicled in his other articles.

5. Williams and Schultz, "Dealing with the Disturbing."

6. Hayward, "Politics of Living History."

7. Nancy Webster, "Interpreting Religious Events and Festivals."

8. Bell, "Skeletons in the Closet," 103.

9. Ibid., 102.

10. The issue of delicate balance is addressed in Patterson, "Conner Prairie Refocuses."

11. Hayward, "Politics of Living History."

12. See also Fried, "History of Character Interpretation," 3.

13. For a discussion on the various benefits and drawbacks of different types of first-person, third-person, scenario, and scripted presentations, see Stover, "Interpretation of Historical Conflict," 232–63.

14. Plimoth Plantation, "Outline for Evaluation Criteria"; group discussion, Plimoth, April 20, 1991.

15. MacCannell, *The Tourist*, 105.

16. Peter Cazaly, UCV, questionnaire response, October 2, 1994.

17. Jill Costa and others, Plimoth group, April 20, 1991.

18. Larry Erickson and others, Plimoth group interview, April 20, 1991.

19. Interview with Dave Cloutier, OSV, April 19, 1991.

20. Eddie Grogan, taped questionnaire response, November 17, 1994.

21. The history of the slave interpretation at CW is recounted in Ellis, "Decade of Change." Two other articles by Ellis, "Museums and Race" and "Re: Living History," briefly discuss the development of African American interpretation at CW and highlight some of the challenges that black Americans face in interpreting and confronting the history of slavery.

22. Ellis, "Decade of Change," 18.

23. Ellis, "Re: Living History," 22; Ellis, "Museums and Race." The development, triumphs, and tribulations of these early programs is chronicled in Zwelling, "Social History Hits the Street."

24. Zwelling, "Social History Hits the Street," 12.

25. Stover, "Interpretation of Historical Conflict," 210–31.

26. Telephone interview with Christy Coleman Matthews, August 28, 1994.

27. Conversations with Jeremy Fried, July 28, 1994, and Christy Coleman Matthews, August 28, 1994.

28. Fried, "History of Character Interpretation."

29. This event has been reconstructed through conversations with CW staff and observers, including Christy Matthews, D. Stephen Elliott, Conny Graft, Larry Earl, and Dave Harvey, and the following newspaper accounts: "Tears and Protest at Mock Slave Sale"; "Slave Auction Re-Enacted in Colonial Williamsburg"; and "Slave Sale Educates and Angers." Dave Harvey, the conservator of metals and arms at CW, published a thoughtful observer account of the incident to MUSEUM-L@UNMVMA.BITNET on October 12, 1994, under the subject heading re: reenactments.

30. *Courier Times*, October 11, 1994.

31. Ibid.; conversation with Larry Earl, CW, April 21, 1995.

32. "Tears and Protest at Mock Slave Sale."

33. Korn, "Evaluation of the 'Becoming Americans' Theme," 57.

34. See Stover, "Interpretation of Historical Conflict," 248; Marsh, *Eye to Eye*, 43.

35. Stover, "Interpretation of Historical Conflict," 249.

36. Gordinier, "Exhibit Job Description."

37. Comment by Jeff Scotland, during group discussion, Plimoth, April 20, 1991.

38. Group discussion, Plimoth, April 20, 1991. See also Nancy Webster, "Interpreting Religious Events and Festivals."

39. Jeff Scotland, during group discussion, Plimoth, April 20, 1991.

40. Conversation with Richard Pickering, Plimoth, March 19, 1992. See also Nancy Webster, "Interpreting Religious Events."

41. Conversation with B. J. Pryor, CW, July 28, 1994.

42. Peter Cazaly, UCV, questionnaire response, October 2, 1994.

43. Larry Erickson and others, Plimoth, April 20, 1991.

44. Conversation with John Kemp, Plimoth, October 25, 1991.

45. Conversation with Donna Evans, Old Barracks Museum, February 14, 1995.

46. Durham, "Trips into Black History."

47. CBS News "Sunday Morning," television broadcast, February 14, 1993. Many thanks to Christy Matthews for sharing her taped copy of the segment with me.

CONCLUSION

1. Stone and Edwards, *1776!*, 38.

GLOSSARY

1. Term used by CW interpreters.
2. Term used by CW interpreters.
3. Coined by Sanders, "Thoughts on Effective Living History," 10–11.
4. Robertshaw, "From Houses into Homes."
5. Coined by Jeff Scotland, Plimoth.

Printed sources are listed in the Bibliography. For information on interviewees and respondents to questionnaires, see Appendix 3, Participants.

Ahern, Dale. "Where History Really Lives." *American Education* 16, no. 7 (August/ September 1980): 17–24.

Alderson, William T. "Answering the Challenge." *Museum News* 53 (November 1974): 9, 63.

Alderson, William T., and Shirley Payne Low. *Interpretation of Historic Sites*. Nashville: American Association for State and Local History, 1985.

Alexander, Edward P. "A Fourth Dimension for History Museums." *Curator* 11, no. 4 (December 1968).

———. *Museums in Motion: An Introduction to the History and Functions of Museums*. Nashville: American Association for State and Local History, 1979.

Allen, Lawrence A. "Basic Concepts and Assumptions about Adult Learners." In Collins, *Museums, Adults, and the Humanities*, 73–78.

Allen, Mel. "Seventy-Two Hours in 1870." *Yankee*, December 1979, 62–67, 141–46.

Allgore, Catherine. "Not Going as Tourists: Immersion into a Pilgrim Community, 1627." Association for Living Historical Farms and Agricultural Museums *Proceedings* 14 (1994): 63–66.

Alsford, Stephen, and David Parry. "Interpretive Theatre: A Role in Museums?" *Museum Management and Curatorship* 10 (1991): 8–23.

Anderson, Jay. "Immaterial Material Culture: The Implications of Experimental Research for Folklife Museums." *Keystone Folklore* 21, no. 2 (1976–77): 1–13.

———. "Living Histories: The Symbiotic Relationship of Living History and Historical Film." Association for Living Historical Farms and Agricultural Museums *Proceedings* 16 (1994): 18–23.

———. "Living History." In Jay Anderson, *Living History Reader*, 3–12.

———. *A Living History Reader*. Vol. 1, *Museums*. Nashville: American Association for State and Local History, 1991.

———. "Living History: Simulating Everyday Life in Living Museums." *American Quarterly* 34 (1982): 290–306.

———. *The Living History Sourcebook*. Nashville: American Association for State and Local History, 1985.

———. "Sweet Liberty: The Promise of Living History." Association for Living Historical Farms and Agricultural Museums *Proceedings* 16 (1994): 24–28.

———. *Time Machines: The World of Living History*. Nashville: American Association for State and Local History, 1984.

Anderson, Jonathan L. "Sainte Marie De Gannentaha: An Expression of Seventeenth Century North America." *Living History* 3, no. 1 (1986): 10–13.

An Annotated Bibliography for the Development and Operation of Historic Sites. Prepared by the Historic Sites Committee, American Association of Museums. Washington, D.C.: American Association of Museums, 1982.

Armstrong, Sharon. "Living History at Sainte-Marie among the Hurons." *History and Social Science Teacher* 18, no. 4 (May 1983): 241–43.

Arth, Malcolm. "Program Formats for Humanities Themes." In Collins, *Museums, Adults, and the Humanities*, 165–76.

Axtell, Roger E., ed. *Do's and Taboos around the World*. 3rd ed. New York: Wiley, 1993.

Baker, Andrew, and Warren Leon. "Old Sturbridge Village Introduces Social Conflict into Its Interpretive Story." *History News* 41 (March 1986): 7–11.

Baker, Augusta, and Ellin Green. *Storytelling: Art and Technique*. New York: Bowker, 1977.

Baker, James. "Looking Back – Looking Around – Looking Ahead." Association for Living Historical Farms and Agricultural Museums *Proceedings* 13 (1993): 12–18.

———. "Worldview at Plimoth Plantation: History and Theory." Association for Living Historical Farms and Agricultural Museums *Proceedings* 13 (1993): 64–68.

Balling, John D., and John H. Falk. "A Perspective on Field Trips: Environmental Effects on Learning." *Curator* 23, no. 4 (1980): 229–40.

Barnes, Frank. "Living History: Clio — or Cliopatria." *History News* 29 (September 1974): 202–3.

Barthel, Diane. "Nostalgia for America's Village Past: Staged Symbolic Communities." *International Journal of Politics, Culture, and Society* 4, no. 1 (1990): 79–93.

Barto, David. "Teacher as Actor: Henry David Thoreau, from Room One-Eleven to Walden Pond and Beyond." Paper presented at the Annual Meeting of the National Council of Teachers of English, Philadelphia, Pa., November 22–27, 1985. ERIC Document ED 268 530.

Bauman, Richard. *Story, Performance, and Event: Contextual Studies of Oral Narrative*. New York: Cambridge University Press, 1986.

Beattie, Geoffrey. *TALK: An Analysis of Speech and Non-Verbal Behaviour in Conversation*. Milton Keynes, England: Open University Press, 1983.

Becker, Carl Lotus. *Every Man His Own Historian*. New York: Crofts, 1935.

Beeman, Ardis. "Historical Mindset: Its Development and Its Application." Association for Living Historical Farms and Agricultural Museums *Proceedings* 12 (1992): 96–99.

Bell, Ian. "Skeletons in the Closet: Choosing a Past for Our Sensitive Present." Association for Living Historical Farms and Agricultural Museums *Proceedings* 13 (1993): 101–3.

Benedict, Paul L. "Historic Site Interpretation: The Student Field Trip." American Association for State and Local History Technical Leaflet 19. *History News* 26 (March 1971).

Bennett, Tony. "Museums and 'the People.'" In Lumley, *Museum Time Machine*, 62–84.

Berlin, Isaiah. *The Crooked Timber of Humanity: Chapters in the History of Ideas*. New York: Knopf, 1991.

Berlo, David K. *The Process of Communication*. New York: Holt, Rinehart and Winston, 1960.

"Beyond the Classroom." *History Today* 40 (November 1990): 4–5.

Bicknell, Sandra, and Susie Fisher. "Enlightening or Embarrassing? Drama in the

Science Museum, London, United Kingdom." In *Visitor Studies: Theory Research and Practice*, 6:79–87. Jacksonville, Ala.: Visitor Studies Association, 1993.

Birney, Robert C. "An Evaluation of Visitor's Experience at the Governor's Palace, Colonial Williamsburg, Virginia." *Academic Psychology Bulletin* 4 (March 1982): 135–41.

Bitgood, Stephen. "A Comparison of Formal and Informal Learning." Technical Report No. 88-10. Jacksonville, Ala.: Center for Social Design, [1988].

Bitgood, Stephen, and Ross J. Loomis. "Introduction: Environmental Design and Evaluation in Museums." *Environment and Behavior* 25, no. 6 (November 1993): 683–97.

Black, Nikki. "How Museum Visits Can Strengthen Family Ties." *Museum News* 69 (September/October 1990): 88–89.

Blumenfeld, Alan, et al. "Applied Theatre Techniques (summary)." Association for Living Historical Farms and Agricultural Museums *Papers* 8 (1988): 37–38.

Bolton, Robert. *People Skills: How to Assert Yourself, Listen to Others, and Resolve Conflicts*. New York: Simon and Schuster, 1979.

Bordewich, Fergus M. "Williamsburg: Revising Colonial America." *Atlantic*, December 1988, 26–32.

Borun, Minda. "Do You Read Me?" In Nichols, *Museum Education Anthology*, 175–76.

Bradley Commission on History in Schools. *Building a Curriculum: Guidelines for Teaching History in Schools*. Washington, D.C.: Educational Excellence Network, 1988.

Breen, T. H. *Imagining the Past: East Hampton Histories*. Reading, Mass.: Addison-Wesley, 1989.

Breneman, Lucille N., and Bren Breneman. *Once upon a Time: A Storytelling Handbook*. Chicago: Nelson-Hall, 1983.

Brown, Kathleen. "Tourist Trends for the '90s." *History News* 48 (May/June 1993): 4–7.

Brown, Patricia Leigh. "Away from the Big House: Interpreting the Uncomfortable Parts of History." *History News* 44 (March/April 1989): 8–10.

Bruneau, T. J. "Communicative Silences: Forms and Functions." *Journal of Communication* 23, no. 1 (March 1973): 17–46.

Bruner, Jerome. *Toward a Theory of Instruction*. Cambridge, Mass.: Harvard University Press, 1966.

Buerki, Robert A. "Interpreting Nineteenth-Century Pharmacy Practice: The Ohio Experience." *Journal of American Culture* 12, no. 2 (1989): 93–102.

Bultena, Gordon, Donald R. Field, and Renee Renninger. "Interpretation for the Elderly." In Machlis and Field, *On Interpretation*, 88–95.

Burcaw, G. Ellis. "Can History Be Too Lively?" *Museums Journal*, December 1980, 5–7.

Butler, Rick. "Historians to Stage Revealing Court Martial." *Sunday Star Ledger* (N.J.), March 31, 1991.

Callender, Don W., Jr. "Reliving the Past: Experimental Archaeology in Pennsylvania." *Archaeology* 29, no. 3 (July 1976): 173–77.

Cameron, Duncan. "How Do We Know What Our Visitors Think?" *Museum News* 45 (March 1967): 31–33.

————. "A Viewpoint: The Museum as a Communications System and Implications for Museum Education." *Curator* 11, no. 1 (March 1968): 33–40.

Canadian Museum of Civilization. *Evaluation of the Live Interpretation Program.* Quebec: Division de la vérification et de l'évaluation, Canadian Museum of Civilization, 1992.

Carmody, Martin. "Brandywine Christmas and Beyond." *Brandywine Battlefield Park Associates Newsletter*, January 1991, 1.

Carnahan, Frances. "Plimoth Voices." *Early American Life* 22 (June 1991): 2–5.

————. "Time Travelers." *Early American Life* 21 (June 1990): 2–3.

Carnegie, Dale. *How to Win Friends and Influence People.* Rev. ed. New York: Pocket Books, 1981.

Carroll, James. "Pilgrimage to Plymouth: America's Home Town Comes into Its Own as Thanksgiving Nears." *New York Times*, November 4, 1984.

Carson, Cary. "From the Bottom Up: Zero-base Research for Social History at Williamsburg." *History News* 35 (January 1980): 7–9.

————. "Living Museums of Everyman's History." *Harvard Magazine*, July/August 1981, 22–32.

Case, Victoria, and Robert Ormond Case. *We Called It Culture: The Story of Chautauqua.* Garden City, N.Y.: Doubleday, 1948.

The Challenge of Interpretation. [Williamsburg, Va.]: Colonial Williamsburg Foundation, 1991.

Chapman, George D. "Living History Stew: A Recipe for Historical Interpretation and Public Interaction." *Living Historian* 6, no. 1a (Spring 1992): 13.

Cherem, Gabriel Jerome. "The Professional Interpretor: Agent for an Awakening Giant." *Journal of Interpretation* 2, no. 1 (1977): 3–16.

Chiodo, John J., and Robert L. Klausmeier. "'V.T.': The Extra Step in Classroom Roleplaying." *Social Studies* 75, no. 3 (May–June 1984): 122–23.

Clark, Glenn. "Research and Interpretation." *Interpretation*, Summer 1989, 1.

Cohen, Erik. "A Phenomenology of Tourist Experiences." *Sociology* 13, no. 2 (May 1979): 179–201.

Cole, Charles C. *Active Group Learning: A Selective Study of Effective Public Humanities Programs.* Minneapolis, Minn.: National Federation of State Humanities Councils, 1985. ERIC Document ED 256 253.

Cole, Doug. "Visitor Orientation: Need and Effectiveness." Association for Living Historical Farms and Agricultural Museums *Proceedings* 7 (1983): 64–68.

Cole, Toby, and Helen Krich Chinoy. *Actors on Acting: The Theories, Techniques, and Practices of the Great Actors of All Times as Told in Their Own Words.* New York: Crown, 1949.

Collins, Zipporah W., ed. *Museums, Adults, and the Humanities: A Guide for Educational Programming.* Washington, D.C.: American Association of Museums, 1981.

Condon, John C., Jr. "When People Talk with People." In Mortensen, *Basic Readings in Communication Theory*, 45–63.

Cooney, Julia A. "No Farbies Here: The Feast of the Hunters' Moon." *Living History* 3, no. 1 (1986): 14–17.

Craig, Tracey Linton. "Reinterpreting the Past." *Museum News* 68 (January/February 1989): 60–63.

———. "Retreat into History: Visitors to Maine's Washburn-Norlands Leave the Twentieth Century to Re-create 1870's Downeast Family Life." *History News* 38 (June 1983): 10–18.

Crosson, David. "Museums and Social Responsibility: A Cautionary Tale." *History News* 43 (July/August 1988): 6–9.

Crowley, Carolyn Hughes. "Out of the Maine Stream." *Saturday Evening Post*, May/June 1993, 82–84.

Csiksentmihalyi, Mihaly. *FLOW: The Psychology of Optimal Experience*. New York: Harper and Row, 1990.

Deakin, Carol C. "Re-enactors and History: Attention to Detail Can Insure Accurate Re-enactments." *History News* 41 (May/June 1986): 14–20.

Deetz, James. "The Changing Historic House Museum: Can It Live?" *Historic Preservation* 23 (January–March 1971): 51–54.

———. *In Small Things Forgotten: The Archeology of Early American Life*. Garden City, N.Y.: Anchor, 1977.

———. "The Link from Object to Person to Concept." In Collins, *Museums, Adults, and the Humanities*, 24–34.

———. "The Reality of the Pilgrim Fathers." *Natural History* 56, no. 6 (November 1969): 32–44.

———. "A Sense of Another World: History Museums and Cultural Change." *Museum News* 59 (May/June 1980): 40–45.

Dewar, Keith. "Monitoring and Evaluation of Sender Competence in Personal Service Interpretive Programs." Ph.D. diss., Department of Geography, University of Waterloo, 1991.

Dierking, Lynn D. "First-Person Interpretation: Perspectives on Interpreter-Visitor Communication." Association for Living Historical Farms and Agricultural Museums *Proceedings* 15 (1996): 237–41.

Duncan, Starkey, Jr. "Some Signals and Rules for Taking Turns in Conversation." *Journal of Personality and Social Psychology* 23, no. 2 (1972): 283–92.

Durham, Michael S. "Trips into Black History: Southern States Lead the Way in a Movement That's Transforming Landmarks into Tourist Attractions." *Orlando Sentinel*, February 21, 1993.

Eakins, Barbara Westbrook, and Gene Eakins, "Sex Differences in Non-Verbal Communication." In Samovar and Porter, *Intercultural Communication*, 297–344.

Ecroyd, Donald H. *Living History*. N.p.: Eastern National Park and Monument Association, 1990.

———. *Talking with Young Visitors in the Parks*. N.p.: Eastern National Park and Monument Association, 1989.

Egan, Kieran. "Relevance and the Romantic Imagination of Students." *Education Digest* 57, no. 4 (December 1991): 50–52.

———. "Teaching the Romantic Mind." *English Journal* 83, no. 4 (April 1994): 16–25.

Ekman, Paul. *Unmasking the Face*. Englewood Cliffs, N.J.: Prentice-Hall, 1975.

Elder, Betty Doak. "Drama for Interpretation." *History News* 36 (June 1981): 8–16.

Ellis, Rex. "A Decade of Change: Black History at Colonial Williamsburg." *Colonial Williamsburg* 12, no. 3 (Spring 1990): 14–23.

———. "Museums and Race: A Case Study at Colonial Williamsburg." Association for Living Historical Farms and Agricultural Museums *Proceedings* 12 (1992): 79–81.

———. "Re: Living History: Bringing Slavery into Play." *American Visions*, December–January 1993, 22–25.

Fairclough, John. *A Teacher's Guide to History through Roleplay*. London: English Heritage, 1994.

Falk, John H., and Lynn D. Dierking. *The Museum Experience*. Washington, D.C.: Whalesback Books, 1992.

Falk, Sally. "Changes in Black America on Conner Prairie Program." *Indianapolis Star*, [late February 1991]. Photocopy of newspaper article.

Farish, Stephen. "Wigs, Whigs, and Corporate Gigs." *PR Week*, May 30, 1991, 6–7.

Farmelo, Graham. "Drama on the Galleries." In *Museums and the Public Understanding of Science*, edited by John Durant, 45–49. London: Science Museum, 1992.

Farm Museum Directory: A Guide through America's Farm Past. Lancaster, Pa.: Stemgas, 1993.

Field, Donald R., and J. Alan Wager. "Visitor Groups and Interpretation in Parks and Other Outdoor Leisure Settings." In Machlis and Field, *On Interpretation*, 11–23.

"Finding History in Day-to-Day Life with the Pilgrims." *New York Times*, January 27, 1991.

Fischer, David Hackett. *Albion's Seed: Four British Folkways in America*. New York: Oxford University Press, 1989.

Fisher, Robin Gaby. "Lesson in Living History: Actor Teaches Gill Students Douglass' Power of Thinking." *Star Ledger* (Newark), October 21, 1993.

Floyd, Candace. "Drama for Training." *History News* 36 (June 1981): 17–19.

Follin, Mike. "Historical Mindset: Interpreting the Essence." Association for Living Historical Farms and Agricultural Museums *Proceedings* 12 (1992): 100–103.

Fortier, John. "The Dilemmas of Living History." Association for Living Historical Farms and Agricultural Museums *Proceedings* 10 (1989): 1–19.

———. "Managing a Moment in Time." in Jay Anderson, *Living History Reader*, 35–45.

———. "Thoughts on the Re-creation and Interpretation of Historical Environments." In Third International Congress of Maritime Museums *Schedule and Papers*. Mystic, Conn.: Mystic Seaport Museum, 1978.

———. "What to Do after the Architect Leaves." *Gazette* (of the Canadian Museums Association), Spring 1976, 6–13.

Franco, Barbara, and Millie Rahn. "Who's Teaching History?" *History News* 42 (September/October 1987): 7–11.

Fried, Jeremy. "The History of Character Interpretation at Colonial Williamsburg." April 25, 1993. Four-page leaflet.

Gable, Eric, Richard Handler, and Anna Lawson. "On the Uses of Relativism: Fact,

Conjecture, and Black and White Histories at Colonial Williamsburg." *American Ethnologist* 19, no. 4 (November 1992): 791–805.

Gahlhoff, Sonia, and Kathleen A. Henwood. "Educational Outreach Packets: How to Make Local History More Accessible." *History News* 42 (May/June 1987): 36–40.

Garbarino, Merwyn S. *Sociocultural Theory in Anthropology: A Short History*. Prospect Heights, Ill.: Waveland, 1983.

Gardner, Howard. *Frames of Mind: The Theory of Multiple Intelligences*. New York: Basic Books, 1983.

Gardner, Toni. "Learning from Listening: Museums Improve Their Effectiveness through Visitor Studies." *Museum News* 64 (February 1986): 40–44.

Gartenhaus, Alan R. *Minds in Motion: Using Museums to Expand Creative Thinking*. Davis, Calif.: Caddo Gap Press, 1991.

Geertz, Clifford. "Blurred Genres: The Refiguration of Social Thought." *American Scholar* 49 (Spring 1980): 165–79.

Gentile, John S. *Cast of One: One-Person Shows from the Chautauqua Platform to the Broadway Stage*. Urbana: University of Illinois Press, 1989.

George, Alberta Sebolt. "Living History at Old Sturbridge Village: A Method of Portraying the Past." September 1983. Photocopy.

———. "Living History at Old Sturbridge: Why the Medium Works." *Living Historian* 5, no. 2 (April/May 1991): 1, 18.

Gibson-Quigley, Sandra, and Susan Rowden. "Social Change in America, 1790–1840: Teaching about Life in the New Republic." *Magazine of History* 2, no. 2 (Winter 1986): 22–30.

Glassberg, David. *American Historical Pageantry: The Uses of Tradition in the Early Twentieth Century*. Chapel Hill: University of North Carolina Press, 1990.

———. "History and the Public: Legacies of the Progressive Era." *Journal of American History* 73, no. 4 (March 1987): 957–80.

———. "Living in the Past." *American Quarterly* 38 (1986): 305–10.

Glaze, Bernadette M. "Role Writing to Understand the Past." Prepared through the Northern Virginia Writing Project. ERIC Document ED 240 551.

Goffman, Erving. "Facial Engagements." In Mortensen, *Basic Readings in Communication Theory*, 64–90.

———. *Frame Analysis*. New York: Harper and Row, 1974.

———. *The Presentation of Self in Everyday Life*. New York: Anchor, 1959.

Gonis, George. "History in the Making." *History News* 40 (July 1985): 12–15.

Gordinier, Glenn. "Exhibit Job Description: Roleplaying." Training materials, Mystic Seaport Museum, 1983.

———. "Guidelines for Roleplayers Meeting on the Streets." Training materials, Mystic Seaport Museum, 1983.

Graburn, Nelson. "The Museum and the Visitor Experience." In Nichols, *Museum Education Anthology*, 177–82.

Gramann, James H., Myron F. Floyd, and Alan Ewert. "Interpretation and Hispanic American Ethnicity." In Machlis and Field, *On Interpretation*, 161–77.

Green, Timothy. "Modern Britons Try the Iron Age, Find They Like It." *Smithsonian*, June 1978, 80–87.

Green, Vicki Ann. "An Oral History of a Field Trip: A Study of Participants' Historical Imagination in 'Action' and 'Artifact within Action.'" Ph.D. diss., Department of Social and Natural Sciences, University of Victoria, 1992.

Greene, Jack P. "The 'New History': From Top to Bottom." *New York Times*, January 8, 1975.

Grinder, Alison L., and E. Sue McCoy. *The Good Guide: A Source Book for Interpreters, Docents, and Tour Guides*. Scottsdale, Ariz.: Ironwood Press, 1985.

Gutek, Gerald, and Patricia Gutek. *Experiencing America's Past: A Travel Guide to Museum Villages*. Columbia: University of South Carolina Press, 1994.

Hall, Edward T., and William Foote Whyte. "Intercultural Communication." In Mortensen, *Basic Readings in Communication Theory*, 1973.

Ham, Sam Houston. "Familiarity and Adaptation: A Study of Family Attendance at Interpretive Activities." Ph.D. diss., Department of Wildland Recreation Management, University of Idaho, 1982.

――――. "Sorting Out Wild Ideas: Interpretation and Research Are Necessary Partners." *Interpretation*, Summer 1989, 15–16.

Handler, Mimi. "How Do We View the Past?" *Early American Life* 21 (April 1990): 15–19, 67.

Handler, Richard. "Overpowered by Realism: Living History and the Simulation of the Past." *Journal of American Folklore* 100 (July–September 1987): 337–41.

Handlin, Oscar. "Living History." *New York Times*, March 6, 1971.

Hanson, Susan Atherton. "The Flip Side: Using Popularizers within the Museum Site Context." Association for Living Historical Farms and Agricultural Museums *Proceedings* 13 (1993): 78–82.

Hayakawa, S. I. *Language in Thought and Action*. 3rd ed. New York: Harcourt, Brace, Jovanovich, 1972.

Hayes, Jennifer, and Dorothy Schindel. *Pioneer Journeys: Drama in Museum Education*. Charlottesville, Va.: New Plays Books, 1994.

Hayward, Ann. "The Politics of Living History." Association for Living Historical Farms and Agricultural Museums *Proceedings* 14 (1994): 35–39.

Hayward, D. Geoffrey, and Arthur D. Jensen. "Enhancing a Sense of the Past: Perception of Visitors and Interpreters." *Interpreter* 12, no. 2 (1981): 4–12.

Hayward, D. Geoffrey, and John W. Larkin. "Evaluating Visitor Experiences and Exhibit Effectiveness at Old Sturbridge Village." *Museum Studies Journal* 1, no. 2 (Fall 1983): 42–51.

Heighway, David. "The Don Quixote Syndrome." Association for Living Historical Farms and Agricultural Museums *Proceedings* 17 (1995): 166–68.

Hiemstra, Roger. "The Implications of Lifelong Learning." In Collins, *Museums, Adults, and the Humanities*, 120–30.

――――. "The State of the Art." In Collins, *Museums, Adults, and the Humanities*, 61–72.

Hilke, D. D. "Family Learning in Museums." *Marriage and Family Review* 13, no. 3/4 (1989): 87–129.

Hilker, Gordon. *The Audience and You: Practical Dramatics for the Park Interpreter*. Washington, D.C.: National Park Service, Department of the Interior, 1974.

Historical Society of Pennsylvania. "Partners with the Past." Promotional flier from a first-person program, ca. 1990–91.

Historic Fort Wayne. Materials from their interpreter's manual, 1984–86.

"History Goes on Stage: How Theatre Techniques Aid Local History." *History News* 36 (June 1981): 7–19.

Hodgson, John. *The Uses of Drama*. London: Eyre Methuen, 1972.

Hodgson, John, and Ernest Richards. *Improvisation*. London: Eyre Methuen, 1974.

Holbrook, Hal. *Mark Twain Tonight!: An Actor's Portrait*. New York: Ives Washburn, 1959.

Holzer, Harold. "Disarmingly Abe." *Americana* 19 (February 1992): 43–47.

Hood, Marilyn G. "Comfort and Caring: Two Essential Environmental Factors." *Environment and Behavior* 25, no. 6 (November 1993): 710–24.

———. "Getting Started in Audience Research." *Museum News* 64 (February 1986): 25–31.

———. "Leisure Criteria of Family Participation and Non-Participation in Museums." *Marriage and Family Review* 13, no. 3/4 (1989): 151–69.

Hooper-Greenhill, Eilean. *Museums and Their Visitors*. London: Routledge, 1994.

Horvath, August T., and Lin Bin. "From Reality to Hyperreality: Simulation and Images at Greenfield Village." *Communication Research* 18, no. 1 (February 1991): 103–14.

Hudson, Kenneth. *Museums of Influence*. New York: Cambridge University Press, 1987.

Hurst, Carol Otis, and Rebecca Otis. "Living History in the Classroom." *Teaching PreK–8* 23, no. 2 (October 1992): 80–82.

Interpretation for Disabled Visitors in the National Park System. Washington, D.C.: National Park Service, [1986].

Interpretation: Key to the Park Experience. Washington, D.C.: National Parks and Conservation Association, 1988.

"The Interpretive Challenge." *Interpretation*, Fall 1989. Special issue.

Jackson, Norman L. "An Analysis of Hal Holbrook's Development and Performance of the Role of Mark Twain." Ph.D. diss., Department of Theater and Cinematic Arts, Brigham Young University, 1981.

Johnson, Cathy. "Creating a Persona — with Particular Attention to 'The Ladies.'" Pre-publication copy of an article destined for *Muzzleloader* magazine, 1993.

———. *Living History: Drawing on the Past: A Re-enactor's Sketchbook of Artifacts and Sites*. Excelsior Springs, Mo.: Graphics/Fine Arts Press, 1994.

———. *Who Was I? Creating a Living History Persona*. Excelsior Springs, Mo.: Graphics/Fine Arts Press, 1995.

Jones, Dale. "Living History in the City." *History News* 50 (Summer 1995): 10–13.

Jones, Dale, and Kate Stover. *Interpretive Resource Programming Guide: A Listing of Historical Performers, Interpreters, and Craftspeople*. [Baltimore]: Historical Interpretation Committee of the Association of Living Historical Farms and Agricultural Museums, 1992.

Kabagarama, Daisy. *Breaking the Ice: A Guide to Understanding People from Other Cultures*. Needham Heights, Mass.: Allyn and Bacon, 1993.

Kaplan, Stephen, Lisa V. Bardwell, and Deborah B. Slater. "The Museum as Restorative Environment." *Environment and Behavior* 25, no. 6 (November 1993): 725–42.

Karp, Walter. "Putting Worms Back in Apples." *American Heritage*, August/September 1982, 33–43.

Kay, William Kennon. *Keep It Alive! Tips on Living History Demonstrations.* U.S. Department of the Interior, National Park Service, 1970.

Kehr, Janet R. "Historical Mindset: To Be What You Were When." Association for Living Historical Farms and Agricultural Museums *Proceedings* 12 (1992): 104–6.

Keller, Clair. "Roleplaying and Simulation in History Classes." *History Teacher* 8, no. 4 (August 1975): 573–81.

Kelsey, Darwin P. "Harvest of History." *Historic Preservation* 28 (July–September 1976): 20–24.

Kemp, John. "World View and the Interpreter." Association for Living Historical Farms and Agricultural Museums *Proceedings* 13 (1993): 68–72.

Kilgore, Kathleen. "Real Pilgrims Throw Their Trash out the Window." *Yankee*, November 1983, 62–72.

King, Margaret J. "The Theme Park Experience: What Museums Can Learn from Mickey Mouse." *Futurist* 25, no. 6 (November–December 1991): 24–34.

Knox, Alan B. "Basic Components of Adult Programming." In Collins, *Museums, Adults, and the Humanities*, 95–111.

Knutson, C. "Recruiting and Interpreting." *Moderne Aviso* 3, no. 3 (1994): 10–11.

Korn, Randi. "An Evaluation of the 'Becoming Americans' Theme." Prepared for the Colonial Williamsburg Foundation, September 1994.

———. "Introduction to Evaluation: Theory and Methodology." In *Museum Education: History, Theory, and Practice* (Reston, Va.: National Art Education Association, 1989): 219–38.

———. *Living History Sunday: Visitor Responses to Living History at Pennsbury Manor.* Alexandria, Va.: Randi Korn and Associates, 1990.

———. "Studying Your Visitors: Where to Begin." *History News* 49 (March–April 1994): 23–26.

Kropf, Marcia Brunit, and Inez S. Wolins. "How Families Learn: Considerations for Program Development." *Marriage and Family Review* 13, no. 3/4 (1989): 75–86.

Krugler, John D. "Behind the Public Presentations: Research and Scholarship at Living History Museums of Early America." *William and Mary Quarterly*, 3rd ser., 48 (July 1991): 347–86.

———. "The Godiah Spray Plantation: Living History and the Historian, 1966–1984," draft, [1991?].

———. "Homes of the Heroes: The Challenges of Interpretation." Paper presented for the Annual Meeting of the Society for Historians of the Early American Republic, Charlottesville, Va., July 22, 1989.

———. "Keeping the Illusion of Historical Accuracy: Is First Person Interpretation History or Historical Fiction?" August 23, 1991.

———. "Living History: An Oxymoron." Talk given to the Phi Alpha Theta Regional Conference, April 7, 1990.

———. "Stepping outside the Classroom: History and the Outdoor Museum." *Journal of American Culture* 12, no. 2 (1989): 79–85.

Lacy, Thomas J., and Julie Agar. "Bringing Teachers and Museums Together." *Museum News* 58 (March–April 1980): 50–54.

Lambert, W. A. *The Elements of Effective Communication.* Washington, D.C.: Acropolis Books, 1974.

Lang, Michale. "Marketing Historic Resources." M.A. thesis, University of Calgary, 1991.

Leichter, Hope Jensen, Karen Hensel, and Eric Larsen. "Families and Museums: Issues and Perspectives." *Marriage and Family Review* 13, no. 3/4 (1989): 15–50.

Leon, Warren, and Margaret Piatt. "Living History Museums." In Leon and Rosenzweig, *History Museums in the United States*, 64–97.

Leon, Warren, and Roy Rosenzweig, eds. *History Museums in the United States: A Critical Assessment.* Urbana: University of Illinois Press, 1989.

———. Introduction to Leon and Rosenzweig, *History Museums in the United States*, xi–xxvi.

Leone, Mark P. "The Relationship between Artifacts and the Public in Outdoor History Museums." *New York Academy of Science Annals* (1981): 301–13.

———. "Sketch of a Theory for Outdoor History Museums." Association for Living Historical Farms and Agricultural Museums *Proceedings* 10 (1989): 36–46.

Levstik, Linda S. "Living History — Isn't." *History News* 37 (May 1982): 28–29.

Lewis, Ralph. *Manual for Museums.* Washington, D.C.: National Park Service, Department of the Interior, 1976.

Littlejohn, Margaret, and Gary E. Machlis. *A Diversity of Visitors to the National Park System: The National Park Service Visitor Services Project.* [Moscow, Idaho]: University of Idaho Cooperative Park Studies Unit, 1990.

Living History Foundation. "Character Outline (form)." February 1988.

"Living History: Getting Closer to Getting It Right." *Early American Life* 21 (June 1990): 18–25.

Loomis, Ormond. *Sources on Folk Museums and Living Historical Farms.* Bloomington, Ind.: Folklore Forum, 1977.

Lowenthal, David. "The American Way of History." *Columbia University Forum* 9, no. 3 (Summer 1966): 27–32.

———. "The Dying Future, the Living Past." Association for Living Historical Farms and Agricultural Museums *Proceedings* 13 (1993): 3–11.

———. "The Dying Future, the Living Past." Photocopy of keynote address, "A Future for the Past," given at the Association for Living Historical Farms and Agricultural Museums twentieth anniversary annual meeting, June 18, 1990.

———. *The Past Is a Foreign Country.* New York: Cambridge University Press, 1988.

———. "Pioneer Museums." In Leon and Rosenzweig, *History Museums in the United States*, 115–27.

Lumley, Robert, ed. *The Museum Time Machine: Putting Cultures on Display.* London: Routledge, 1988.

Lynch, Kevin. *What Time Is This Place?* Cambridge, Mass.: MIT Press, 1972.

McCalmon, George, and Christian Moe. *Creating Historical Drama: A Guide for the*

Community and the Interested Individual. Carbondale: Southern Illinois University Press, 1965.

MacCannell, Dean. *The Tourist: A New Theory of the Leisure Class.* New York: Schocken Books, 1976.

Machlis, Gary E. "Ethnography as a Research Tool in Understanding Visitors." In Machlis and Field, *On Interpretation,* 44–64.

———. "Interpreting War and Peace." In Machlis and Field, *On Interpretation,* 235–44.

———, ed. *Interpretive Views: Opinions on Evaluating Interpretation in the National Park Service.* Washington, D.C.: National Parks and Conservation Association, 1986.

Machlis, Gary E., and Donald R. Field. "Getting Connected: An Approach to Children's Interpretation." In Machlis and Field, *On Interpretation,* 65–74.

———, eds. *On Interpretation: Sociology for Interpreters of Natural and Cultural History.* Rev. ed. Corvallis: Oregon State University Press, 1992.

Machlis, Gary E., and Maureen McDonough. *Children's Interpretation: A Discovery Book for Interpreters.* Washington, D.C.: National Park Service, 1978.

Machlis, Gary E., Donald R. Field, and Mark E. Van Every. "A Sociological Look at the Japanese Tourist." In Machlis and Field, *On Interpretation,* 96–114.

Mackintosh, Barry. *Interpretation in the National Park Service: A Historical Perspective.* Washington, D.C.: History Division, National Park Service, Department of the Interior, 1986.

McQuarie, Bob. "'Experiences in History': A Museum Time Machine for Teaching History." *Social Education,* January 1981, 56–59.

Majewski, Janice. *Part of Your General Public Is Disabled: A Handbook for Guides in Museums, Zoos, and Historic Houses.* Washington, D.C.: Smithsonian Institution Press, 1987.

Malcolm-Davies, Jane. "Acting the Part Properly." *Times* (London), December 12, 1989.

———. "Keeping It Alive." *Museums Journal,* March 1990, 25–29.

———. "Keep It Live." *Environmental Interpretation,* July 1990, 22–24.

———. "Live Interpretation Conference, Springfield, Ohio." *Heritage Interpretation* 45 (Summer 1990): unpaginated.

Mandell, Patricia. "Details, Details, Details: At Plimoth Plantation, the Quest for Authenticity Never Ends." *Americana* 17 (November/December 1989): 48–54.

Mandle, Roger. "Adult Programming Approaches." In Collins, *Museums, Adults, and the Humanities,* 177–97.

Marsh, Peter, ed. *Eye to Eye: How People Interact.* Topsfield, Mass.: Salem House, 1988.

Marshall, Howard Wright. "Folklife and the Rise of American Folk Museums." *Journal of American Folklore* 90 (October–December 1977): 391–413.

Massialas, Byron G., and Jack Zevin. *Teaching Creatively: Learning through Discovery.* Malabar, Fla.: Krieger, 1983.

Mastromarino, Mark A. "Interpreting American Agricultural Fairs: Challenges and Opportunities for Living History." Association for Living Historical Farms and Agricultural Museums *Proceedings* 12 (1992): 90–95.

Matelic, Candace Tangorra. "Not Message but Method: Interpretive Training

Exercises Focusing on Communication Skills." Association for Living Historical Farms and Agricultural Museums *Papers* 8 (1988): 209–18.

———. "Through the Historical Looking Glass." *Museum News* 58 (March/April 1980): 35–45.

Matelic, Candace Tangorra, Patricia Sadler, and Marty Perkins. "Research for Interpretation: Translating Research into Written Materials." Association for Living Historical Farms and Agricultural Museums *Papers* 8 (1988): 3–8.

Mehrabian, Albert. "Communication without Words." In Mortensen, *Basic Readings in Communication Theory*, 91–98.

Melton, Arthur W. "Some Behavior Characteristics of Museum Visitors." *Psychological Bulletin* 30, no. 9 (November 1933): 720–21.

Miller, Cecilia. *Giambattista Vico: Imagination and Historical Knowledge*. New York: St. Martin's Press, 1993.

Miller, James William. "Museums and the Academy: Toward Building and Alliance." *Journal of American Culture* 12, no. 2 (1989): 1–6.

Moore, Willard B. "Folklife Museums: Resource Sites for Teaching." *Indiana English Journal* 11 (Winter 1976): 3–10.

Morris, Desmond, Peter Collett, Peter Marsh, and Marie O'Shaughnessy. *Gestures: Their Origins and Distribution*. New York: Stein and Day, 1979.

Mortensen, C. David. *Basic Readings in Communication Theory*. New York: Harper and Row, 1973.

Moscardo, Gianna M., and Philip L. Pearce. "Historic Theme Parks: An Australian Experience in Authenticity." *Annals of Tourism Research* 13 (1986): 467–79.

Munley, Mary Ellen. "Asking the Right Questions: Evaluation and the Museum Mission." *Museum News* 64 (February 1986): 18–23.

———. "*Evaluation Study Report: Buyin' Freedom.*" An Experimental Live Interpretation Program, March 20–May 1, 1982. Prepared for the Department of Social and Cultural History, National Museum of American History, Smithsonian Institution. Washington, D.C.: The author, 1982.

———. "Intentions and Accomplishments: Principles of Museum Evaluation Research." In *Past Meets Present: Essays about Historic Interpretation and Public Audiences*, edited by Jo Blatti, 116–30. Washington, D.C.: Smithsonian Institution Press, 1987.

"Museum Theater: Many Roles, Many Players, Many Places, Many Reasons." *Journal of Museum Education* 15, no. 2 (Spring/Summer 1990). Special issue devoted to museum theater.

Mystic Seaport Museum. Training materials for roleplayers, 1983–86.

Naylor, Lois Anne. "Living History Farms and Museums." *Better Homes and Gardens*, August 1990, 126, 128.

Neff, Merry. "The Interpreters of Old Fort Wayne." *Early American Life* 14 (August 1983): 58–63.

Nichols, Susan K., ed. *Museum Education Anthology: Perspectives on Informal Learning, a Decade of Roundtable Reports*. Washington, D.C.: Museum Education Roundtable, 1984.

O'Connell, Peter. "Adult Education and the Museum Experience." *History News* 43 (September/October 1988): 10–17.

———. "May the Force Be with You." In Nichols, *Museum Education Anthology*, 96–100.

O'Connell, Peter, and Patricia A. Lavin. "A Living History Museum." *Social Education*, April/May 1986, 284–87.

O'Toole, Dennis. "Keynote Address." Association for Living Historical Farms and Agricultural Museums *Papers* 8 (1988): 72–75.

Pahl, Ronald. "Forsooth! An Exploration into Living History." *Social Studies* 85, no. 1 (January–February 1994): 21–24.

Patterson, John. "Conner Prairie Refocuses Its Interpretive Message to Include Controversial Subjects." *History News* 41 (March 1986): 12–15.

Pearce, P. L. "Tourist-Guide Interaction." *Annals of Tourism Research* 11 (1984): 129–46.

———. *The Ulysses Factor: Evaluating Visitors in Tourist Settings*. New York: Springer-Verlag, 1988.

Peart, Bob. "Interpretation in Informal Learning." *Journal of Interpretation* 11, no. 1 (1986): 33–40.

Personal Training Program for Interpreters. Washington, D.C.: National Park Service, Division of Interpretation, 1976.

Peterson, David. "History, Pseudo-History, and Living History." Association for Living Historical Farms and Agricultural Museums *Proceedings* 12 (1992): 47–51.

———. "There Is No Living History, There Are No Time Machines." *History News* 43 (September/October 1988): 28–30.

Piatt, Margaret. "Character Analysis Worksheets." Old Sturbridge Village, 1984–85.

———. "How the Grasshopper Sprang from the Soil and Hopped into the Twenty-first Century." Association for Living Historical Farms and Agricultural Museums *Proceedings* 13 (1993): 19–23.

———. "An Outline of Theatrical Forms Used in History Museums as Interpretive or Educational Methods." 1986.

———. "Role Acting: A Training Approach at the London Town Publik House." Ca. 1978.

Piatt, Margaret, and Dale Jones. "Planning Effective Living History Performances." Outline materials for "A Union of Spirits: A Conference for Interpreters." Farmers' Museum, Cooperstown, N.Y., March 22–23, 1991.

Piatt, Margaret, and Jane Schwerdtfeger. "Reading and Writing about History." *History News* 46 (January/February 1991): 5–11.

Pickering, Felicia. "Constitutional Convention Became Living History." Bucks County (Pa.) *Advance*, January 2, 1992.

Pitcaithley, Dwight. "Historic Sites: What Can Be Learned from Them?" *History Teacher* 20, no. 2 (February 1987): 207–19.

Pitman-Gelles, Bonnie. *Museums, Magic, and Children: Youth Education in Museums*. Washington, D.C.: Association of Science-Technology Centers, 1981.

Plimoth Plantation. "Outline for Evaluation Criteria: Colonial Interpretation, 1991."

———. "Plimoth Plantation Welcomes You." 1991. Descriptive brochure and site map.

———. Training Manuals.

"Plimoth Plantation." Videocassette. Glastonbury, Conn.: Video Tours, 1989.

Pond, Kathleen Lingle. *The Professional Guide*. New York: Van Nostrand Reinhold, 1993.

Porter, Richard E., and Larry A. Samovar. "Basic Principles of Intercultural Communication." In Samovar and Porter, *Intercultural Communication*, 5–22.

Postman, Neil. *Amusing Ourselves to Death: Public Discourse in the Age of Show Business*. New York: Penguin, 1986.

Pritchard, Diane Spencer. "Fort Ross: From Russia with Love." In Jay Anderson, *Living History Reader*, 49–53.

Quinn, Sondra. "Theater Techniques as a Method of Interpretation for Adults." In Collins, *Museums, Adults, and the Humanities*, 257–70.

Rath, Frederick L., Jr., and Merrilyn Rogers O'Connell, eds. *Interpretation: A Bibliography on Historical Organization Practices*. Nashville: American Association for State and Local History, 1978.

Rayner, Sue Sturtevant, and Judithe Douglas Speidel. "Learning Theories and History Museums." *History News* 42 (July/August 1987): 23–26.

Regnier, Kathleen, Michael Gross, and Ron Zimmerman. *The Interpreter's Guidebook: Techniques for Programs and Presentations*. Interpreter's Handbook Series. Stevens Point, Wis.: UW-SP Foundation Press, 1994.

Richmond, Pete. "John Goodman Is Some Babe." *Gentlemen's Quarterly*, April 1992, 170–75, 230.

Rigsby, Frances. "Shipwrecked Spaniards: The Museum of San Agustin Antiguo Presents an Educational Program for Gifted School Children." *History News* 41 (January 1986): 26–29.

Risk, Paul H. "The Interpretive Talk." In Sharpe, *Interpreting the Environment*, 159–75.

———. "On-Site Real-Time Observational Techniques and Responses to Visitor Needs." In Uzzell, *Heritage Interpretation*, 2:120–28.

Robertshaw, Andrew. "From Houses into Homes: One Approach to Live Interpretation." *Journal of Social History Curators' Group* 19 (1992): 14–20.

Robinson, Gilbert. "The Historical Interpreter/Reenactor: Their Role Defined, Their Importance Restated." *Living Historian Quarterly, 1990 Events Annual* 4, no. 1 (Spring 1990): 11a–11b.

Ronsheim, Robert D. "Christmas at Conner Prairie: Reinterpreting a Pioneer Holiday." *History News* 36 (December 1981): 14–17.

———. "Is the Past Dead?" *Museum News* 53 (November 1974): 16–18, 62.

Roos, Pieter N., and Carolyn B. Wilkinson. "Operating Instructions for the Visitor: An Outline for Museum Orientation Exhibits." *History News* 47 (July–August 1992): 20–23.

Roth, Stacy Flora. *Communicating in First-Person: Perspectives on Interpreter/Visitor Interaction*. Langhorne, Pa.: The author, 1992.

———. "Communication Skills Necessary for First-Person Interpreters." Association for Living Historical Farms and Agricultural Museums, *Proceedings of the 1992 Conference and Annual Meeting* 15 (1996): 242–54.

———. "Conveying Women's Issues in Live Interpretation." Paper presented at Pennsbury Manor Fall Forum on Women's History in Southeastern Pennsylvania, October 31, 1992.

————. "Incorporating Women and Women's Issues into Interpretive Programs at PHMC Sites." Notes/outline for a workshop presented to the Pennsylvania Historical and Museum Commission Interpreters Conference, Harrisburg, Pa., March 8, 1993.

————. "Incorporating Women's Issues into Interpretive Programs." *Tapestry: The Newsletter of the Pennsylvania Federation of Museums and Historical Organizations* 2, no. 2 (Spring 1993): 5.

————. "Sense and Sensibility: Thoughts on Interpreting Ugly and Uncomfortable Issues." Notes for a talk given at the Union of Spirits Conference, Old Sturbridge Village, March 1993.

Ruane, Michael F. "Deathwatch: 1864 Trial, Execution to be Re-enacted at Fort." *Philadelphia Inquirer*, August 2, 1990.

Ruckman, John. "Living History Is Far More Effective Than Static Displays." *Living Historian* 4, no. 4 (Winter 1991): 4.

Ryan, Joseph J. "Early Morning Mist." *Social Studies* 77, no. 5 (September/October 1986): 214–15.

Ryan, Peter M. "Typology of Living History Formats." 1987.

Samovar, Larry A., and Richard E. Porter, eds. *Intercultural Communication: A Reader*. Belmont, Calif.: Wadsworth, 1991.

Sanders, Tom. "Thoughts on Effective Living History: Interpretive Suggestions." *Midwest Open-Air Museums Magazine*, Spring 1990, 10–11, 21.

Sanderson, Jane. "Jefferson's Descendant Becomes a Living Memorial." *People Weekly*, January 26, 1987, 80–81.

Sarnoff, Dorothy. *Never Be Nervous Again: Time Tested Techniques for the Foolproof Control of Nervousness*. New York: Ivy Books, 1987.

————. *Speech Can Change Your Life*. New York: Dell, 1972.

Schafernich, Sandra. "On Site Museums, Open Air Museums, Museum Villages, and Living History Museums." *Museum Management and Curatorship* 12 (1993): 43–61.

Schama, Simon. "Clio Has a Problem." *History News* 47 (1992): 10–13.

Schechner, Richard. *Between Theater and Anthropology*. Philadelphia: University of Pennsylvania Press, 1985.

Schimmel, Nancy. *Just Enough to Make a Story*. 2nd ed. Berkeley, Calif.: Sisters' Choice Press, 1982.

Schlebecker, John T., and Gale E. Peterson. *Living Historical Farms Handbook*. Washington, D.C.: Smithsonian Institution Press, 1972.

Schlereth, Thomas J. *Artifacts and the American Past*. Nashville: American Association for State and Local History, 1989.

————. "The Historic Museum Village as a Learning Environment." *Museologist*, June 1977, 10–18.

————. "History in the Making." *History News* 40 (July 1985): 12–15.

Schramm, Wilbur. "How Communication Works." In Mortensen, *Basic Readings in Communication Theory*, 28–36.

Screven, C. G. "A Bibliography on Visitor Education Research." *Museum News* 57 (March/April 1979): 56–59, 86–88.

———. "The Museum as Responsive Learning Environment." *Museum News* 47 (June 1969): 7–10.

Sebolt, Alberta. "Old Sturbridge Village Teacher-Training Program." In Collins, *Museums, Adults, and the Humanities*, 313–37.

Seeman, Charlie. "Living History or Living Culture? One Alternative to Historical Re-creation." *History News* 44 (January/February 1989): 42.

"Seventy-Two Hours in 1870." *Yankee*, December 1979, 62–67, 141–46.

Shannon, Terri M. "Introducing Simulation and Role Play." In *Strategies for Active Teaching and Learning in University Classrooms: A Handbook of Teaching Strategies*, edited by Steven F. Shomberg, 27–34, 91–94. Minneapolis: University of Minnesota, 1986. ERIC Document ED 276 356.

Sharpe, Grant W., ed. *Interpreting the Environment*. New York: Wiley, 1976.

Sharrer, G. Terry. "Hitching History to the Plow." *Historic Preservation* 32 (November/December 1980): 42–49.

Sheldon, Amy, and Joan M. Jensen. "Gender, Language, and Historical Interpretation." *Oral History Review* 17, no. 2 (1989): 92–96.

Shepard, Clinton. "Interpretation: Techniques or Theory." *Parks and Recreation*, July 1987, 44–47.

Sherfy, Marcella. "Honesty in Interpreting the Cultural Past." *Parks*, January–March 1979, 13–14.

———. "Interpreting History." Photocopied reprint of an article that appeared in a National Park Service publication *In Touch*.

Sidford, Holly. "Stepping into History." *Museum News* 53 (November 1974): 23–34.

Silverman, Lois. "Johnny Showed Us the Butterflies: The Museum as Family Therapy Tool." *Marriage and Family Review* 13, no. 3/4 (1989): 131–50.

———. "Our Children Were Shy at First: An Evaluative Study of Living History at Pennsbury Manor." Unpublished report, January 1989.

Skobalski, Marnie J. "Issues in Open Air Museum Management: Planning, Marketing, and Interpretation." M.A. thesis, University of Calgary, 1992.

"Slave Auction Re-Enacted in Colonial Williamsburg." *Courier Times* (Bucks County, Pa.), October 11, 1994.

"Slave Sale Educates and Angers." *Star Ledger* (Newark, N.J.), October 11, 1994.

Smith, Brendan. "Interpreting to School Children at Plimoth Plantation: Learning Theory and Case Study." Graduate research paper, Cooperstown Graduate Program, 1993.

Snow, Stephen Eddy. *Performing the Pilgrims: A Study of Ethnohistorical Role-Playing at Plimoth Plantation*. Jackson: University Press of Mississippi, 1993.

———. "Theatre of the Pilgrims: Documentation and Analysis of a 'Living History' Performance in Plymouth, Massachusetts." Ph.D. diss., New York University, 1987.

Sorenson, Sharon. "Three in One: How Dee Ashpaugh Stitches Depends on Who She Is at Conner Prairie That Day — Mrs. Biddleton, Mrs. Campbell, or Widow Bucher." *Americana* 11 (September/October 1983): 52–56.

Spolin, Viola. *Improvisation for the Theater*. Evanston, Ill.: Northwestern University Press, 1985.

———. *Theatre Games*. Evanston, Ill.: Northwestern University Press, 1985.

Stanislavsky, Constantin. *Building a Character*. New York: Theater Arts Books, 1949.

Stephens, Terry. "The Visitor — Who Cares? Interpretation and Consumer Relations." In Uzzell, *Heritage Interpretation*, 2:103–7.

Steps in Time: Scenes from 1840 Baltimore, Teacher Manual. Baltimore: Baltimore City Life Museums, 1988.

Sternberg, Patricia. *Sociodrama: Who's in Your Shoes?* New York: Praeger, 1989.

Stevens, Mary Lynn. "Wistful Thinking: The Effect of Nostalgia on Interpretation." *History News* 36 (December 1981): 10–13.

Stillman, Diane Brandt. "Living History in an Art Museum." *Journal of Museum Education* 15, no. 2 (Spring/Summer 1990): 8–10.

Stone, Peter, and Sherman Edwards. *1776! A Musical Play*. New York: Bantam Books, 1972.

Stover, Kate F. "Interpretation of Historical Conflict in Living History Museums." M.A. thesis, John F. Kennedy University, 1988.

———. "Is It REAL History Yet? An Update on Living History Museums." *Journal of American Culture* 12, no. 2 (1989): 13–17.

Sussman, Vic. "From Williamsburg to Conner Prairie: Living History Museums Bring Bygone Days to Life but Not Always Accurately." *U.S. News and World Report*, July 24, 1989, 58–62.

Teaching History at Colonial Williamsburg. Williamsburg, Va.: Colonial Williamsburg Foundation, 1990.

"Tears and Protest at Mock Slave Sale." *New York Times*, October 11, 1994.

Tilden, Freeman. *Interpreting Our Heritage*. Chapel Hill: University of North Carolina Press, 1977.

"Touch It, Feel It." *Economist*, August 19, 1989, 75.

Tramposch, William J. "'Put There a Spark': How Colonial Williamsburg Trains Its Interpretive Crew." *History News* 37 (July 1982): 21–23.

Trenouth, Peter. "Pilgrim Summer." *English Journal* 75, no. 5 (September 1986): 24–29.

Turner, Victor, and Edith Turner. "Performing Ethnography." *Drama Review* 26, no. 2 (1982): 33–50.

"Turning Back Time in Maine." *Yankee*, June 1988, 34–42.

Uzzell, David, ed. *Heritage Interpretation*. 2 vols. New York: Belhaven Press, 1989.

Vance, Tom. "Developing a First Person Program at a Small Site." Association for Living Historical Farms and Agricultural Museums *Papers* 8 (1988): 161–80.

Vanderstel, David G. "A Behavioral Approach to Living History: The Search for Community in the Past." Association for Living Historical Farms and Agricultural Museums *Papers* 8 (1988): 76–87.

———. "Death, Racism, and Intemperance: A Social Historian's Perspective on Living History and the Interrelation of Controversial Issues." Association for Living Historical Farms and Agricultural Museums *Proceedings* 12 (1992): 70–73.

———. "Humanizing the Past: The Revitalization of the History Museum." *Journal of American Culture* 12, no. 2 (1989): 19–25.

Van Ments, Morry. *The Effective Use of Role-Play: A Handbook for Teachers and Trainers*. New York: Nicholas, 1989.

Vukelich, Ronald. "Time Language for Interpreting History Collections to Children." *Museum Studies Journal* 1, no. 7 (Fall 1984): 43–50.

Wall, Alexander J. "History through Drama: A Program at Old Sturbridge Village." *New England Galaxy*, Spring 1967, 64–68.

Wallace, Michael. "The Future of History Museums." *History News* 44 (July/August 1989): 5–8, 30–33.

———. "Mickey Mouse History: Portraying the Past at Disney World." In Leon and Rosenzweig, *History Museums in the United States*, 158–80.

———. "Visiting the Past: History Museums in the United States." In *Presenting the Past: Essays on History and the Public*, edited by Susan Porter Benson, Steven Brier, and Roy Rosenzweig, 137–61. Philadelphia: Temple University Press, 1986.

Walsh, Kevin. *The Representation of the Past: Museums in the Post-Modern World*. New York: Routledge, 1992.

Webster, Harriet. "On Stage at Plimoth Plantation." *Americana* 8 (November/December 1980): 64–70.

Webster, Nancy. "Interpreting Religious Events and Festivals." Association for Living Historical Farms and Agricultural Museums *Proceedings* 14 (1994): 50–53.

Welsch, Roger L. "Very Didactic Simulation: Workshops in the Plains Pioneer Experience at the Stuhr Museum." *History Teacher* 7, no. 3 (May 1974): 356–64.

West, Bob. "The Making of the English Working Past." In Lumley, *Museum Time Machine*, 36–63.

"When Israel Was in Egypt's Land . . ." *Past Times*, January/February 1991, 2–4. Calendar and newsletter of the Chicago Historical Society.

White, Eugene E. *Practical Public Speaking*. 3rd ed. New York: Macmillan, 1978.

Williams, Bonnie. "Playing in the Stream of History: A Flexible Approach to First-Person Interpretation." Association for Living Historical Farms and Agricultural Museums *Proceedings* 15 (1996): 255–61.

Williams, Wayne, and Edward N. Schultz. "Dealing with the Disturbing: Interpreting Pain and Suffering." *Legacy*, March/April 1996, 28–30.

Woodall, Martha. "Walking in the Light of Quaker History." *Philadelphia Inquirer*, November 9, 1991.

Woods, Thomas A. "Beyond Color and Motion in Museums: Inductive Methods and Conceptual Interpretive Objectives." Association for Living Historical Farms and Agricultural Museums *Proceedings* 10 (1989): 60–70.

———. "Criteria for Reviewing Historic Sites: A Pilot Review of the Minnesota Historical Society's Program at the Forest History Center." Association for Living Historical Farms and Agricultural Museums *Proceedings* 13 (1993): 73–77.

———. "Living Historical Farming: A Critical Method for Historical Research and Teaching about Rural Life." *Journal of American Culture* 12, no. 2 (1989): 43–47.

———. "Perspectivistic Interpretation: A New Direction for Sites and Exhibits." *History News* 44 (January/February 1989): 14, 27–28.

Woods, Thomas A., and Joan M. Jensen. "The Challenge of Public History." *Oral History Review* 17, no. 2 (1989): 97–102.

Yellis, Ken. "Dying 'Interstate': World View and Living History at Plimoth Plantation." Association for Living Historical Farms and Agricultural Museums *Proceedings* 13 (1993): 59–63.

———. "Not Time Machines but Real Time: Living History at Plimoth Plantation." Association for Living Historical Farms and Agricultural Museums *Proceedings* 12 (1992): 52–57.

———. "Real Time: The Theory and Practice of Living History." Draft of an unpublished paper, October 1, 1990.

———. "Real Time: The Theory and Practice of Living History." Draft of an unpublished paper, August 24, 1991.

———. "Real Time: The Theory and Practice of Living History at Plimoth Plantation." Draft of an unpublished paper, February 3, 1990.

Zwelling, Shomer. "Social History Hits the Street: Williamsburg Characters Come to Life." *History News* 35 (January 1980): 10–12.

need for interpreters to understand, 54

History on the Hoof, 42, 210 (n. 2), 212 (n. 10)

Holbrook, Hal, 18, 34–35

Hood, Marilyn G., 121, 181

"Hooks," 86–93; verbal, 86–88; questions as, 87–88; objects as, 88; activities as, 89–92; dialogues as, 90, 93

Hopkins, Stephen: portrayed, 90, 96, 129, 132, 142

Hostility: reactions to, 69, 86

Housewifery: portrayed, 54, 59–60, 72, 84, 89, 90, 96, 140, 151

Hudson, Carson, 91 (ill.), 130, 215 (n. 14). See also Historical Diversions

Humor, 35, 100–102, 120–21, 127, 132; nineteenth-century, interpreted, 101; adult visitors and, 120–21

If Looks Could Kill, 35–36

Imagining the Past, 23

Improvisational theater: compared with first-person, 52; exercises, 56, 113

"Information overload," 121, 149

Intercultural communication, 127

International Museum Theater Alliance, 205 (n. 5)

Interpersonal communication: techniques, 32, 69, 71–73; process of, 67–68; effect of historical authenticity on, 67–69; visitors and, 67–69; historical gender and class restrictions on, 69; multidisciplinary aspects of, 69–75; and archaic vocabulary and concepts, 71–73; nonverbal aspects of, 73

Interpretation: goals and objectives, 20, 41, 42, 52–53, 55, 68, 134, 161–62, 179–80; affected by modern perspectives, 23, 178–79; business/sales model, 35, 76; history and philosophy, 205 (n. 2)

Interpreters, 3–4; motivation of, 3; importance of skilled, 5, 24, 28, 35, 54, 180–81, 208 (n. 40); definition of, 9–11; women and minority, 23–24;

affected by first-person process, 55; appearance of, 85, 113–15; responsibilities for directing conversation, 89; ideal characteristics of, 181

Interpreter's Guidebook, 100

"Interpretive Impetus," 3

Intimacy: projecting, 111–12

Jackson, Norman L., 34–35

Jeacle, Jean, 90, 213 (n. 19)

Jefferson, Thomas: portrayed, 15 (ill.), 98, 146

Jenkinson, Rick, 47, 116

Johnson, Cathy, 212 (n. 5)

Jones, Dale, 46–47

"Jumping the Broom," 17 (ill.), 18

Kashatus, William, 18, 62, 97, 114, 152, 220 (n. 35)

Kay, William Kennon, 31

Kelleher, Tom, 101–2, 112–13, 142 (ill.), 174, 206 (n. 15), 214 (n. 19)

Kemble, Fanny: portrayed, 34, 47

Kemp, John, 2 (ill.), 32, 58, 68, 78–79, 93, 96, 97, 175, 206 (n. 1), 209 (n. 33)

Knott's Berry Farm, 200

Krugler, John, 26

Laborers, Irish: portrayed, 102, 113

Lane, William: portrayed, 88

Language barrier, 125

Language in Thought and Action, 161

Learning: intergenerational, 122–23, 143; children and, 133–55 passim; models of, 136–40; inquiry and, 138; styles of, 138–39; disabilities, visitors with, 158–59

Leon, Warren, 33

Lincoln, Abraham: portrayed, 34, 143–44, 219 (n. 19)

Lincoln, Robert, 34

Lincoln-Douglas debates, 22 (ill.)

Lincoln Log Cabin State Historic Site, 42, 92 (ill.), 200

Lincoln Presenters, Society of, 219 (n. 19)

Living history: significance of, 1–2,